The Bright New Dawn

Louise Beker

Copyright © 2012 Louise Beker
All rights reserved.
ISBN: 978-0-473-20867-7 (Paperback)
ISBN: 978-0-473-20868-4 (E-book)

Published by: Louise Beker
Edited by: Eve Hogan, Robyn Pearce
Cover Design: Damonza.com

info@louisebeker.com
www.louisebeker.com
www.facebook.com/louisebeker.author

All rights reserved. No part of this publication may be reproduced, stored in a retrieval system, or transmitted in any form or by any means, electronic, mechanical, photocopying, recording, or otherwise, without the prior permission of the publishers.

DEDICATION

For Mum,

with love and honoring.

'Put your ear down close to your soul and listen hard.'

Anne Sexton

ACKNOWLEDGMENTS

Sincere and grateful thanks and acknowledgment to:
Eve Hogan, earth angel extraordinaire - special thanks for your editing, feedback, belief and encouragement; The remarkable Robyn Pearce, very grateful thanks for your valued input, editing and friendship; Deep and heartfelt gratitude to Chuck and Lency Spezzano and Psychology of Vision for teaching invaluable healing principles and creating a better world; for Ancient Egypt inspiration, sincere and grateful acknowledgement to the work of Colin Wilson; Damonza.com many thanks for the fabulous cover design and making the process so easy.
My many Angels - for your friendship, love and support:
Sheree Carbery, Meegan Hirst, Ange Todd, Norma Dutton and
Di Traveler (Thank you all for feedback).
Justine Farnsworth, Patricia Kyle, Anna Baldwin, Nikki Emmerton (fabulous cook!), Ross Hyslop – thank you for your enduring friendship and making England such a special place for me. Scott Jolly, Gina Hunt (another fabulous cook!), Tania Ikin, Phil Murray, Peter Gregg, Catherine Winn, Gill and Barry Williamson, Liana Clements, Steve Walls, Kendall Langston, Kristen Nash, Kelsen Butler, Zahira, Angie and Vince, Rajyo Markman, Rachel Phelps, and Lisa Revell – thank you all, for a multitude of great and beautiful reasons. And to Dawn Allan and Catherine Newton – for generosity of time and spirit, along with advice.
Thank you all so much for touching my heart along the way.
To the many clients who support my work and who have become friends to me, a humble and very grateful thank you.
Vic Jones, thank you beyond words.
Vicki Beker, Mark Greenlaw, Rob Smith, Tracey Thompson and
Rosina Beker – with love and appreciation.
Margaret Sanders...deep gratitude, respect, and love - for your guidance and contribution to my life...always remembered.
And to my family: Dad, deepest love and appreciation;
Mum – in dedication; Karen, Garth and Cherie – huge love and gratitude. Anna, Claire, Alexandra, Francis and Christina – a joy and inspiration to me...a sincere wish for a better world for you to inherit;
And to little Izzy, who kept me company as I tapped away
on the computer.
A heartfelt thank you to all.

Chapter One

She knew she was alone. That was one of the few certainties in life she understood perfectly. Perched high up on the Cliffs of Moher, the icy Atlantic breeze blew into her face, stinging her eyes and causing her dark hair to fly about wildly in the air. Deep in thought and contemplative, the connection to her outer world was diminishing as if a shutter were closing over a lens. There was so much deadness inside her.

In reality, Isadora Bright had been dying slowly for many years. Now she simply wanted it over and done with. Reflecting on her life for a moment, a stockpile of memories tumbled through her mind that she observed with numb detachment, noticing the futile cycles and patterns endlessly playing out. It seemed there was a consistent theme of her being always on her own and never feeling quite enough. Was it possible she had been an appallingly bad human being in a previous life, she wondered. At one point she had suspected so and spent large amounts of time and money attempting to improve and fix her failed self. But somehow after the long line of professional and New Age experts, and her slide into the bottom of a tequila bottle, she realized the answers were never coming, nor was the fixing.

Having pondered the philosophical reality that arriving into life was a very solitary experience, as was exiting, she knew to her bones that there was something inherently wrong about spending so much of existence on her own. Her blueprint was clearly flawed and subsequently so was her destiny, leaving her wandering on earth like a random stray. Life had become like a boring imprisonment in a twisted maze that looped her hopelessly around in circles. She didn't want to live like this anymore. And she certainly didn't want the unending meaninglessness that followed her everywhere like the stench of a rotting corpse.

It was God's fault, Isadora decided. And the great Creator hadn't seemed particularly bothered about putting in a benevolent appearance to tell her things were all okay, because they weren't, and they never would be. God was a coward, Isadora thought.

'Damn this and damn you,' she declared loudly, as if the untamed air over the cliff would carry her message across the Atlantic Ocean right to the ears of the Great Almighty. Whatever the Great Almighty really was.

I believed in you. I know I pretended not to, but I did.

Christ, what a pointless exercise, she admonished herself again. Her thoughts were entirely futile, which was why she knew it was time to finally silence them for good. God was like a child's imaginary friend that one was supposed to give up at the age of five or something, much like a fairy tale character. Either that or the great leader was like a seriously bad Chief Executive Officer of Company Earth: never showing up, missing all the meetings, leaving the place in a state of total chaos while attending to the more pressing concerns of eighteen holes of golf, then lingering over drinks at the nineteenth without conscience or consideration. God was negligent, Isadora decided. Although despite the Creator's apparent incompetence and complete lack of intervention, including the blatant absence of *miracles* flowing her way, there was nothing she could do anymore. She sighed heavily. It was time to hand in her human resignation. It was time to leave earth, a planet she never seemed to quite belong to.

Inhaling the freezing Irish air and feeling something like a mild frost form in her throat, she leaned a little closer towards the cliff edge. Plumes of thick fog rolled in beneath her. For the briefest moment Isadora remembered the magic of being a child again, gazing at stars in the night. They had enchanted her, like a million happy homes in the sky, and she had been quite certain that she came from one of them, because surely those twinkling lights held the secret of exactly what she was missing. Although whatever that was she really couldn't say, but the absent ingredient had sadly not been in the house, the porch of which her five-year-old backside had been sitting upon.

As the years had passed by, Isadora's young adult mind continued searching, only to reach the tragic conclusion: if she was never from earth, then she was never likely to find where she belonged on earth or anyone to belong with. And the evidence to date had certainly stacked up in that direction. Love eluded Isadora like the average person trying to reach the top of Everest without oxygen. It was the same precarious affair. Beautiful and inspiring from a distance, but inevitably a bloody indecent climb in treacherous conditions the reality of it actually turned out to be. The end result was generally within the parameters of terrible disaster, or death…typically a frozen one. And the wasteland of snow-covered bodies lying scattered in the ascent appeared to be largely hers, marking the locations in her lifetime where the great mountain of heartbreak had claimed her yet again.

'As if,' Isadora snorted out loud in disgust at herself 'I've never even made it to base camp. I've been nothing short of a failure,' she thought, staring numbly out at the ocean.

The rough February seas relentlessly pounded the cliffs below. The air was misty and damp late on the Irish winter's afternoon with the temperatures plummeting and the sky losing light fast. She became suddenly aware her nose felt frozen and shuddered, toying numbly with the zip on her thermal jacket. How cold her entire body felt.

Nobody will see me go.

It would be a blessing for everyone, she thought.

If her life was a play then it had run like very bad Shakespeare, a tragic farce at the end of which she didn't get to take a bow and return to an alternative happy real-life story. Yet it no longer mattered. Not today, not again. There would be no more cycles of heartache and despair, and no more hoping for things to be any different.

Just some peace.

Isadora felt her aching weary limbs as she began to stir her body off the cold wet grass. These days she was tired too easily. And cold all the time – so cold. It was as if the life force was being sucked right out of her.

It's my soul. You don't want to be here anymore, she lamented quietly, rising from the ground and taking a long moment to look at the wild ocean and the chiseled out cliffs through the mist. They were spectacular. Dark in color, stratified layers of different rock, and geometrically straight all the way down as if large chunks of land had been sliced away with a giant blade and drifted off out to sea. She caught herself admiring the beauty of it all for a moment and stubbornly reminded herself not to get distracted from what she was about to do.

She had picked the location in County Clare specifically. Flying into Shannon International Airport earlier in the day Isadora had secured a hire car and was at the Cliffs within several hours of landing. She had left her job in London several days earlier before organizing the flight and was operating in a surreal state, as if she were a ghost occupying a body she didn't belong in. Only the keenest observers would have detected how disconnected from herself she really was. Unbeknown to Isadora she was suffering badly from depression. She had avoided people and communicating for a number of weeks, with a general winding down feeling like the blips on a heart rate monitor steadily declining to a flatline.

Now there remained one more thing she needed to do before leaving, one more conversation to have. So she directed her voice to the rapidly forming mist.

'Do you exist, God? If you do, *why* didn't you help me when I needed you? I prayed. I even begged. You must have known I needed help, you must have known what I needed and wanted. You know all my heartbreaks and how it has been for me. Surely you could have done something, surely that was in your power.' Isadora felt an aching sadness stirring in her heart and began to inch closer to the edge of the cliff, leaning out a little to peer through the enveloping mist to the crashing waves far below.

'Did I matter at all?' she whispered, beginning to choke back sobs. 'Where were you?' Her knees gave way as she dropped to the ground overcome by the feeling of pain inside her chest. A sudden gust of wind flying off the ocean pushed her forcibly backwards from the edge of the cliff. The air was palpably electric as Isadora knelt clutching her chest, hearing the noise of the wind beating fiercely into her thermal jacket and feeling her eye sockets burning from the blasting cold air. Anger unexpectedly welled up from deep within her.

'Damn you!' she yelled. 'Damn you!! DAMN YOU!!' The echo of her voice carried across the ocean on the wind into a dark void. 'I needed you! Where were you?! I needed you.' Warm salty tears flowed down her face.

'I must have failed you. I failed with this life, and I'm sorry, I'm so sorry,' she whispered, feeling pain surge in her heart one more time. 'Forgive me,' she clawed her fingers into the earth dragging her body closer to the cliff edge. 'Forgive me, God. Forgive me.'

Isadora surrendered completely, she was ready and there wasn't a soul to stop her. Her mind ceased its chatter and a calm descended upon her. She felt an indescribable peace and for one of the first times she could recall, felt no fear, no anxiety or struggle, and nothing she had to do or be anymore. Just stillness. Her head was bowed low as she prepared herself for her final fall from grace.

Even the wind seemed to become still as if pausing to observe.

Chapter Two

She tapped the shut-down menu on her computer with relief, watching the apple slowly dissolve in the center of the screen. For a moment, Julie admired her beautifully manicured nails coated in soft pink lacquer, before sliding her slim elegant fingers off the keypad. The office was ghostly quiet with all but one other work colleague having long exited the building into the darkening night.

She was tired. Lately Julie felt cold all the time and was dying for some sunshine. London was miserable in February and a large proportion of its many occupants with disposable income had also had enough of the long dark winter. Booking holiday packages left, right and center, had become dreary daytime fodder for her. Canary Islands and more Canary Islands.

Let's all go eat fish and chips in the damned Canaries, she thought. Honestly, if she had to book another soul to Lanza-bloody-rotie she would stand on her desk and scream. Julie felt like having a tantrum, and beneath her iron clad professional exterior she was certainly capable of one. Possibly entitled to one too. Her brain was overloaded from copious amounts of detail and polite people-pleasing and today was no exception.

The German family had just about finished her off. She had spent almost an hour and a half with them arranging a holiday to Fuerteventura. But that was after they decided against Portugal,

Morocco, and Grand Canaria holiday packages, and after Julie had cancelled all the flights she had painstakingly spent booking and holding for the other destinations.

Trust me to get the only Germans on the planet that parked their brains with their car this morning.

It was culturally uncharacteristic of them to be so unplanned and unstructured, she thought.

Putting on her long camel-colored woolen coat, she wrapped a black scarf around her neck before reaching into her handbag and plucking out her cellphone. Three missed calls from Laney. That wasn't good.

Julie had excellent intuitive ability, but when it came to her younger sister she was downright psychic. Of course, some of that was also a combination of simply knowing her sibling so well. And frankly she had run out of enough fingers and toes to count the number of times Laney had let her down. Badly. So today it was less of a case of clairvoyancy and more simply one of good odds that she wasn't phoning her to impart glad tidings.

Farewelling her colleague she made her way to the front door of the travel agency, pressing the return connection on her cellphone as she exited the building to a slap of cold air on her face. Her nose tip began to freeze in the time it took her sister to pick up the call at the other end.

Within thirty seconds of conversation Julie could feel her blood begin to boil.

'You're damn well kidding me, Laney! What do you mean you've changed your mind. You can't, everything is booked.'

She listened seething for several minutes to the weak apology. It was a man, of course. It was always to do with a man. She didn't feel forgiving and hung up on Laney by the time it took her to reach Baker Street underground station.

Unbelievable! Little minx.

Julie was spitting tacks. She had ten days before they were supposed to be leaving for a holiday together. She was desperate for sunshine and some time away from London. This couldn't be happening.

She needed a back up plan and a new travel buddy fast. It was a shame that George wasn't available. Actually, it was more a shame that George wasn't dead. For the briefest of moments Julie felt a tinge of sadness and her heart stirred with old feelings. She squashed them in a second.

There had to be someone else.

The ticket machine sucked in her tube pass and spat it out again, opening the gates to let her through as she felt the warmer air in the underground station with a sense of relief.

Come to think of it, there was someone she could try.

She paused to retrieve her cellphone once more before heading down the escalator and began scrolling through her contacts list.

No point in mucking around. She would make the call now.

Chapter Three

'Isadora, wait.'

She heard the voice strangely all around her, a voice that was kind and calm. Yet she hadn't heard a vehicle pull up. Who knew her name? Her head remained hung and her breathing almost stopped. Peripherally she glanced out to her right and noticed a glowing light off in the thick fog. As her mind suddenly ignited back into gear she wondered if a car had driven up the road without her hearing. She had been very careful where she parked. Was it a ranger? Surely not.

Who knows me? Who knows I am here?

'We do. We know you, Isadora.' She heard the voice again, and felt the kindness in it.

Who's we? She thought. *Who the hell is we?!* And surely she hadn't spoken out loud. Was she having some sort of pre-death schizophrenic experience? The hairs on her neck rose instantly as her adrenals surged and her survival instinct ironically returned. She wanted to look but felt frozen with fear flooding back into her body.

'No need to fear, Dear One.'

There was the voice again.

Isadora mustered the courage to speak but her head remained in a fixed position staring over the cliff at the dark misted void, hearing the sound of the ocean way below.

'Who are you?'

'We are your friend,' the voice responded. It sounded so warm and kind that she found her fear subsiding and turned to locate its source.

'We are very bright. Do not look directly.'

She could see a dazzling light radiating from within the thickly formed fog and blinked a number of times as she adjusted her eyes and averted her gaze. Whatever it was, it seemed to be way off in the distance but it was large and she guessed its central core to be at least fifteen feet high and oblong in shape. There appeared to be wing formations behind it - there were two sets out to each side, and one set lower to the ground, with the largest pair at the top having a wingspan up to twelve feet in diameter. The pair beneath was narrower in diameter, and the base pair looked like large feet trailing down from the middle set of wings. They were sparkling with diamond, silver and gold, intermittent and merging colors. The body of light moved in fluid waves, at its center glowing orange and gold and throwing off a softer radius of light many meters into the mist around it.

My God, is that...

Shocked, she noticed there appeared to be a face and long golden hair but undefined features. Isadora couldn't guess how far a distance it was from her exactly as its circumference was so large, but figured it had to be at least forty meters away. Yet the voice seemed right next to her, and oddly, inside her head too. Its light was extraordinarily beautiful and dazzling, with an incredible intensity, and could have blinded her without the mist to buffer it. Isadora felt an indescribable kind of love emanating from it that rapidly dissolved her fear and made her almost euphoric in its presence. The light, she noticed, reached from the center of the energy source and ran directly through and beyond her. All the icy cold in the air around her had rapidly vanished and her body began to tingle all over with warmth that penetrated right into her bones.

She softened, feeling drawn towards it. 'Who are you, really? What are you?' she said stunned.

'We are eternally your friend, Isadora. We are Seraphim.'

'Seraphim? What is Seraphim?' she asked, more curious now. Turning her whole body, still seated on the ground, she faced the light as the melodic voice continued.

'We are part of the Angelic Realm. We are Prime Creator's highest order of Angelic servants.'

'Are you serious?' she stuttered, condemning her elementary response. After all, how often did a giant angel appear in her world.

'We are ever truthful and understand this is much for you to take in. We heard your cries. We have felt your suffering and your pain in this life.' Isadora noticed the colors at its center changing from orange to a vibrant indigo blue and purple.

'We feel all the suffering of humanity and we transmute this negative energy in service of Prime Creator.' The voice was soft and beautiful.

'You mean, Gggod?' Isadora stumbled over the word.

'Yes, Dear One. This is one of the many references to the all pervading Source.'

'Oh,' was all she could think to say, suddenly feeling very humbled and uncomfortable.

After some hesitation she continued. 'So why are you...appearing here, before...me?'

'Because dear Isadora, our deepest prayer is that you remain here to fulfill your earthly purpose, and we seek your assistance. The suffering on this planet has become great, so much pain and struggle. Humanity has lost its way, it has forgotten.' The radiant light pulsated blue and green.

'Forgotten what?'

'Forgotten they chose this. Forgotten they chose their life, chose all of it. That it was the greatest joy for their soul to reside in this dimension and experience. They have forgotten their greatness, their power and ability to create beauty and love; forgotten the heart of the Creator resides always within them - there is no separation. Every soul has chosen this life, you cannot come to earth without already being perfect. You are already perfection. Yet you would call yourself a failure and consider being here a mistake in the face of the greatest gift and opportunity.'

'What gift and opportunity?'

'Life, in physical form.'

Isadora paused. 'Look, that all sounds great in theory, but I can't say that I see it quite the same way from here.'

'Of this we are aware.'

Shrinking on the spot, she was suddenly overcome with guilt and shame.

'Do not condemn yourself further with guilt. Change the thought. Understand the mistake as simply what it was and change the thought direction to a positive one. Waste no more precious time and life in guilt.' The Seraphim continued gently. 'We understand the yearning for home. You believe deep down you are far from source and your soul longs to be back, yet as we say, there is no separation. The journey and growth here on earth is best for you on all levels. Recognizing this is where you are and that you chose this experience endows you with the power and ability to create consciously. Knowing you have chosen this life, chosen all of it...and you have done so for a purpose, will help you release the negative thoughts that have held you back and brought you to this precipice. What is required of you, what we ask of you now Isadora, is Faith.'

'Faith?'

'Yes. A return to Faith will expose you to endless experiences based on new and creative thoughts. This is much for you to take in and we must depart soon. But will you stay now? Stay and assist us in a great service. We ask this of you with deep love, appreciation, and reverence for your soul.'

'I...I...well I don't understand any of this. I doubt that I can assist you in any way. I'm just one simple person and not a particularly effective one at that,' Isadora responded, confused and overwhelmed.

'Oh Dear One, if only you could see what we can. If only you knew the magnificence of who you are...of each and every soul here on earth.'

'But why this soul? Why me?!'

'Because you don't really wish to end this life, do you Isadora. Above all what you most wish for is *to Live,* and to live fully, deeply, profoundly, and freely...*with Love.* It is your love for life that has brought you this far. And it is your passion turned painfully back on yourself through mistaken thoughts, blame, guilt, condemnation and a sense of worthlessness, that has led you to believe there is no other way out but to end life in this physical form. Yet you have purity and yearning in your heart. It has always been with you - and any undertaking that is ever to amount to anything requires this. You never forgot. You have simply believed too much in the illusions of this world, yet have always known there is something greater in existence. You *do* believe, and you have courage and heart beyond measure.'

Isadora was quiet as she absorbed the words, feeling tears rolling softly down her face. 'I don't feel particularly courageous. I'm standing on a cliff ready to end my life. That's not courageous, it's cowardly,' she hung her head in shame. 'I just couldn't take it here anymore. I've been knocked down, betrayed and abandoned, more times than I could take. I couldn't feel more of a failure. It has been too hard...feeling this much is too hard.' She was fighting to hold back a reservoir of tears.

'Every soul has meaning and purpose on this earth and every soul is loved deeply without exception. You said you could not take it anymore Isadora, but we say it is not the experiences you cannot take,' the voice responded lovingly, 'it is the grinding down of your faith through your own perception, to the point that it is all but gone. It is the loss of your faith that crushes your spirit and that you cannot live another day without. You have taken each event in your life and made it have a meaning that is fearful and devoid of love. The past has continued to rule your present, despite it being gone, and this is a large burden for you to carry. It has caused in you a sense of defeat, a separation from your truth and a loss of faith. So now you are required to *trust* again. We will send you one amongst us to guide you. They have been with you before and you will know this. You have all the support you need and always have had. You are never alone, and you have never been alone. We have always loved you and will forever more. Understand this. You need only choose your thoughts more wisely to direct your life. And now we depart.' Isadora noticed the beautiful light beginning to fade and began to feel an unexpected sense of panic.

'But what will I do?' she said scrambling to her feet. 'You haven't told me what you want me to do? Where do I go now?' Emotion rose in her voice. All the warmth and colors of the Seraphim were beginning to draw back as they appeared to be sucked right into the core of the giant angelic being. The wind blew once more off the coastline pushing her body forcefully inland and she started moving toward the vanishing light.

'Tell me. What do you want?' she yelled, throwing her arms up in the air.

'Faith Isadora, find your faith again. We will guide you. Love, peace and blessings to you...always,' she heard the voice drifting off in the wind. 'Faith...find your faith...'

Isadora stared long into the mist after the light had disappeared.

Eventually she returned to the cliff edge to take one last look and was overcome with horror at what she had almost done.

Jesus, did I almost jump off this cliff?! What the heck was I thinking?!

Her body shook as tears of relief stung her eyes and for a moment she paused to reflect on the events that had just occurred. She needed to get far away from these cliffs right now. If what the angelic being had said was true, she had almost made her greatest mistake ever. She could still feel the warmth in her body, it was real. The angel's appearance had actually happened.

Taking a final tear-stained look through the fog at the two hundred foot drop, she turned and moved quietly towards the vehicle.

Chapter Four

He figured she was one of them the moment she walked into the bar. He had a sixth sense about these things. Likely he had inherited it from his Grandmother who always claimed to see spirits, and sometimes had prophetic visions. Paddy had learned to listen to everything his Grandmother said with great care as he grew up. She had saved his life a number of times. Like the day she told him not go out on the O'Flannagan's boat and it had capsized that same afternoon, drowning his schoolmate Fergal. He never doubted her gift after that. Sadly Granny was gone now, but he still liked to think she was watching over him.

He had inherited some of her gift to be sure and he could sense the woman was a troubled soul the moment she walked into O'Hagan's bar. Exactly how troubled he wasn't sure, but he felt compelled to find out. Paddy watched her order a large meal with an extra side of roast potatoes, bread, and a pint of Guinness. It wasn't even twelve noon and she was showing signs of an exceptionally large appetite for a skinny lass.

She was comfortably seated at a table near the crackling open fire. Waiting patiently until she finished her meal, Paddy watched her quietly from a distance for some time. She had sad eyes. A striking green color - but they were sad. She had suffered loss, he would bet on it.

Maybe it was his Grandmother directing him from afar, but it suddenly seemed very important that she didn't leave O'Hagan's bar until she'd had a spot of uplifting Irish company. He ordered two pints of Guinness and approached her with a warm engaging smile.

'Paddy Sullivan. I'm pleased to meet you,' he said boldly setting the pints down and sitting on the chair opposite her. He had always had a great gift of being able to corner the ladies.

She looked startled, like he'd just punctured her private bubble.

'Isadora,' she said quietly.

She wasn't looking as thrilled as he had hoped. He would have to pull his greatest Irish charm out of his butt, that was clear. 'Isadora, a pleasure to meet you. Now what brings you to this beautiful land?'

'Just some sightseeing.' Her response was unmoved.

'Sightseeing, you say? Cliffs of Moher, yes?'

The woman was clearly feeling discomfort under his intense stare and he watched her promptly swallow back a third of the pint of Guinness. Paddy considered himself a master conversationalist and launched into a blow-by-blow account of his former travels, including a trip to the Middle East where he'd enjoyed the heat and marveled at the Pyramids and the Sphinx. Isadora appeared happy to sit back and listen. Maybe it was the alcohol beginning to warm her blood and her temperament, but he could tell within ten minutes she was enjoying his company. He felt certain of it. When she wasn't nervous and looking like a startled sparrow she was actually very radiant, although a little older than he had first thought. Possibly five or six years older than his youthful twenty eight years. Managing to make her laugh a number of times revealed a different and more relaxed woman. He finished up the tale of his Middle Eastern adventure. 'So if you ever get a chance to go to Egypt, you simply must. You really haven't lived until you've been there.'

'I'm quite sure I haven't lived much at all, Paddy. Perhaps I shall. Besides, I've always wanted to go there.' She smiled more brightly than before.

He knew the moment when an open door was before him and he seized the opportunity like a child reaching for the candy floss. On his feet in a flash, he motioned her to follow. When she remained fixed he nudged her arm, encouraging her out of the chair.

'Well come on, I have to show you some real Irish sights while we still have some daylight.'

'I can't...I...'

'I what?' Paddy responded matter-of-factly. 'I'm the perfect guide and gentleman. Would be an utter waste to visit these parts and not let me show you around.'

'Well I...'

'Well nothing. Come on, I'm parked out front. Can't have a guest in our great country looking gloomy. It's terrible publicity for Ireland.' His accent was lyrical.

A tiny smile creased her face as she collected her jacket from the back of the chair and followed Paddy out of O'Hagan's into the cold, where he hurried her toward a muddied four-wheel drive parked out front.

'Now buckle up, Miss Isadora, I just got my license last week.'

She looked at him, horrified.

'I'm kidding, just kidding. You Kiwis are a gullible bunch aren't you,' he said.

'How did you know where I'm from?' Isadora raised her eyebrows.

'I met a lot of Kiwis and Australians traveling in the Middle East. There's really no hiding that New Zealand accent, or anything at all from me Isadora, to be sure,' he added, searching her eyes for a moment longer than necessary.

***

Paddy proved his tour guide expertise. First they drove North to the Karst limestone landscape in Burren, then to the Buttaray castle, and finally into the charming town of Ennis where another pint of Guinness washed down the dust of the back roads. He had managed to make her laugh a lot and was feeling particularly chuffed about it, so when he went very quiet on the drive back to the village Isadora found the silence unusual.

'So, just a real flying visit to Ireland then?' He finally spoke again as they had almost reached O'Hagan's again. 'You did say you have seen the famous Cliffs of Moher, yes?'

'Yes, I did yesterday, before finding Molly's Bed and Breakfast.' She motioned her head to indicate the location over the road from the pub.

'You know, those cliffs have certainly claimed their share of casualties,' Paddy continued pointedly.

'Oh, really?' She looked uncomfortable again.

'Well, we lose a few over the side you know. Some accidental, but most on purpose. People just up and jump right off. Hard to believe why someone would do such a thing, isn't it,' he said glancing sideways at her and watching her squirm nervously. 'I don't think there is any honor in taking your own life. Not to mention the unbelievable devastation to family and friends, leaving all that terrible guilt and grief like a form of punishment.'

'Terribly sad,' she muttered, avoiding eye contact with him and turning her head away toward the fading light.

'Aye, Isadora. To be sure. I think we all have a responsibility to live our lives, and not only for ourselves. Besides, life's too grand to throw away, surely. You just have to take a moment to feel the breeze on your face, swim in a glorious ocean, smile at the eyes of another…it's simple. You have to give things a crack and if you get knocked down have faith that there's something else good around the corner. Least, that's the way I see it,' he said as they pulled up in front of Molly's Bed and Breakfast. 'But I expect you know that. You look like someone who has a lot of living to do.'

She avoided his penetrating eyes.

'Well, here's your bed for the night,' he finished with a wink.

'Thank you, Paddy, for everything. I mean that.'

'Was my great pleasure, Isadora.' He was aching to give her a hug because something told him she needed one, but she was already out of the vehicle, so he wound down his window. 'And remember Egypt, Kiwi. You must go there,' he said watching her head off across the road pulling her jacket tightly around her.

His instinct had been right, she was a jumper. He could feel it to his bones. Why a woman so pretty would even consider such a thing he couldn't fathom, but she hadn't gone through with it and she wouldn't now, of that he was certain.

Paddy quietly thanked his Gran as he drove off into the night.

Chapter Five

Having arrived at the village the previous night dazed and in shock, Isadora had been too exhausted for anything but sleep. Thankfully Molly, the rosy-cheeked older woman at the Bed and Breakfast establishment she had found, had fixed her up with a room. She'd also told her she could get a great meal at O'Hagan's over the road. And she had.

The lunch earlier in the day had been spectacularly good. She'd wanted to order more food and then Paddy had shown up. She thought about her day as she followed the crimson carpeted stairs for the second night to her room. It was cozy with a double bed covered in a pink floral bed cover. She smiled as she looked at the kaleidoscope before her. So many European Bed and Breakfasts she had stayed in seemed to have bright pink and red flowery bedspreads or curtains, or both. Still, it was cheerful, she thought, noticing an old-fashioned doily with dried pink and red flowers in a vase sitting on the only dresser in the room.

By the time she climbed into bed her eyelids were already falling shut, but in the last thirty seconds before she fell into a deep sleep she thought about Paddy. He had the wildest spriggy brown hair she'd ever seen. She had trusted him; her intuition had told her she could. As she felt herself drifting off she recalled his electric blue eyes filled with intensity, staring into her soul, compelling her to embrace her life again. Somehow he'd guessed the reason for her trip to the Cliffs. Exactly how, she couldn't say, but he had imparted the preciousness of each moment of living to her. Thinking about his words, and before slipping into a restful slumber, her last feeling was one of gratitude for having met him.

***

Sometime in the hours before dawn, Isadora stirred awake. She was sure she heard a voice speaking but for a while she couldn't even remember where she was. As her memory finally placed her in a bed in County Clare, Ireland, she became aware of an orange light glowing in her room. She hadn't left the curtains open. And when she had looked out the window the previous night there were no signs of buildings or street lights below.

'Greetings, Dear One' said a melodic voice from the corner of the room.

Isadora sat bolt upright as she drew the bedding tightly around her. She immediately noticed a soft glowing image similar to the Seraphim that had appeared to her, but so much smaller. It was more human in size and the light, although dazzling, with the same undulating waves of gold, silver, and orange in its core, was easier on her eye. It even had a beautiful gentle face, but its wings appeared to be folded down.

'They don't fit in your room.'

'I'm sorry?!' said Isadora stunned.

'My wings. They don't fit in your room.'

'Oh.' Her jaw dropped. After a slight pause it dawned on Isadora that the thing in the corner, that appeared to be an angel, had read her mind.

'Yes, I know your thoughts. I know everything about you, Isadora.'

'You're the Seraphim emissary, right?' She was aware of loving energy radiating from the light and her fear dissolved rapidly.

'That is true. I am an angel. Part of the Seraphim. You can call me Seraph. I am your guide and lovingly at your service,' it said in a soft voice.

She tried desperately to comprehend what was happening to her and remembered the Seraphim telling her whoever they were sending had been with her before and she would know, which confused her.

'Yes Isadora, I have been with you before.'

'I don't know that. I don't know you,' she responded a little suspiciously. 'When?'

'Think Isadora. Remember.'

'Okay. It's your voice and the way I hear you both inside and outside my head at the same time.' She hesitated before a look of surprise formed on her face. 'I *have* heard you before.'

'This is also true. Do you remember when?' The angel said softly.

Isadora paused for a minute. Seraph was silent, allowing her the time and space for her memories to flow back. She noticed the angel's core color changing from orange to yellow. 'I remember,' she said triumphantly. 'My car accident. You were there with me then, weren't you.'

'I was.'

'You were the voice I heard twenty minutes before I had the accident.' Isadora began to recall the traumatic experience from the previous decade like it was yesterday. 'You said *No, not here*, didn't you. I've never forgotten that. I was so certain someone was in the car with me that I looked straight at the passenger seat expecting a person to be sitting there. It sounded like a direct order?' Isadora's curiosity was fully engaged as she began seeking answers from many years ago.

'The corner you initially swerved on was not a good place to have an accident. Our calculations and awareness informed us that your earth body would not survive. I had to intercede radically.'

'Oh,' responded Isadora, feeling more confused. 'So you didn't want me to have the car accident there, but further down the road?'

'This is correct. Your soul had chosen the accident, Isadora. We could not alter that choice. However, I could intervene to ensure your survival.'

'Really? And why was that?' She was suddenly feeling a little annoyed at the concept that she had *chosen* her car accident.

'Because it was not your time, Isadora. It was not your time then, just as it was not your time yesterday. You have far too much to do here on earth. Far too much,' Seraph said softly.

'So you're saying it was *my* choice to have the car accident?' she replied agitatedly, ignoring his words and continuing like a dog that had just snatched onto a bone.

'Indeed.'

'Well perhaps you could explain to me why I would choose that?'

'Isadora, there are so many things you do not understand about the true nature of human existence. It would be impossible to try and convey them all. In short, your soul required the experience for its own unique reasons. You could say for healing. You wanted to know and experience yourself more deeply. You wanted a higher understanding of yourself and life. So let us just say that on this occasion you were fast-tracking your growth.'

'Wow, and I thought I was just an incompetent driver.'

'Well, possibly a little of that too.' The angel chuckled. 'Your concentration could have been better. But tell me what you remember of the accident?'

'Okay.' She leaned back against her pillow, more relaxed. 'Twenty minutes or so after I heard your voice in the car, I was on a straight stretch of road and I looked down to change the music. The next thing I knew, I was swerving across the road heading towards a lake. I recall very clearly that it felt like slow motion as I traveled across the road and I had all the time in the world to think about my entire life. I knew I might not survive the accident and yet I can recall very clearly that I had a choice to live - I had a choice to stay or to go.'

'And what did you think of your twenty one years of life at that point?'

'Honestly? I wasn't very impressed. It was clear that something was missing. I don't think I realized until then how empty I felt inside.' Isadora looked down sadly at the patterns on her bold bedspread.

'You're doing great, Isadora. And what else?' The angel's voice was so kind.

'I became aware I wasn't in my body, I was *behind* my body. What I mean is, my body was driving the car, but I was behind myself, in the back seat of the car. I realized then that I wasn't actually my body…who I *really am* just inhabits it. It was a pretty profound moment. There was this whole other aspect to life, to me, to being alive, something more than just my body. And then I chose.'

'What did you choose?

'You know the answer to this,' she stared at the angel. 'I chose Life. I yelled, *I want to Live, I want to Live* - and then I was back in my body turning the wheel of the car to avoid the concrete wall that separated the road from the lake. The car smashed into the wall side-on, eventually skidding to a halt. It was a write-off, yet I walked away with only minor whiplash,' she paused. 'You know, I could never figure out how I managed to turn the steering wheel fast enough that day. It seems impossible in hindsight.'

'Well, I gave you a hand, Isadora.'

'Really?'

'Yes, really.'

'Wow. Thank you,' she responded quietly.

'A pleasure dear one, always in loving service. Now you really need to get some more rest. I will visit you again, often. And at times you will hear my voice guiding you.'

'I have more questions, though,' she began to feel suddenly very sleepy.

'The answers you seek will all come in time.'

'Seraph?' Isadora used the angel's name for the first time. 'The Seraphim yesterday referred to itself as *we* all the time. Why was that?'

'Well, it was more than one Seraph. It was a collective of Thrones from the highest Triad of the Angelic order. Quite an honor really. It's very rare for so many to combine as one energy and appear on earth. And we had to produce all that fog so only you could see us.'

'But why did you show yourselves…to me?' Isadora asked shyly.

'Oh, I think you could refer to it in human analogy as *shock and awe*.' Just one little angel like me appearing on my own probably wouldn't have impressed you enough. You humans receive miracles all the time and it's often not enough. Like you forgot the experience of your car accident and the splendor of another chance at life. You needed the big wow factor, Isadora. Besides, you've been praying a lot for a long time, and we listen.'

'So what do I do now?'

'Follow my guidance and your own intuition. Trust each moment and allow your life to unfold. Sleep. Tomorrow you will return to England. Now I must go. I hope you enjoyed your day today, Isadora.'

'Yes I did. I met Paddy. He was nice.' She was feeling so sleepy now.

'Paddy, a very good and wise soul.' Seraph's core was changing to a vibrant purple indigo color.

'You know him?' She yawned feeling her eyelids becoming heavier.

'Indeed. I arranged for him to show you around.'

'That's nice,' Isadora slurred.

She never saw the angel disappear. She was fast asleep before that happened.

Chapter Six

Julie had tried calling three times over the past twenty-four hours without success. She had emailed her work address too, but had received an automated response saying that Isadora was no longer with the company.

So where the hell is she?

It had been six weeks since they had last spoken and come to think of it she had sounded a little flat on the phone. But Julie had put that down to her missing the new boyfriend who was away on a trip. Harold, was that his name? Damn, she couldn't recall. Isadora was probably on her honeymoon with him by now. She was such a dark horse it wouldn't surprise her if that were the case at all.

Of course, things could have gone the other way too. Isadora did seem to have a knack of attracting men that ended up completely stuffing her around. She was just too nice a person, Julie thought. Not like her, she reflected. She had once thrown a stiletto in a fit of rage at a cheating boyfriend and almost punctured his cheek. She grimaced at the thought.

I could have ruined my gorgeous shoe. Absolute travesty.

Still, Julie justified that as a woman you had to have a bit of mongrel in you to combat the weak genetics of some men and survive them. She had learned early and mostly never looked back. Her motto in relationships was to always withhold ten percent. That way not only did she remain a mystery to her men, more importantly she could never be completely hurt by them. Mostly this had worked. Mostly.

Except for George. He had taken her completely by surprise, both in his arrival and his departure from her life. She had thought him *The One,* conceded the precious ten percent, and had paid for it dearly.

Never again! And part Italian…I should have bloody known.

But she had fallen in love with him, quite profoundly. He was older, distinguished, charming, passionate, and always made her feel like a million dollars and the only woman in the world. Of course, she discovered, he made his wife feel the same. That news in itself was something she could have almost handled, even forgiven, but leaving her because he had conceived a child to another lover was more than her dignity and her heart could take. George was a classic male cliché and she had fallen for him completely - which embarrassingly placed her in the category of being a classic female cliché. She couldn't have been more appalled, particularly as she had always prided herself on spotting deception after an earlier great heartbreak that slipped through her defensive net had left her bedridden for weeks.

George had left her bedridden for days.

Eventually, after a number of dramatic intervention calls from her gay friend and work colleague Xavier, she had crawled out of her dark bedroom and into the bottom of a gin bottle. This was progress, despite the fact that gin made her cry. At least she had begun to feel again, and thankfully Xavier loved to listen to a woman weep. He said it reminded him of when his parents used to make love. Julie had never dared get him to elaborate.

By the time she had blasted through the anger and denial stages, she was spraying on her tightest pair of black denims and sexiest top and was back in a bar gyrating against the pelvis of the hottest man she could attract. And Julie could always attract the hottest man, no exception.

With the healing almost complete, she arrived back at work to a bottle of Dom Perignon on her desk with a beautifully handwritten note from Xavier that simply said *'Gloria Gaynor and I are proud of you. Welcome back darling!'*

She had promptly booked the ten-day holiday to Egypt, factoring in that hundreds of dark swarthy men staring at her would surely boost her battered ego. And she had coaxed her sister Laney to join her without revealing a smidgeon of her wounded soul. That was three weeks ago. Now she was in a bit of a pickle. There was no way she was going to travel alone, especially not with blonde hair in Egypt. She should have asked Isadora in the first place. She would make a perfect traveling companion: quiet but easily led. Her intuition was screaming at her Izzy was the best person to take.

If she could just get hold of her.

Chapter Seven

She slept soundly until eight in the morning, but then spent an extra half hour in bed reflecting on the strange conversation with Seraph before moving a muscle. Ever practical, Isadora was glad she had brought an overnight bag with a little makeup and skincare. She was the kind of person who if told a nuclear bomb was about to explode, would bring out a suitcase and start packing for different weather possibilities. Although on this occasion she hadn't needed to think too far ahead.

She gingerly made her way naked and cold to the window and pulled the curtains open wide. She hadn't bothered to open them yesterday because she'd slept so late and was so darn hungry she had showered and bolted for O'Hagan's Bar without a thought. Now she was pleasantly surprised at the beautiful and picturesque view of fields of deep green grass blending into rolling hills.

God, I forgot how much I love wide-open spaces and lush green grass.

She had forgotten the value of nature and how healing it was for her. The natural earth had so many remedies. The grey London cityscape was very depressing in comparison.

'Perfect,' she said with a smile, absorbing the view before heading to the shower.

Throwing on her soft pink turtleneck sweater with her jeans and boots for the second day running, she made her way downstairs to reception and pressed the buzzer. Molly Flannigan appeared in the same bustling manner as she had the night before.

'Ah, you're awake, lass. I expect you'll want some breakfast. You need a good feeding up, my girl. We'll fix up the bill later. I don't want you passing out on me,' she said with mock concern.

'Thank you,' Isadora responded, following Molly through to the breakfast room.

She devoured her large cooked breakfast as she had the meal the day before. The Irish breakfast was legendary - they considered the first meal of the day the most important for building energy. She was not disappointed and even had seconds, which seemed to please the Irishwoman immensely. It was as if Isadora's value as a person increased exponentially the more food she consumed. If Molly had been a stockbroker dealing in the commodity of human fat, Isadora's share price would most certainly have just rocketed in value.

She tucked a couple of delicious looking muffins into a napkin before departing the dining room at speed. She had a plane to catch.

***

Sometime in the night she'd had another visitation from Seraph, she was sure of it. But having been so darned tired and deeply asleep she didn't have a clue what the angel had said to her. So when she boarded the plane at Shannon headed for Heathrow Airport, Isadora had the uneasy feeling that she may have missed an important message. She was beginning to feel anxiety resurfacing at the thought of returning to London. It was the kind of discomfort that had plagued her on and off for many years, since her dysfunctional long-term relationship with Tom.

It had developed as a destructive kind of emotional pattern inside her that over time became tripped with relative ease. It was never just a mild anxiety attack when it struck. It whipped in via her stomach like a gigantic Midwestern tornado, with a ferocity that left her reeling. Biological acid and negative thoughts were its weaponry and neither made Isadora feel particularly well, or very good about herself.

However the conversation on the cliff with the Seraphim had certainly made her aware that she had to do some serious work on replacing her negative thoughts. Despite this new resolve she was quaking in her boots by the time she stepped onto the plane. Flying had also become a major challenge in recent years, although on the flight over from England several days ago it hadn't been quite so bad. Back then she hadn't cared if the plane dropped into the ocean. Now she did.

I'll be fine, she told herself as she shuffled down the aisle to find her seat, because she now had friends in very high places and surely they could pilot a 747 Jet. The main thing was that she was not alone. If she repeated this like a mantra to herself, much like the chanting she had been taught in yoga classes, it would be a piece of cake. Surely.

First to arrive in her row, she stowed her carry-on bag in the overhead compartment and took her allocated window seat.

'Oh bugger,' she said looking out the window and noticing the plane's engine directly below. 'Just what I need. Not.' Rolling her eyes to the heavens, she noticed anxiety beginning to surface at the thought of flying in turbulence. It was in bumpy air that Isadora would grip on to the arm rests, stare blankly into space, and deploy the power of prayer at its most intense level.

She began the only repetitive inner mantra she could think of '*I'm not alone, I'm not alone*' to distract herself before take off, praying that the angels could clear the skies, or at least direct the plane through calm airspace.

'Is this seat taken?' A tall dark-haired man leaned in from the aisle motioning to her handbag lying in the seat beside her.

'I'm not alone.' The words flew out of her mouth before she could snatch them back and for a moment she cringed in her seat with horror. To add to her embarrassing outburst, the man was totally good-looking. He raised an eyebrow, looking a little perplexed and causing Isadora to feel compelled to redeem herself.

'What I mean is, I was traveling with a friend…girlfriend, but she's still in Ireland. The seat is free.' She squirmed inwardly at her gibberish and quickly snatched up her bag, wishing she could put a zipper on her mouth.

'Thanks.'

He had an easy smile and looked like a nice man. Although she always seemed to think that initially only to discover she had it all hideously wrong. But his brown eyes were definitely kind. They had the same twinkly kindness that Paddy had. As he slid his way into the seat beside her she couldn't help but notice the expert fit of his jeans on his lean and strong-looking physique. His thick black jumper fitted snuggly on his broad chest and his short black hair appeared to be styled with some product.

God, he smells good.

Feeling awkward, Isadora turned to look out the window as though there were something of interest outside. *Alas, the engine,* she sighed to herself. She was surprised she couldn't hear the thunderous laughing of angels as the plane began to taxi down the runway and prepare for take off. How hysterical for them.

Oh well, at least she had worn her pretty pink jumper today *yet again*, and the same jeans tucked inside her suede boots that she had worn solidly the last two days. She leaned down to take a subtle sniff of her top. But really, what else had she to wear? It wasn't as if she'd packed for a European ski vacation. At least she had applied a little make-up and was looking reasonably feminine in her outfit.

Thank God for small mercies.

In any case, why was she worrying about what she looked like, or the plane crashing, or anything for that matter. Yesterday she had almost jumped off a two hundred foot cliff, on purpose! With that simple thought and restored perspective, she realized it was enough to simply be alive. Sure, her life was an unknown, but wasn't that actually part of the adventure of it.

Staying quietly in her thoughts for some time, Isadora relived the surreal events of the past two days, as the plane finally paused on the runway and began building speed for take off. Her stomach lurched. For a minute, she focused on calming her mind and relaxing again, taking a deep full breathe as she had been taught in yoga classes and exhaling long and slow.

'Nervous flyer?' The handsome man asked, jolting her from her inner space.

'Just the take off. And the landing. Oh, and any turbulence in the air.' She turned shyly to look at him. Wow, he was even better up close. A nice strong jawline, beautiful lips and...*stop it*!

'So...pretty much the whole flying experience,' he smiled again. 'I'm Josh.'

'Isadora,' she said a little shyly.

'Do you live in Ireland, or were you visiting?'

'Just some travel. You know, weekend trip, see some sights.'

'Cliffs of Moher?'

'Yes,' she looked at him with a quizzical expression.

'Most visitors flying into Shannon go and see the cliffs. They're pretty spectacular. I just took a look at them yesterday.'

'Are you on a holiday?'

'No, it's a work trip. I'm an engineer. I was just checking on a finished project. I've been over here for a few days.'

'Oh, what was your project?' Isadora asked becoming suddenly aware that the plane was in the air and she hadn't noticed it lifting off.

Josh was captivating, chatting easily about his work and life in general. It transpired he was American by birth, with some Hopi Indian descent to which he credited his love of the land and a strong gut instinct. It was information and an openness that surprised Isadora. He'd lived in London for three years, was busy and successful with his work, but missed spending time in nature. Isadora was guessing by his timeline of University study and years in Arizona and abroad that he must be around the mid-thirties in age. Surprisingly she couldn't see a wedding ring on his finger. Surely a guy like that would have been snapped up years ago, she thought to herself. Women could be quite predatory, after all. But she'd never had that *bag him and tag him* kind of mentality.

God, how unappealing. She screwed her face up.

Isadora had witnessed first hand the femme fatale sizing up men with the *'he's mine'* attitude, in pursuit with calculated precision, much like a predatory animal. To her it seemed like a reversal of the sexes, only the hunter was cloaked with a sweet sickly smile and designer dress. Only the strong survived and reproduced and she had clearly missed that clever feminine gene as well. In fact, she'd mostly been a casualty of it – that or the guy who chewed women up for breakfast and spat them out. Neither scenario was a good deal and she had sampled them both to a PhD level, which partly explained why she was where she was in life.

Deeply romantic at heart, Isadora knew she could only be with a man for love, pure and simple. Otherwise she was destined to wander the planet aimlessly on her own, which was evidently the way things had been going.

That or jump off a cliff. She grimaced inwardly at the thought.

Her choices with men to date had certainly not been the greatest. She clearly had a blind spot when it came to her selection process.

'So what about you, Isadora? You know all about me now and I know nothing about you...except perhaps that you're from somewhere in the Southern Hemisphere?' There was his lovely smile again, twinkling like a toothpaste commercial.

'Yes, New Zealand...Land of the Long White Cloud.'

'Of course. And Lord of the Rings,' he added, and they were off on a whole new topic. He loved all types of film too.

It was some time into the flight when Isadora was in mid-sentence about her favorite actors when the *fasten seatbelt* light came on. The plane began to bump about in the air. Instantly losing her train of thought she promptly dug her fingers into both armrests.

Josh was quick to notice her discomfort.

'Hey, it will be all right. I'm an engineer, trust me.'

'Sure,' said Isadora, who was focusing intensely on her churning stomach as the plane started to drop into a succession of air pockets. '...when we land.'

'Try focusing on your breathing,' he said laying his hand on top of hers. 'We'll be through this in no time.'

Although surprised at the action, his hand was enormously comforting. She felt herself calm down, becoming aware of her slowing breath. Remaining silent, she stared straight ahead as the plane buffeted a few minutes longer and eventually evened out.

'Are you okay?' He leaned into her, surprising her completely by squeezing the back of her hand in a supportive gesture.

'Yes, much better thanks,' she said, throwing him a small smile in appreciation. 'You know, I didn't used to be this bad flying.' For a moment Isadora remembered a time when being thirty thousand feet in a plane brought her happiness.

'No? What happened?'

'I'm not sure. Life. A few shocks along the way,' she said quietly staring at the seat in front of her, unable to make light of things. He paused for a while, listening patiently to her silence. She half expected him to tell her to *'Harden up,'* as Tom would have done on one of his softer more complimentary days. But he didn't say a word, just waited to see that she had finished speaking. She was amazed. And even more amazing to her was that he still had his hand on hers...and she liked it there.

'Hey, it's not like people don't get hit with uncertain events at times. It's just...well, I guess a couple of them slipped through the net and landed in my nervous system.' She shrugged her shoulders and looked away again, suddenly feeling very exposed and fighting down the impulse to bolt from his understanding gaze. Miraculously the pilot announced their approach into London Heathrow. She found herself thanking her angel, but was disappointed to feel Josh lift his hand, slightly awkwardly, off hers.

'Well, you're almost on the ground again. Now it's back to London and work,' he said.

'Actually, no.' She absorbed the fact quietly. 'I resigned from my job recently, so life is a bit of a blank canvas at the moment.'

'Lucky you. More travel?' He smiled at her, looking directly into her eyes.

'Very probable.'

'Somewhere hot?'

'Absolutely,'

'By boat,' he suggested.

And they both laughed.

Isadora barely noticed the plane descending for the runway.

Chapter Eight

The touch down at Heathrow occurred without a hitch and Josh and Isadora chatted easily with each other all the way to the baggage carousel. He was not like she might have expected – the good-looking, big-ego type. Instead she found herself relaxing more and more, losing her initial self-consciousness. By the time it came to part she really didn't want to say goodbye.

'Well, Isadora, I really enjoyed meeting you.'

'I did too.'

'Look, I hope you don't think this forward of me, but can I get your number? I'd like to take you out for dinner sometime, if you'd like to?'

If I'd like to? He's kidding, right.

'Well...sure. That would be nice.' Her heart began to race as he pulled out his cellphone and entered her number.

She hadn't cared about her phone before she left for Ireland. Actually, she hadn't cared about anything, least of all herself, so she hadn't bothered to take it with her – it was back in her flat. But as she watched his fingers hastily tapping the screen she now wished she had it on her.

'I'll call you. Have a safe journey home,' he said simply before turning and walking away.

Yes, but did he enter the right number?!

She almost skipped to catch her train from Heathrow to Paddington Station where she could connect with the Northern Line to Golders Green. Boarding a carriage, she found a quiet corner where the nearest person was several rows away. Much of the journey was spent staring out the window watching houses and land merge into a blur, thinking about his hand resting on hers. It was hard to forget the feeling, but then she wasn't really trying to forget it at all.

He actually wants to see me again.

If he wanted to see her again then he would definitely do something about it. All she needed to worry about was what she would wear. So she did worry. Within five minutes she had whipped herself into another state of unrest, but it was infinitely more than was necessary. She liked him, that was all. So why the big fuss?

In another five minutes it was downright panic, but panic about what exactly?

Her breathing now erratic, her mind was beginning to slide down the familiar black hole of terror. It was like taking a hydro-slide ride in pitch darkness with cut glass sticking in the sides all the way down. It was her own living hell and the angels unfortunately hadn't removed it with their visit.

I need a lobotomy.

Isadora attempted to slow her breathing. Now everything was irrationally out of control and she knew it. This wasn't how she used to be. If only she could remember a time when she was calm and together.

Think of a beach. I just need to imagine I'm lying in the sun on a beach relaxing.

Why was this happening to her? This irrational overwhelming anxiety. And so frequently. Why?

But she knew why.

She remembered all the times that he had told her she was

nothing, that she was weak. He had called her horrible names, even angrily dragged her around the house by her feet. He'd stuck his fist in her face threateningly far too often – many times more than the acceptable zero. But he had never hit her, ever. At least not visibly; not in a way that left bruises on her skin. At times she thought it would have been easier if he had, leaving some tangible evidence of damage. Instead, every ounce of her light loving spirit had shut down under the assault of his cruel verbal blows.

Eventually she couldn't hear her own voice inside her head. She couldn't see anymore - his sight had become hers. She saw herself through his own damaged critical eyes, and every word he spoke about her became her truth. Every jarring jagged word. She was a feeble caged bird living on instruction and she was nobody she recognized anymore. But he had loved her, surely. After all, he had been the one who would pick her up and nurture her childlike tears afterward. He had parented her. He had controlled her. He had owned her.

Yes, it would have been far better if she'd had bruises on her skin. Instead, her soul had been stripped bare and buried in some forgotten land.

Who can love me now? Who would ever want this?

Tears welled up in her eyes as she felt an avalanche of pain descending upon her and her breathing becoming small and rapid.

'Isadora.' A kind and familiar voice startled her. 'This is an emotional habit. Keep breathing. Just focus on the moment.' It was Seraph. Only, the angel seemed to be sitting invisibly in the empty passenger seat right beside her. She glanced around the carriage to check if anyone else on the train had heard the voice but it was virtually empty and no one appeared to have noticed.

An emotional habit? Focus on the moment?!

'Yes. Just focus on now; this moment.' There was Seraph's voice again.

Now? I can't breathe, Seraph, I can't breathe.

'Relax. Just relax. Be still.'

I can't relax. I can't be still, because then I will have to feel. I'll have to feel ALL...THIS...PAIN!

Her diaphragm moved rapidly in short sharp repetitions.

'Trust me, Isadora.'

Trust you. TRUST?! Like trust is EASY?!! I can't. I can't be that person again.

'Yes you can. Because if you don't you will always be someone you're not. And that would be far greater pain and suffering. So choose trust. Just choose to trust me, right now. Just this moment, Isadora. That's all there is. Just this moment.'

Just this moment. Just this moment. Just this.... She attempted to slow her rapid breathing, noticing the trees and buildings whizzing by outside. Her hand gripped the seat in panic, her heart was pounding in her chest and she was like a balloon about to burst. But she began to feel Seraph's love, as if the angel were holding her. And her breathing slowed.

'Feel the feelings, Isadora. Release them, let them go.'

God, I feel so vulnerable. I don't want to do this.

'Then feel that, too. Welcome it all.' The angel was reading her thoughts. It paused for a long moment before continuing in a gentle voice. 'Let me carry you today, Dear One.'

The words were simple but they were spoken with such kindness and so needed like monsoon rain after years of withering drought, that they hit like a well-directed lightening bolt. The love flew straight into Isadora's wounded heart, shattering her dark slippery tunnel. The random bits of scaffolding that had been holding her up collapsed in a second. She crumbled.

She crumbled completely, and she wept for the exhaustion of having carried so much for so long. Pain bled from her body like a cut artery. She wanted to shake and scream yet she was frozen inside like a horrified witness to a terrible act.

How could I have done so little? Why didn't I protect myself?

She watched her suffering release with great sorrow, much like a stranger. Tears flowed and emptied from her body. And after some time she became aware of space and expansion. She felt light, as if a great weight had been lifted from her shoulders.

'This, too, shall pass.'

She heard Seraph's voice and bathed in the feeling of peace and the beginning of remembering herself again.

'Rest now, Isadora.'

'Thank you,' she whispered feeling exhausted and humbled.

'No Isadora, thank *You*.'

'I don't understand why you would thank me at all,' she said as several more tears rolled gently down her face.

'Dear Isadora, because surrendering to feeling, to the expression of the soul, is a very beautiful and precious thing on earth. Can't you hear them singing?'

'Who?'

'The other angels.'

She strained to listen to the sound of a choir but could not hear, although the feeling of lightness stayed with her as the train rolled slowly into Golders Green station.

And her heart felt decidedly good.

Chapter Nine

Joshua Hunter drove his black four-wheel drive through the tree-lined streets of Finchley. His fingers tapped the steering wheel as he listened to the music playing on the radio. He was happy. Not only had the project in Ireland been completed on time within budget but he had also met a beautiful woman on the plane, one with haunting green eyes. Clearly she had flying nerves and had experienced some sort of trauma or setback in life, he thought. There was a fragility about her that made him want to wrap her up in cotton wool, although admittedly he also wanted to make love to her. She had certainly had a rapid chemical effect on him. In fact, his attunement to her was so quick and automatically protective that he had placed his hand upon hers when he sensed her anxiety. It had seemed an entirely natural act at the time, much like he would do in any close loving relationship. It was only when he went to remove it that the awkwardness of her being a complete stranger had struck him.

He wanted to know her. That decision was made in their first few moments of meeting. He was drawn inexplicably toward her and knew that must be for a reason. His Hopi descent had ensured his instincts were seldom wrong. He knew how to read and follow signs much like a tracker. His middle name was *'Cheveyo'*, which meant 'spirit warrior'. It was given to him by his grandfather before he passed away. In the Hopi tradition the name was his honor and something he wanted to live up to. But despite his pride in it, he didn't feel hugely connected with being a spirit warrior. Perhaps his Grandfather had screwed up somehow. Josh felt he had always been more of a thinker and more intellectually driven than any sort of 'warrior'. As his vehicle slowed, turning onto his street, he concluded that he was a lover not a warrior. Clearly being a lover made him a little weak at times when it came to women. This had almost got him into trouble on a number of occasions. But he was lucky, there was no doubt about it. And he had always been especially lucky with women, until several years ago at least. But somehow even that had happened for a reason.

Life was a *'Ten'* to Josh. Everything on some level was always perfect, even if the rhyme or reason to it was never truly understood at the time. People did things because they needed whatever outcomes or experiences they created for growth or learning, whether they were aware of it or not. Himself included. Humans were like checkers on a board, the pieces inevitably moved by their own master hand, and life was always unfolding as it did and he grew from it all regardless of how it worked out on the surface. So he never found it necessary to sweat the small stuff. That was his general philosophy and it worked for him. It had resulted in his life being charmed in ways that most people never dreamed of. He was pretty sure that he had attracted ease simply by living with that understanding.

At least, that was about right up until he met Madelaine. Their fundamental philosophical differences were precisely why his relationship with her had eventually hit a large brick wall. They were essentially polar opposites yet he had been strangely drawn to her. She was a controlling and demanding creature, Daddy's little girl, and all that money and attention had corrupted her sweetness. Still, he had found her hard to resist, especially with that long black hair flowing all the way down to her sexy rear. There was something exotic, mysterious and catlike about her. She also happened to be a precision strategist, which was why she was so darn good at her business development job where her powers of persuasion and manipulation had seen her ride to the top of her profession. Of course, occasionally he had wondered if she had literally ridden her way to the top. All those glass ceilings had been placed there precisely for ambitious women like her, yet somehow she had smashed her way through them all. It was quite possible that she had used parts of her anatomy other than her brain to get her there - she was certainly unabashed about her sexuality. He had seen the way some of her male colleagues looked at her at social events and it was more than a general undressing. But he hadn't overly minded because at the end of the day he had been the one taking her home and bedding her. He had never begrudged her success in their eighteen months together. He knew how hard the corporate system was and the balls needed to make it in that world. And Madelaine had balls, there was no doubt about it.

She seemed to know how to work a person into a tight corner and have her way with them. It was how they had ended up together. He hadn't minded her coming onto him in the bar that night, wearing a sexy silky red dress with her hair flowing long and tantalizingly over its low open back. The whole night all he had wanted to do was slide his hand in under her hair and touch the naked skin that lay hidden beneath her mane. Usually he liked to work a little slower with women and get to know them more, but not with Madelaine. Nothing worked slowly with her. She had hooked him with her sultry knowing smile across the bar and he had thrown away any caution in a second. He'd wanted to take her home that night. And he had.

They immediately embarked on a heady passionate relationship. In hindsight this was mostly because she had never ceased to call, text, or visit him from that first morning, bombarding him with attention. She had all the right words and knew completely how to charm him and get her own way, even down to his contact with friends and what he wore to company events. She was also capable of sulking when she didn't get her own way or if she felt he'd let her down. At these times she would suddenly and completely cut the barrage of attention. The silence was always deafening to Josh, having by this stage become entirely accustomed and somewhat addicted to her constant contact and their sex life. He would feel a strange and deep sense of loneliness without her and inevitably buckled, just to see her again and to feel that passion. His easy-going nature had been mincemeat in the face of her clever might. He was hooked.

Eventually Josh had cottoned on to the fact he was no man with Madelaine, he was more the woman...and quite possibly her bitch. The sense of being a controlled piece of well-oiled machinery in her world began to grate on him more and more. Their arguments became an increasing ugly fixture, much like a house infiltrated and overrun with cockroaches. And bug bombs were no answer to their infestation of dysfunction. In order to escape her completely he needed to overcome the sick psychology of addiction. After six months all her black widow strategies had slowly failed and he had exorcised her. He exited with finality and hadn't seen her for almost a year, until recently, when he had bumped into her at a bar near his workplace on a Friday evening.

Despite her being as alluring as ever he had felt entirely in control and at ease having conquered his Madelaine-demons, so he hadn't minded when she came over to talk to him at the crowded bar. He hadn't minded at all. He was also entirely strong enough to deal with looking at her long flowing hair, at her pouting sultry lips and the low-cut dress that accentuated the curve of her breasts - breasts he knew every millimeter of. What he had neglected to remember however was her nerve. She had simply grazed her hand over the crotch of his trousers, suggested they get a room, and his manhood had promptly followed her straight into the nearest hotel.

He hadn't seen or contacted her since leaving her wild tousled hair and body in the bed they had passionately romped in. It was what it was, he thought before closing the door on the way out. He had not heard a word from her since then and he liked it that way. What he liked more now though, was that at long last he had met another woman he was attracted to. He wanted to get to know her.

Josh pulled up in front of his home on the tree-lined street of Finchley. Yes, he was happy. Life held new promise at every turn and spring was on its way again.

Chapter Ten

Isadora disembarked from the Northern Line at Golders Green Underground Station, picking up food provisions and heading off in the direction of her flat. It was a ten minute walk for her which took her towards the edge of the Hampstead woods. Breathing in the chill mid-winter air she noticed the trees in the park looking barren and devoid of all foliage. Something seemed to keep them going in the absence of nurturing conditions, she thought to herself. Clearly trees were well endowed with faith in the cycles of life – after all, she'd never seen a tree uproot itself in winter and fearfully charge off to drown itself in a lake. They patiently waited, naked and vulnerable, weathering wind and snow, seemingly content with their lot and certain in the knowledge the sun would eventually shine again. Nature had so many answers, she reflected, as her boots clip-clopped along the pavement.

Nearing the small lane she saw the house. Isadora had responded to an advert almost nine months ago. It was for a self-contained upstairs attic flat on the top floor of a large family home. She had hoped for a place where she could have her own space and privacy and found it perfect. The home itself was owned by an older German woman, Brigitte, who had lived there on her own since the passing of her husband a number of years earlier. She was pleasant but kept to herself, which suited Isadora just fine. Occasionally the woman's grown children and grandchildren would visit. Both her son and her daughter were concert violinists, which Isadora found fascinating. She often spent time considering how much discipline would have been required from an early age for them to create such successful careers in their craft. She didn't have any specialized gift or talent and was a little envious. The height of her skill seemed to be more along the lines of organizing a luncheon for a group of board members, setting transatlantic meetings, and booking flights and accommodation for other successful and busy people. Despite her recent position having been as an Executive Assistant for a Chief Executive of a company, it was not the most soulful or exciting work on the planet. It was certainly not fulfilling for Isadora. She had long sensed, somewhere inside her, that she was destined for something quite different.

As she quietly entered the house there was no sign of Brigitte but she had left post out. Isadora collected it before making her way upstairs with a sense of relief to be back. She paused halfway up to rifle through her mail, which included a flyer from a local massage practitioner.

'Okay, I get it,' she said looking around as if talking to the air. 'I'll make an appointment.'

Reaching the top of the stairs, she glanced around at her quaint and comfortable accommodation. It included a small kitchenette and bathroom. Immediately ahead was her brightly painted yellow bedroom equipped with double bed, television and wardrobe. A beautiful colored glass bowl from her trip to Prague sat atop a large dresser containing much of Isadora's clothing. A big bay window, cut into the attic ceiling, allowed a flood of light into the room. It looked out onto a spacious back garden filled with winter-barren trees, shrubs, and slightly overgrown grass.

She placed her post on the dresser and dropped her bag on the floor, looking around at the familiar territory for a moment before collapsing in a heap on her bed. It was so soft and inviting. Shards of the late afternoon sun cut through the window, embalming her body in light and warmth. She felt like a cat stretched out.

No place to be. Thank God I can just rest.

Allowing the weariness to consume her tired body she drifted off into a deep mid-afternoon slumber.

***

It was dark when Isadora awoke, hearing a familiar voice gently whispering her name. She was slightly disoriented but recognized the voice of her angel once again.

'Isadora, you will be leaving England soon.'

'What?' she responded sleepily.

'You need to give Brigitte notice. You'll be traveling abroad,' Seraph said gently.

'Where? Why? For how long?' Isadora began hastily waking up.

'It's all arranged. You'll be contacted soon. Follow the signs.'

'What? Is that all you're going to give me?'

'No. Your flight must be an open-ended return one.'

'That's it?! That's seriously all you're giving me?'

'I'm just a guide, Dear One, not a Travel Agent,' Seraph responded.

'Aren't you becoming quite the comedian.'

'Well, you're developing a sense of humor, Isadora. Remember, an open-ended return flight. Give your notice - and comfort too.' The Angel's voice rang musically through her ears.

'Comfort?'

'Yes, Isadora. You will understand.'

'Okay,' she screwed up her face, deciding to accept the enigma of the dialogue.

'Wonderful. Signs of trust.'

'Working on it. Seraph, what happened to me on the train today?'

'You were releasing shock and trauma from your body. Events of the past few days caused substantial nervous energy to build up. If you hadn't released it from your body, where do you think it would go?'

'I'm not sure. Nowhere. I guess it must stay in my body.'

'This is correct. It's stored in your cells as unresolved energy. This does not lead to a happy body or happy living, as I think you now understand. In time the unresolved energy can cause disease or depression, therefore it is better to discharge it.'

'And how exactly do I discharge energy again?

'Think of a bird having just flown mistakenly into a windowpane Isadora. You will observe how afterward the shock is evident as it sits quivering and shaking before flying again.'

'So that's how an animal gets rid of shock energy? They shake it out?'

'It is one way.'

'But not humans?'

'Sometimes humans do, but not always.'

'So if I'm not sitting shaking after a shock of some sort, what's another way?'

'By feeling all the feelings, Isadora. By simply being with them and allowing them to flow without judging or getting attached to a story about what they mean or why you are experiencing them. Then you have the conditions for the negative energy to discharge at a deep level, as you did today. This is an excellent way to create space for better patterning and experience.'

'It happened so fast,' Isadora said recollecting in amazement.

'Yes, it will when you allow the feelings without blocking them or attaching to a story about their reason for being. They could derive from an experience or multiple experiences at any point in your life. However, whatever triggers them is simply an access point for healing. In the end, they are simply feelings, a form of energy. Allow them to flow like a river and wash negativity away.'

'I guess that makes a little sense to me.'

'It makes sense to you because you know all this. I'm not telling you anything you don't already know or remember, on some level.'

'Well I certainly felt much better afterward.'

'You felt better because in feeling fully you returned your awareness to the present moment and inhabited your body in totality. This required you to soften, which sadly seems to have become quite a crime these days in humanity. Many humans now simply avoid feeling as if their life depended upon it, which is really very ironic. Quite the opposite is true. It's much healthier to feel and release anything undesirable safely than to remain dissociated.'

'I guess I must have a lot of unresolved energy in my body then.'

'Indeed, there is more. But as you say on earth, *Rome was not built in a day.*'

'Well I guess I have that to look forward to then.'

'One step at a time Isadora. Go slowly and be easy on yourself. You are surrounded by love and many blessings, always. Farewell for now.'

After the angel had disappeared again she lay on the bed for some time, pondering the conversation, and began to understand at least in part why she had been feeling so bad for such a long time. She must have had so much unhealthy energy stored up in the cells of her body that she was like a walking emotional time bomb. No wonder she struggled now with even little stresses in life. Her body was in a constant state of hyper-vigilance, just waiting for the next trigger. It was like a packed cupboard that couldn't fit a single thing more inside and she needed to clear it out fast. Isadora began to feel anxious about the state of her physical system. She sure did need some fixing.

'Isadora, please relax. Worrying about negativity simply adds negativity. True healing energy does not fix, it *allows*. Nature has its own wisdom and heals with time.' Seraph's words lit up her mind in an instant.

So I don't need to fix this? There's nothing I need to do?'

'No, Isadora.'

'Nothing at all?'

'Just *Be.* You're perfect as you are.'

'Perfect as I am? You're really sure about that, Seraph?'

'Relax, Dear Isadora. Trust. Healing comes when the time and conditions are right – you must simply be willing and the path will be laid before you.'

Chapter Eleven

Julie sat alone in the restaurant staring into space, but behind the blank eyes her mind was working with the kind of persistent detective work found in criminal investigation television shows.

Where the hell is Isadora?

She was evidently no longer in the same job and she hadn't responded to the phone messages left for her. She was living in Golders Green but Julie didn't have an address. Now there were exactly ten days to go before the departure date for Egypt and it was possible she would have to cancel the trip.

One thing she knew for certain, Isadora was one of the world's most organized women. It was her precision attention to detail that had made her excel in top Executive Assistant roles, so if she had received her voice messages then she would call her straight back. She was as reliable as a Swiss watch, so for some reason she hadn't received them or something had happened to her cellphone. If only she could recall the name of that German woman whose house she lived at. Christ, what kind of a friend was she. She couldn't remember any of Isadora's idiot boyfriend's names either. Although to be fair she had a hard enough time recalling the names of her own.

Where is she?

Julie reflected on her friend for a moment. She had known her since High School days where they had sat together in English class and spent a lot of time gossiping about boys and philosophizing over the meaning of life. Julie had leaned markedly toward the boy talk and Izzy, as she affectionately called her, seemed fixated on understanding life and existence. In their conversations they had discovered that by an odd fluke they once inhabited the same family home in their early childhood. Isadora's family had moved in right after Julie's had moved out. Equally coincidental was the shared experience of the house holding a negative history for both families. Mrs Jamieson had moved her daughters into the home where her new partner John lived. His previous wife had suffered extreme depression and sadly walked into the ocean one day, purposefully drowning herself and leaving John to fend for himself and his three young daughters on his own. Until he met Julie's mother.

She sighed a moment at the memories. Life was certainly full of unexpected twists and turns and it could sometimes be quite cruel. Isadora's mother had also suffered depression in the house, eventually succumbing to a breakdown and leaving suddenly - which effectively made the home like a pit of maternal abandonment. She'd never spoken about it, but Julie could clearly see that Isadora's relationship with her mother had been severed badly and her young emotional world left hanging in a most critical way.

As they were growing up, Julie sensed that Isadora lived her life as if she were balanced precariously upon a perpetually moving platform. Everything was temporary or transitory and not to be trusted. She was a nervous creature with not particularly good self-esteem - an understandable development, given that her most fundamental relationship had been ripped away at a time of great innocence and need. Julie reasoned it was why Isadora had become so meticulously organized in life and then made a career out of it. It was her way of at least appearing to have some control, if not entirely feeling it. Practicality had been Isadora's crutch; boys and developing the art of flirtation had been Julie's.

She picked her cellphone up off the table and scrolled through the contacts to locate Isadora's number again.

One more try.

Pressing the phone to her ear she heard the ringing several times. To her great delight, Isadora answered.

'Izzy, it's Julz.'

'Hi, Julz. It's good to hear from you.'

She sounded sleepy to Julie. 'Where have you been? I've been trying to get hold of you. I emailed and left you messages as well.'

'I'm sorry. I haven't checked my phone for messages yet. I've been away…in Ireland.'

'Oh. Well didn't you take your phone with you?'

'No I left it behind…accidentally.'

Julie heard the hesitation suggesting she had just invented a lie and decided Isadora was sounding cagey and guarded about Ireland too, if that is really where she had been at all. She decided to park the information.

'The emails I sent to your work address kept bouncing back…?'

'Yes. I quit my job.'

'You quit your job?! To the Chief Executive of a Fortune 500 company?' Julie said surprised.

'Well you can't do the same thing forever, Julz. It was time for a change.'

Julie was thinking that eleven months in a job wasn't exactly long-haul but decided against saying anything. If Isadora didn't have a job then it meant she was likely free to travel. That was the important thing for the moment.

'So you're not doing much right now?'

'No, not doing much. Need a hand stuffing travel brochures into envelopes or something?'

'Honey, that's very funny. We find email these days works just fine, especially for the rainforests.'

'I was kidding.'

'Of course darling, but oddly enough I have an even better idea. How about two weeks under the burning sun of Egypt away from this horror story of a winter?' Julie could hear a pause that seemed just too long.

'You're serious? A trip to Egypt?' Isadora responded quietly.

'Of course I'm serious. I'm a Travel Agent, for God's sake. I've had the trip planned with my sister Laney and she just bailed out on me. Damn man-honeymoon phase. The cheek! But it's a superb deal, Izzy. Great airfare and everything is organized. So how about coming with me instead? It will be so much fun…girls on tour!'

'Egypt, huh?'

'Yes, brilliant, hot, exiting Egypt! I remember at school you were always going on about the pyramids. So now's your chance to see them up close and personal.'

Julie heard the dull thud of unenthusiastic silence for a number of seconds.

'Weird.'

'Weird is not exactly the response I was looking for, Izzy. What in the blazes is weird about it?'

'Nothing, Julz.' Isadora hesitated again. 'Look, you're absolutely right. I have always wanted to visit the pyramids.'

'So can I take that as a yes?' Julie sensed she just needed a little nudging over the finish line.

'Yes. That's a yes.'

'Brilliant. Brilliant, Izzy. That's perfect! It's going to be just amazing.'

'I'm sure it will be interesting.'

'Interesting? Interesting?!' For goodness sakes, woman! You need to lighten up and get a little excited. Now come in and see me at the Travel Agency, okay? I'll arrange everything and give you the details.'

'Okay, that's fantastic, Julz. Give me a day to sort some things out here and I'll figure out a time to come in on Friday.'

'Perfect. No backing out now, Izzy. I'm looking forward to seeing you. Bye for now.'

Julie was feeling slightly uneasy as she disconnected the call. Something was up with Isadora. She sounded flat and suspiciously as though she was hiding something. She would have to dig around and find out what was going on. The main thing for now, though, was that she was joining her on holiday.

Julie smiled like the cat that got the cream as she stood up and put her coat on. The trip was going ahead and finally something was going right. Yet her instincts told her she was going to have to keep a close eye on Isadora and find out what was really going on in her life. She slung her handbag over her shoulder with a new and determined glint in her eye. If there was one thing she excelled at, it was finding the doorway to people's hidden secrets and walking right on in. She would extract whatever information Isadora was hiding. If not before their departure, then in Egypt. Of that she was certain.

Wrapping her scarf snuggly around her throat Julie exited the restaurant into the night with a renewed sense of purpose.

Chapter Twelve

Isadora had been half asleep when she heard the muffled ringing of her cellphone. She had almost forgotten where she'd stashed it before departing for Ireland but managed to trace the sound to her underwear drawer. Before she picked up the call she noticed three missed calls, two voice messages, and an unread text.

Please, God, let one of the calls be from Josh.

But the calls had been from Julie Jamieson.

After finishing talking with her old school friend she sat in stunned silence. Man, those angels sure had everything mapped out very neatly for her. It was a little strange and all too much to comprehend at the moment. She had literally started living again on a wing and a prayer. It was now almost incomprehensible to her that two days earlier she had nearly ended her life. But she really had nothing to lose at all by throwing herself into the great unknown and following the trail that was appearing magically before her.

Isadora reflected on the fact that her future destination was Egypt. As child she had been quite obsessed with Egypt, often staring at pictures in the family encyclopedia of the Great Pyramid of Giza and the Sphinx. She would frequently daydream about being there in person. As the years passed, she had subsequently undertaken much personal research about them. Seraph had told her to *follow the signs*, Paddy had said she really hadn't lived until she had been to Egypt; now Julie was inviting her on a fully planned trip. It almost felt like a conspiracy.

'I don't really have a choice. Do I, Seraph?'

'You always have choices.' The angel's response was in her mind.

'Right, sure. I have a choice not to go to Egypt,' she said.

'Why of course you have the choice not to go. But didn't you always have a dream to see the Pyramids? Didn't you spend a lot of time researching them? Besides, think of what you'd be missing,'

'Okay, okay. You win.'

'No Isadora, you win. Now get some sleep.'

'You're beginning to sound like my mother,' she responded lightly.

'Really? Are you quite sure about that?' Seraph spoke with a serious tone, surprising her.

'Are you trying to make a point about something, Seraph?'

'Not unless you wish me to, Isadora. Now get some sleep, and blessings to you.'

Seraph's voice disappeared again giving Isadora no time to pursue the meaning behind the curious remark. She had too much else to consider and organize in any event, so she dismissed thinking about it again, instead focusing on Josh as her eyelids became heavy.

I wonder if he'll contact me?

She screwed her face up.

Oh…darn.

Sitting bolt upright up in the bed, her hand fumbled blindly around in the dark on her bedside table in an urgent effort to locate her cellphone.

I haven't read that message.

Securing the phone, she scrolled hopefully to the text from the unnamed number and clicked on it, staring at the words.

Isadora watched the light fade out on the screen of her phone before calmly placing it back on the dresser and sliding back down under the covers.

Unbelievable. It IS a conspiracy.

But she couldn't help smile as she closed her eyes, resigning herself to the fate awaiting her abroad. Recalling once more the feeling of Josh's hand on hers and his kiss on her cheek, Isadora drifted contentedly into a deep and restful sleep with the words from his text at the airport floating through her mind.

'I think you'd love Egypt.'

Chapter Thirteen

Brigitte Steinberg finished tidying the breakfast dishes away and poured herself another cup of tea from the porcelain pot. It had been some time since she had seen Isadora. The young woman had been abroad for a long weekend. She was aware she was back because the post left out for her had disappeared, but that was her only clue. She was certainly a quiet tenant, Brigitte thought. She had never had a single friend come to visit her in nearly nine months of living upstairs, and she didn't seem to go out that much. It was a little odd for someone her age - she was really in her prime and such a pretty woman after all. Still, Brigitte reasoned that not being native to England she probably didn't find it all that easy to meet people and make friends. Her own children had been relatively quiet when younger too, but that was mostly because they were always at home practicing on their violins.

It was curious, though. Her isolation was definitely odd.

You had to keep an eye on the quiet ones, you really did, she thought. Solitude had a funny tendency to breed strange thoughts in a person's head. After all, these days she struggled with unusual thoughts in her mind too. Life had been lonely and silent since Luther's passing. Very lonely.

Sighing heavily, she glanced up at the calendar above the fridge.

As if I need to check the date.

She was momentarily startled to feel tears begin to form in her eyes and hastily dabbed them away with a tissue before sitting down with her cup of tea, absentmindedly shuffling it around by the handle. It was exactly two years and dwelling on it hadn't brought him back. She was preparing to take her first mouthful of Earl Grey when she heard sounds of movement on the staircase. Pausing, her cup half in the air, she listened intently to the footsteps and waited until the woman stuck her head somewhat sheepishly around the corner and stepped into the kitchen.

'Hi, Brigitte.'

'Hello dear.'

'Is this an okay moment to have a chat?'

'Yes of course. Did you have a nice weekend away?' Brigitte said, placing her cup back down and thinking Isadora looked pale, underweight, and very tired.

'It was…great, thanks.'

'Why don't you take a seat and I'll pour you a tea.'

'Oh, I…'

But Brigitte was already on her feet getting a cup and saucer and filling it from the pot on the kitchen bench. After all, it would help take her mind off things for a while. She sat the filled cup down on the table and could clearly see nervousness in Isadora's eyes.

'Is everything alright dear?' She sat back down, suddenly feeling a little concerned about what exactly she wanted to talk about.

'Well, I'm so terribly sorry Brigitte, but I need to give you two weeks notice on the flat.'

'Oh dear, I'm very sorry to hear that,' and she really was. 'Can I ask why?'

'I'm going overseas for a while to travel and I'm not sure when I'm coming back.'

'Oh.' It was all Brigitte could think to say as she felt the heaviness of her heart once more and the threatening tears. She gathered her wits a moment. 'Why don't you know when you're coming back, Isadora?' She watched her hesitate nervously again.

'I just need to get away for a while. To be free, I guess.'

'Free of what, dear?' Brigitte's lip began to quiver as she watched Isadora take a small sip of her tea. As quiet as she was, she knew and trusted the younger woman. Now she would have to face another stranger in her home and hearing that today of all days was more than she could take.

'I'm not sure, if I'm really honest. Free of everything, I think.' Isadora stared at her cup.

Brigitte could feel emotions surging underneath like a fountain had just been switched on inside her. She hadn't really cried properly; she'd had to be strong for her children after all. She simply had to be or everything inside her would collapse like a house of cards. Now having been this way for several years, eventually everything just stayed conveniently numb. Unable to look at Isadora sitting across from her, she hastily stood up, taking her half full cup and emptying it down the sinkhole without thought.

'I'm so sorry, Brigitte. I have enjoyed living here, but I have to do this.'

'You have to do this?' she whispered quietly, feeling the fountain moving up her chest.

'Brigitte, I really am sorry. Are you okay?'

He had to be free too…forty one years, gone. All gone.

'Brigitte?'

The fountain hit her throat and a tiny choked sob escaped like the first bubble on the surface of a simmering pot of water.

And then another.

She heard the scraping of the chair behind her as Isadora stood up. Her footsteps nearing her, a hand placed ever so gently on her back.

'Brigitte? What is it?'

And there it was, after years of holding back, the fountain finally emerged with all its might.

Brigitte Steinberg's first tears caused her shoulders to shake up and down in tiny movements as she attempted initially to restrain them, with the movements becoming bigger and bigger until her shoulders moved freely.

Then she sobbed more loudly until she howled. And she howled as if her whole life depended upon it.

Chapter Fourteen

Isadora shut the door quietly behind her. She left the house feeling shaken and somewhat ashamed. Brigitte's sad revelation had left her stunned. To think she had lived with her for nearly nine months and had absolutely no idea what that poor woman had quietly contended with. Then she'd almost added an extra weight to her burden in the weekend.

She'd been on her way to Julie's workplace before descending into the kitchen and unwittingly popping the cork on Brigitte's deepest pain. The woman's distress had been intense but Isadora had eventually managed to get her to sit down, slowly curb her tears, and finally reveal the tragic tale of her husband.

You were right, Seraph. She did need comfort. I understand now.

Luther Steinberg had been a noted University lecturer and a bright loving husband and father, right up until his car accident when his world had changed in a few simple heartbeats. Confined to a wheelchair, he had become increasingly depressed despite Brigitte's devoted attempts to keep his quality of life and spirits up. Eventually, on his darkest day exactly two years ago, he had wheeled his chair and his shrunken body into the woods across the road and shot himself, terminating his own existence, and to a large extent that of his beloved wife of forty one years.

Isadora felt plagued with deep guilt as she walked at pace back to the underground station. How many lives did one person really affect through their actions? Everything seemed to count. Every action or choice wove people in different ways; created feelings and impacts that one simple choice could have changed. It was abundantly clear to her now that had she taken her own life on the cliff that day the effects would have rippled out far and wide in ways that affected many. Yes, it was her life and she had the freedom to choose, but didn't she also have some sort of accountability to the lives intertwined with her own to do the very best she could with the gift of her life? Weren't there possibilities beyond that fated day and event that were available to her if she gave them the chance.

My God, what did I almost do?

Was there an echo into time and space with every choice? She certainly impacted the lives of those she touched with every action, just as others' actions, or lack of them, had impacted her. If she had made that final decision to jump she would most certainly have influenced the web of life, causing more sorrow than she could have ever imagined. What legacy would she have left to those she cared for?

Another wave of guilt rippled through her.

The angels had advised her guilt was a mistake, to simply change the thought to a more positive one; that she had real power and ability to create her life in any way she chose. So wasn't it better then to create good for herself and for others by thinking and being positive? There had to be some real power and truth in that, which meant that there was power and truth in her own life. One simple life made an enormous difference to many, she was beginning to see that now. Her life made a difference, so she had to make sure it had positive loving people in it.

She could see the Golders Green underground station in sight now.

If someone isn't treating me well, I need to exit fast. It's pretty simple really.

Like Hayden. After three months of a loving time together he had one little window of opportunity when she was away from London organizing conference details abroad and he'd accidentally slipped himself back inside his ex-girlfriend. But he still had the good grace and generosity to meet Isadora at the airport and take her back to his place to make love to her too. She stung a little at the thought. He had left to play poker with his friends that night smiling and hugging her tightly before departing, but Isadora later discovered with shock and horror that his card game had in fact been *poke-her*, not poker.

She was lucky to find out the truth because his very generous other woman had found it in her heart to text Isadora some appalling messages from his phone, designed to create a wedge. Including that he was now engaged to the previously unknown woman. Of course, Hayden didn't know that his phone had been borrowed at the time. Nor was he aware he was now apparently engaged.

Poor silly Hayden.

Some women may have driven round to his house and spray-painted something obscene on his wall, or at the minimum tracked down the other woman and ripped parts of her hair off. But the sad fact remained that whoever she was, she may have used handcuffs – in the form of manipulation or her body - but he had gone willingly. Therefore, given that he clearly didn't think enough of her, the likely place to lay any relationship blame or failing was inevitably with herself. And after the effects of Tom she always did, quite brutally. The most unkind cuts of all were the ones she gave herself. Eventually the succession of painful experiences piled on top of each other had driven her down a long dark tunnel, concluding on the Cliffs of Moher.

However, it was now suddenly abundantly clear to Isadora where the real mistake lay. It was in her interpretation of events and the meaning she had given them. If she'd thought more highly of herself she would have easily been able to see that Hayden was weak and insecure. His choice of woman was based on that. And although it hurt like the blazes, he had freed her for something far greater and more worthy of her heart.

Why wasn't I able to see things this clearly before?!

'Because you weren't ready to, dear Isadora.' Seraph's lilting voice ran through her mind. 'You just didn't value yourself enough.'

Her heart lurched with a deep sadness at the truth of the words. Nearing the underground station she paused, hearing the sound of her phone ringing in a muted tone from somewhere in the bottom of her handbag.

Great, that will be Julie.

Digging around, she located the vibrating object.

'Hello,' she said, partly out of breath from being on the move.

But it wasn't Julie at all. Isadora heard the deep familiar voice and knew in a split second who it was.

Chapter Fifteen

'Hi, Isadora. It's Josh.'

'Oh.' He heard the surprise in her voice and it threw him for a second.

'Is this a bad time?'

'No, not at all.'

'You sound out of breath?'

'I'm just walking to catch a train.'

'And how is the lady of leisure doing?'

'Very good, thanks. How about you?'

'Well I think a holiday would be nice, and I'm well overdue for it.' Wasn't that the truth, he thought to himself. He'd been working such long hours the past year. 'Look, I wondered if you're free tomorrow evening for dinner?'

'Tomorrow's good.'

'Great. How about I pick you up at seven? You can text me your address when you get a moment.'

'Okay, no problem.' She sounded a little nervous to Josh.

'Perfect. You have a good day. I'll look forward to seeing you tomorrow.'

'And you.'

He heard the phone go silent and felt a strange tingling in his chest. Smiling softly he placed the mobile back down on his desk and turned to look out at the partial view of the muddied Thames River off in the distance below him.

She was different, he could tell. He'd had that feeling once before. However it was a long time ago when he'd been in his final year of engineering studies. When he met Cynthia at university, he'd felt something deep in his chest within minutes of meeting her. Later he had fallen totally in love for the first time in his life. But they had both been so young and he had not had the maturity or wisdom to know that women like her seldom came along, nor did the feelings that came with them. The art world had taken her to New York and his engineering career to places far away from her. Eventually they drifted apart, but Josh had never really felt the same about anyone – after her there hadn't been another woman he'd felt like marrying and having children with.

Sitting down on his desk, deep in reflection for some time, his memories and thoughts were interrupted by the sound of an incoming text message.

Isadora's address. Great.

He picked up the mobile and scrolling into the messages box recognized the slightly familiar number.

'Jesus.' He spat the word out with annoyance, staring at the screen before flinging the phone back to the desk.

His soft reminiscent feelings hardened in a moment.

I need a coffee.

Snatching up his wallet he headed for the door leaving his cellphone on the desk.

It was one message he would not be responding to.

Chapter Sixteen

Isadora climbed the stairs leading out of the Baker Street underground station. She was happy, and the smile on her face was the first genuine and deep one that she'd experienced in months. There was a gorgeous new man in her world and she now had a date with him. She also had an angel in tow bringing her guidance and luck. Life had turned a full three hundred and sixty degrees in a matter of days.

Her boots clipped along the pavement as she approached Julie's travel agency with a radiance in her eyes. Earlier that morning she'd booked herself a nice massage so she would be all relaxed for her date in the evening. What to wear would be the big burning question, she thought, pushing on the door and entering the warmth of her friend's workplace.

Three desks along Isadora could make out Julie's blonde hair bobbing about. She was deep in animated conversation on the phone as she glanced across and noticed her friend in the reception area. Pulling a mock anguished expression she gestured to the empty seat in front of her.

Julie was not only a stunning blonde with shoulder length hair and sparkling blue eyes, but a real professional as well. Although Isadora knew her to be a straight shooter and that she didn't suffer fools gladly, her old school friend was a big softy at heart. Julie had been one of the cool kids growing up, but she'd never let the group mentality or her peers control her. She had still befriended Isadora, who was a quiet teenager and far from cool. Watching her now, Isadora couldn't understand why she hadn't had the courage to talk to Julie long before her trip to Ireland. She could see how isolated she'd let herself become in the past two months. Julie would have barely batted an eyelid at anything Isadora told her. She had skin as thick as the arse of a rhinoceros, but she was also one of the best listeners Isadora had ever known.

Watching her, Julie politely finish up her call and replaced the handset.

'Bla bla fricking bla, just book the damn trip!' she said quietly to Isadora so no one else in the office could hear, shaking her head in annoyance before recomposing herself. 'Damn indecisive people. You need the patience of a saint in this profession, I'm telling you, Izzy.'

Isadora smiled at her theatrics.

'Great to see you girlfriend,' Julie winked, shrugging off any negativity in a second. 'I'm sorry I haven't been in touch for a while, just been so darn busy. Everyone wants to leave England at this time of the year, including me. We have so much catching up to do.'

'Yes we do, Julz.'

'But firstly, let's get this Egypt trip sorted. There will be plenty of time to catch up over a wine or two in the sun. Or is Marguerita still your favorite drink, Izzy?' she said with a cheeky smile, referring to a night out they had been on together which had revealed Isadora's wilder side.

Julie's enthusiasm was infectious as she took down passport details and discussed their accommodation and travel arrangements - right up until Isadora told her she needed an open-ended return ticket. Her tone changed markedly.

'Well, Izzy, what the hell is up with that? Are you planning on hitching up with some swarthy? I mean, an open-ended return ticket. Are you totally serious?'

'I am serious, Julz. It's just something I need to do.' She grasped for some convincing reason. 'I'm at a bit of a turning point in life and I need to get away and just see where life takes me.'

'Yes, but it's the bloody Middle East, darling. Choose South England to go exploring on your own, or fricking Scotland. Not Egypt and Jordan.'

'Look, if it's open-ended, Julz, I get to choose. I can come back with you, or I can stay and explore further. You know how fascinated I always was with Egypt. Now I have an opportunity to experience that, thanks to you.'

Julie stared at her in a state of pause for slightly longer than felt comfortable. 'Is everything okay, Izzy? In your life? I'm sorry we haven't caught up much lately, but seriously, is everything okay? I mean, are you still seeing that guy Horatio, or whatever his name is?'

Isadora smiled. 'His name is Hayden, Julz.'

'Okay, so I was close. Hayden. Are you still seeing him?' Her voice became soft.

'No, I'm not.'

'Oh dear, I'm sorry it didn't work out.'

'That's okay. He was a bit of a weak man anyway.'

'I've had one of those recently, too. It must be the season.'

They both smiled and Julie stared pointedly at Isadora for several seconds as if weighing something up before continuing. 'Okay Izzy, I accept your need to have an open-ended ticket. I can tell you've got something going on you need to work out for yourself. But you have to let me know if you're in trouble or you need anything, okay? I mean that. Do you hear me?'

'I hear you, Julz.'

'Good. And I expect a full report soon about this idiot Hayden, and his address so I can hunt him down.'

Isadora smiled softly. 'He was just insecure and a little lost.'

'Yes, I know the type. And I guess we're all a little lost in our own way. We all need to wake up. Honestly, Izzy, I think the world has gone a bit mad really. But maybe crisis in our lives is just a way of getting a shove to stop sleeping and head in a better direction.' She paused reflectively. 'Unfortunately it's sometimes the most painful things that make us do that.' Julie was quiet and looked distant for a moment before snapping back to her upbeat self. 'Just don't go marrying a Sheikh, Izzy. You'll end up part of some ruddy great harem and I'll never see you again.' She winked.

'As if, Yoda Julz. Anyone ever tell you that?'

'Yes actually, I get it all the time. Counselor Julie Jamieson. If only I could sort my own life out.'

'I think you do okay.'

'Not always, but I do my best.'

'I guess that's all we can do, Julz. I mean, we're human at the end of the day.'

'Some more than others my friend.' Julie looked thoughtfully at Isadora. 'You be careful, Izzy Bright.'

'No sheikhs, Julz. I promise.'

'Good. Then let's do this. Let's go to Egypt.'

'I'm ready. Let's do it.'

Isadora sighed inwardly. She wasn't even sure who she was right now, let alone diving into an Egyptian adventure. But she did know that along with the comfort of having her own personal angel, she had a great friend by her side. So for now, she was prepared to trust whatever lay ahead.

Chapter Seventeen

Sophia Fontaine moved around the room with the softness of a cat, lighting each candle in a ritualistic manner. Slim but strong in stature, with dark hair and smoky long-lashed eyes, her entire being screamed Gypsy from every cell in her body. She was a little curious about the woman who was due for a massage appointment with her in five minutes time. Two of her scheduled clients had just the day earlier cancelled their Friday afternoon appointments – two cancellations at once didn't happen often, so Sophia knew that the client taking the vacated space had been sent to her by spirit for a very specific reason. It was always the way.

Sophia was a third generation healer and clairvoyant, although she never publically advertised the fact that she had the gift of sight. Too many people felt threatened by the mystical realm, or were rather quick to condemn what they did not see or understand. Having recalled being burnt at the stake in a sixteenth century life for her knowledge of herbs and healing plants, and also persecuted and killed for heresy as a twelfth century Cathar in the South of France, Sophia still carried a psychological echo of her incarnations of public ridicule. Hence, she preferred to remain relatively obscure and largely in hiding in her current life. She skirted the periphery of apparent 'civilization' much like a Shaman on the edge of the village. Born and raised in France she had moved to England ten years earlier as directed by spirit, and had since dedicated herself to being a healer in the service of humanity, as her mother and grandmother had done before her.

Some might have considered her life a very lonely existence and viewed her as a largely unfulfilled woman - barren and unmarried – and to many, therefore, inhabiting a life devoid of feminine meaning. But it was not that way for Sophia. In fact, it was largely the opposite. Rather than judging herself as some tragic wasteland of a woman, she tapped a mystically divine and creative energy source every day that left her feeling more like a mother staring permanently into the eyes of her newborn baby. She was vastly more satisfied than most people would ever know or comprehend, but also more misunderstood. However, despite some social ostracism, people still found their way to her door and it gave her the greatest joy to help lift their sorrows and burdens and see the light behind their eyes as they exited her humble home.

Feeling a presence enter the room behind her, she froze suddenly, a lit match in hand, her sensing soul feeling a gentle breeze stir on the other side of the room, causing the candles to flicker simultaneously.

You are most welcome here, and I am lovingly in your service. She communicated in her mind.

Her message conveyed, Sophia smiled to herself, blowing out the low burning match before it reached the end of her long narrow fingers. Assistance had arrived. This would be a most interesting session.

Unsurprised to hear the knock on the door not fifteen seconds later, she turned and directed her thought to the empty space across from her.

Like clockwork, you work like clockwork.

Bowing her head in acknowledgement across the warmed room she softly exited, closing the door behind her and making her way to the front of the house.

Upon opening the door to the younger woman, Sophia was struck by the haunting green eyes staring back at her. She could tell in a moment that the woman's light was most dimmed. She appeared to be not fully in her body and a somewhat fractured soul.

'You must be Isadora Bright,' Sophia said, citing the name the woman had given her over the phone. 'Welcome.'

'Thank you,' she smiled shyly.

'Come this way.'

Sophia lead her down the hallway into her treatment room, explaining in her soft French accent that once she left the room she could place her clothes on the chair, lie face down on the treatment table and cover herself with the warmed towel. She then left her alone to get ready.

No wonder they needed to arrange for two other bookings to cancel.

On Sophia's return, she placed another warm blanket on top of Isadora's slim body before silently saying a prayer and beginning to massage the back of her legs. She worked quietly as soft ocean music played in the background, eventually moving to the back and spending time working her hands into the woman's tight muscles. Tight, rigid, controlling muscles…ones that held her secrets safely tucked inside.

Sophia began to think that no amount of work or intention would begin to shift what needed to leave the woman's body, until finally she observed Isadora's left hand twitching and her rib cage beginning to move in and out in rapid widening waves. Then a shaking motion occurred throughout her whole body, until the sound of sobbing filled the air.

The presence in the room had remained close to the woman as she lay, emptying old emotions from her tired body, but it was the arrival of an additional Spirit Being that was now capturing

Sophia's attention. The room was beginning to glow a deep purple-indigo hue, almost causing her to stop working and watch in awe. She noticed too, that the Angel who had arrived earlier in the room was now drawing back as if in reverence to the new arrival. This was no simple Guide showing up to assist the work. It was something very different; something more magnificent and loving than Sophia had ever encountered in her treatment room before. She watched with fascination as the radiance of the beautiful being surrounded and bathed the frail woman in a powerful healing light. The divine presence caused a wave of humility and gratitude to ripple through her and, gasping inwardly, she finally recognized exactly who and what it was.

It was precisely in that moment that everything about this particular Friday afternoon became very clear to Sophia Fontaine. Isadora Bright was getting assistance from some very high places, which was clearly for a reason. So whatever was looming on this woman's horizon would likely surprise her very much indeed.

Chapter Eighteen

Isadora stared at herself in the mirror for some time. Who was the stranger looking back at her? Had she ever really known this woman? Had she ever truly understood or embraced her? She took a moment to assess her looks, wondering if it was her imagination but the green of her eyes now appeared to have a bright sheen that revealed something more behind them than she had seen before. They were still a little puffy, but they were more radiant than she could recall. Reflecting on the treatment she had received that afternoon, she realized she had never really had a proper massage before. Of course, sometimes her boyfriends had massaged her, but that was different, and decidedly sexual in orientation and outcome.

Something powerful and very clearing had happened to her during the treatment with Sophia Fontaine. She had recalled her earliest memories in life of her mother massaging her chest when she was a sick little girl. Upon searching through her childhood she now realized it was one of the few times she could recall ever having been really nurtured maternally by her mother's hands. It was this knowledge that had caused her tears to flow and filled her with an intense and overwhelming sadness that had lain dormant in her cells for well over two decades.

She had cried for much of the duration of the treatment for the sudden loss of her mother, allowing the ancient grief of her seven-year old self, lodged firmly inside her, to be felt fully for the first time. And she cried, too, for all the suffering and pain carried in her mother's weary body, which had been fused so genetically and entirely within Isadora's young receptive self. Now, understanding for the first time the depth of impact that fundamental relationship had made upon all of her life and her choices to date, Isadora allowed the flow of grief to melt the frozen child. She'd had the curious feeling at the time of someone else in the room watching her, loving her, and urging her to find the courage to claim her life back fully. Seraph was there, but the presence she experienced was different. She had been surrounded and bathed in the most beautiful loving energy, beyond the heart and hands of the compassionate woman massaging her.

Her thoughts drawn back to the present moment, she glanced suddenly at the time.

Hurry, he'll be here any minute.

Isadora assessed her dress choice quickly. The cobalt blue color was nice enough on her. The fabric silky and falling to just above the knees, it moved tantalizingly over her lithe body and curves and had just enough of a plunging neckline to reveal cleavage. Her makeup looked pretty and accentuated the green of her eyes, and she had used a mineral powder to bring a soft brown coloration to her very pale complexion. She finished applying a gloss to her lips, suddenly feeling very nervous and staring back at herself.

I could do with a second opinion. Are angels any good at that?

No, that would be far too crazy and a total waste of Seraph's busy time to enlist in presentation opinions.

This will have to do. You're good enough as you are.

'You're so much more than good enough, Dear One.' She heard Seraph's voice whisper through her mind.

She smiled at the space behind her own mirrored image. Hearing the doorbell from several floors below her, she took a deep breath and composed herself before collecting her handbag and woolen coat and walking as calmly as she could down the two flights of stairs in her three inch stilettoes.

She had almost forgotten how handsome Joshua was as she opened the door to be greeted by his smile and appraising eyes. Her heart rate flew up at the speed of a space shuttle.

He's gorgeous.

'You look beautiful,' he simply said.

'Thank you,' she responded, noticing the slight opening in his light blue-colored shirt, revealing a hint of his manly chest.

It could have been the fact that Isadora was traveling a lot lighter after her tremendous unraveling on the massage table, or the fact that she hadn't been dressed up and feeling feminine for quite some time, but all of sudden she felt rather primal.

He leaned over, giving her a kiss on the cheek and lingering a second. 'Hungry?'

'A little.' But she was not thinking about food.

'Come on, let me get you some dinner,' he said placing his hand gently behind her back and guiding her toward his vehicle.

***

Barely noticing her food, she pushed the rice and last few pieces of fish drizzled in red curry around her plate. They were in a beautiful Thai restaurant. Isadora had been listening intently to every word coming out of Josh's beautifully shaped lips.

My God, I actually want to kiss him.

'So yes, I guess you could say my parents were, and still are, very happy together and I was blessed with a happy home. And how about you, Isadora?'

His direct look and use of her name threw her for a second.

'Oh, I think probably the complete opposite,' she joked, in an effort to hide her real feelings.

'Really? How so?'

'Well they were just…incompatible, I guess. Arguments, and my mother left.'

'She left?'

'Well, actually she had a breakdown. Which is why she left.'

'I'm sorry to hear.'

'Oh, don't be. I was seven. I can hardly remember it at all.'

Josh looked quizzically at her for a little longer than she felt comfortable with.

'Was it a small breakdown?'

'No. It was a big one. She never came back.'

'And you were seven when that happened, yes? That must have been very tough, losing your mother at the age of seven.'

'I don't remember much. I was always a bit of a dreamy child, so I guess I just stayed that way.'

'Dreamy? And you hardly recall? Wow. I would say it has got to leave a resounding memory, and impact for that matter.'

Isadora felt a nervousness and agitation forming in her stomach. She wanted the subject changed quickly. It had already been a big day of memories and she didn't want a nice time with him ruined. But he continued.

'You know, in Native American tradition there is such a thing as 'soul loss'.

'Soul loss?'

'Yes. It can be a painful or traumatic kind of experience such as you encountered at the age of seven.'

Oh God, he's really not going to let this go. She felt tears forming again, which surely wasn't possible after having already ejected a bucket of them out of her eyes during her massage.

'Really,' she said flatly, hoping that would end the conversation.

'Yes, it's said that Soul Loss is a survival mechanism. During a painful or jarring kind of event a piece of our soul, our essence, escapes to protect itself. The Shamans, our healers, say that part of the soul wanders into other realms or realities.'

'Interesting.'

'Look, I'm playing devil's advocate a little here, Isadora. But is it possible that at the age of seven you lost a part of your soul…that it fragmented?'

'I think that's a big call from a small piece of information, Josh.' She spat the response out somewhat defensively, before hastily reminding herself he was not her enemy.

'It's not a small piece of information at all. Besides, I sat with you on the plane, remember. I'm observant.'

'Look,' she sighed, 'if I'm perfectly honest my life *has* moved oddly, like I've been disconnected with a part of myself. It has felt and been frustratingly hard to move forward in any area or way.' She blinked to hold back several tears before they could escape. 'So humor me. If my soul fragmented what would that mean for me?'

'Well, from my perspective I think it would suggest you lost some of your inner light; the brightness of your spirit. Like having some fuses blown in your house, so you're not functioning on full power. That could explain some of your anxiety. You ever thought about that?'

'No. I just figured it was down to losing confidence after some relationship breakups.'

'I don't want to disregard or belittle any events that have occurred in your life, Isadora, but maybe they were just the catalyst to cause you to…feel something you buried a long time ago,' he said, reaching across the table and softly squeezing her hand. 'You can't go through life on half power without eventually noticing some things aren't working. And on the positive side, at least that reveals an area you may be able to recreate.'

'But you're saying I need an electrician before I can recreate.'

She was trying to distract from his hand upon hers.

He smiled. 'An electrician, a Shaman, or maybe just a determined you. Whoever it is, or however you retrieve it, I suspect deep down there's some of your inner light you can claim back. Put it this way, there's a seven-year-old girl who's still waiting for someone to show up for her. Perhaps it's time you found that piece of yourself again, Isadora. Time you collected her from wherever she disappeared to.'

A single tear escaped her eye and slid down her cheek.

'It's just a hunch,' he said, squeezing her hand.

'I wouldn't have a clue how to do that or where to begin.'

'Maybe you don't need to know. I don't even think you have to dredge up old wounds necessarily. I believe awareness is enough. Awareness, and the desire to live your life fully. Simply be willing to have the healing occur, however that comes. People and things will appear in alignment with that and you will know which path to follow.' He placed his free hand on his chest for a moment. 'Trust your heart, your own guidance, and have faith that the way exists for you and you will find it...or it will find you.'

'Are you sure you're really just an engineer? she said with watery eyes and a smile. 'You don't happen to have a priest's collar tucked in your pocket?'

He laughed. 'Perhaps I missed my calling.'

'I think you did.'

Isadora looked into the deep brown eyes of the man sitting opposite her and knew in that moment one thing for certain. She was already beginning to fall for him.

Chapter Nineteen

Josh was quiet as he drove his vehicle around the Hampstead woods towards Golders Green. He was thinking about how much he already felt for Isadora. He hadn't had such a protective instinct for a woman that he could recall, but he certainly did now, and he wanted to kiss her.

'So why Egypt in your text?' She broke his thoughts.

'Because you have time on your hands, you like the sun, and I think the ancient civilization aspect of Egypt would fascinate you.'

And I pictured you there…with me, he thought.

'You do, huh. Have you been before?'

'Once. And I would love to go back.'

'Really?'

'Yes, really. Let's face it, the Pyramids are the world's greatest engineering feat.'

'From priest to engineer in the bat of an eye,' she smiled.

'Oh, I think I can easily wear both hats when it comes to the Pyramids.'

'It's interesting, though. Funny really…' She paused.

He watched her nervously clutch her handbag drawing it closer to her like a shield.

'What is?'

'I'm going there.'

'What? To Egypt?'

'Yes. In just over a week's time.'

'Hell, you move fast on a suggestion. You're kidding me, right?'

'No. My friend Julie is a Travel Agent and she needed a traveling companion. So your text was kind of…prophetic, oddly.'

'Oh.' It was all he could think to say as his heart sank with disappointment. He had mentioned Egypt on a crazy feeling they could go there together sometime. Now he realized his intuition on this occasion was askew, as if he had tuned into the wrong radio station. 'Well that's fantastic,' he countered with bravado. 'How long is your trip?'

'I'm not sure.'

'How so?'

'Well, my ticket is open-ended so I can spend more time away. Perhaps that's where I need to be to find and repair my *fractured soul*.' She turned and smiled at him. 'Besides, I've had a fascination with the pyramids and the Sphinx since I was a little girl, and I promised myself way back then that I would visit Egypt someday.'

'Did you now. That's a long-held promise and very committed of you.'

'Bit of fluke getting the trip really. Right time, right place. In any case, I'd like the opportunity to see Jordan and Israel at the same time.'

'Then you must,' he said, clipping the conversation as he registered the potential duration of her travels and her time away from him. Arriving at the quiet cul-de-sac where she lived he turned onto her road. 'But isn't that a little dangerous, traveling in Jordan and Israel on your own.'

'I'll be fine.'

'You seem pretty sure about that.'

'I am sure. Besides, it's important for me to get away,' she said.

'What do you mean?' He parked the vehicle by the footpath and switched the ignition off, looking at her intrigued.

'I mean that I've reached a crossroads in my life and I just need to let go. I want to find a way to trust myself, trust life, and to find my faith again. Just be free. That's what I mean.'

'But you can be free wherever you are,' he said, unbuckling his seatbelt and turning to face her.

She hesitated a moment. 'Look, before I met you Josh, and I mean *right* before I met you, I was…broken. Really badly broken and not in a great place in myself. So when you were talking about fractured souls in the restaurant, you were probably more on the money than I cared to hear about.'

What in God's name did I just tell him all that for?

'I'm sorry,' he said taking her hand.

'It's okay. I know you were trying to help. And you did. You really have. But I have to get back in the driving seat of my life. I don't want to fall down the same holes I have before.'

Fool. Fool woman. Shut up now.

'I'm sorry you've been feeling this way.' He squeezed her hand, wanting to hold her.

'Thanks, but how could you have known. Besides, my headspace is much better now. I've been receiving some…private coaching…and it has helped me understand that I'm the one responsible for creating my life and reality, so I have the power to change it. All my thoughts and actions shape my life, so it's important I choose them wisely.'

Now zip up. What NOT to say to a man on a first date.

'It sounds like you're on the right track.'

'That's the plan. I'm sorry, this is not what I would have wanted to tell you, but I would rather be honest.'

And blow all my chances with you.

'I appreciate your honesty, and your trust.' He squeezed her hand again. 'I think you are a very courageous and special woman.'

'Thank you, but you hardly know me.'

'I know enough.'

'Well I'm not so sure about that.'

You've now just figured out I'm nuts.

'I am.'

She fell silent for a few long moments and he waited quietly.

'So what about you? You strike me as someone who has a lot of faith, Josh. What does faith mean for you?'

'For me?' He smiled softly and thought carefully about his words before he spoke, staring off into the black night outside.

'Let me see. Faith is the moment when the sun is setting and when the sky is filled with beautiful vibrant colors at the end of another miraculous day that I'm alive. It's when a new day dawns and I feel fresh hope and new possibilities. Faith doesn't judge, it's just real simplicity of love and unconditional acceptance of an experience, whatever it is. It's the realization that no matter where I'm at, I am doing what I'm meant to be doing. And tomorrow I'll be doing what I'm meant to be doing too. Tomorrow will be a Ten, as is right now, this moment. That to me, is faith.'

'Wow. That really is a beautiful way to describe it.'

'Thank you,' Josh paused, looking into her eyes. 'I can tell you I have a lot of faith in where I am right now.'

That dress looks so good on her, he thought.

'So you don't worry about stuff? Things don't get you down?'

'On occasion, sure it does. I'm human, I feel it all. I just don't get too hung up on the things that could potentially bring me down. If I'm angry, or sad, it's okay. I let myself feel the emotion but I avoid getting consumed by it.

'So it's like you are watching it from a distance and it doesn't dominate everything?' she said.

'Yes, that's it. Exactly.' He felt himself leaning in closer to her face.

Such beautiful lips.

'And you can still see life as a ten even though you're aware you are sad or angry or anxious on some level?'

'Yes, because it's always a ten. It is all perfect on some level. Hey, the way I see it I'm at least creating the best scenario, the best outcome, by accepting things as they are and believing in the best. That way I'm not bogging everything down with negativity. I like to think the world conspires to bring me that ten experience through my belief in it…a bit like it brought me you and this moment. This moment is definitely a ten.'

If I could just kiss you…

'You don't think that's a little pie in the sky, like Pollyanna.'

He laughed. 'There's no denial of feeling, just acceptance, that's the key. But I'm sure Pollyanna could still certainly teach the world a thing or two these days.' His pulse was beginning to quicken.

'Probably.'

He could just make out the green of her eyes staring back at him.

Damn it, now.

Blood surged through his body as he leaned into her lips and kissed her full on the mouth, reaching a hand around the nape of her neck and pulling her into him. First kissing her softly and gently, tasting and exploring her, then deeper and more passionately as she opened up to him and aroused him further. He wrapped her slim feminine frame fully in his arms feeling the perfection of their bodies pressed together, and their kissing lasted long into the night.

Chapter Twenty

Isadora slept absolutely soundly that night. She was in a deep peaceful state when light filtered into her eyes.

It's not morning, surely. It can't already be morning.

'It's not morning. It's me.'

The angel's voice may as well have been someone banging on the door.

'Oh dear, I was hoping this wouldn't happen,' Seraph said.

Yawning and still slightly disoriented from the bright angelic light and being woken abruptly, Isadora ignored the angel's remark and tone.

'I haven't seen you for a while, Seraph. You've been quiet. And now you decide to drop in…at four in the morning?' she said checking the time.

'Well you've been busy, and…involved. And angels leave humans alone in their more personal moments.'

'Now there's a relief.'

'For both of us.'

Isadora chuckled at the humor and immediately softened.

'So why am I so honored at this ungodly hour?'

'Every hour is Godly, Isadora. As is every minute and every second. I was just making sure you're okay.'

'Of course I am. I'm wonderful. Everything's great,' Isadora said happily.

'Are you sure?'

'Yes, of course. Why wouldn't I be? I've just had a fabulous night with Josh, which you must know. What's your point, Seraph?'

'I'm just checking that you're...keeping your feet on the ground.'

'Well not really, but isn't that the point? I'm supposed to be trusting and learning to have faith...throwing myself into the unknown and all that. I just met someone nice. Please don't spoil it for me,' she said defensively.

'Of course I won't spoil it for you. That is impossible, Dear One. It's entirely beyond my nature, essence, and my control. Besides, any *spoiling* would be completely down to your own perception. My *point* is simply that given where you have been and how vulnerable your emotions are at present, that I might suggest taking baby steps and not putting the cart in front of the horse...so-to-speak.'

'Are you seriously cautioning me to go slow with a man, Seraph? That sounds like the advice an Agony Aunt in a magazine would give, not some celestial messenger.'

'Well, they're not all bad, the Agony Aunts. Some of them actually channel their advice, well…from us actually.'

'Okay, so I need to go slow or I'm in danger of repeating a similar pattern by leaping in headfirst. That's what you're really saying, isn't it.'

'If it was, dear Isadora, it would not change a thing. In the end, you will do what feels true for you in each moment, according to what you currently know and understand about yourself. And you will learn what you learn. But you have that choice, always. You are master of your own destiny. It is very important you understand this. Be careful the emotions you are feeling are indeed your own and that you're not swept away in the moment without at least being aware of where you are and what you want yourself.' Seraph was beginning to emit a beautiful sparkling green color while speaking.

'So you're saying I'm being swept away by Josh?'

'Oh dear, you've just missed the point entirely.'

'Okay, so pretend I'm really stupid and tell me what your point is.'

'My point is simply that you are master of your own destiny, and it would always be to your greatest advantage to operate with this understanding.'

'So I control my life?'

'Actually, you choose it,' Seraph said.

'What do you mean, I choose it? I would always be happy if I chose it. I'd choose to be wildly successful and rich, and I would travel the world.

'Is that so? That's an interesting choice.'

'And I'd have a beautiful loving relationship.'

'A loving relationship with whom exactly?'

'With my partner.'

'Interesting.'

'What are you saying? What are you saying when you keep using the word *interesting*?!'

'That your response is interesting.'

'Oh. My. God. You are so frustrating,' Isadora exclaimed.

'Actually, might I point out that you're creating the frustration in yourself, not me.'

'Okay, okay! I choose my feelings too!'

'Precisely. Now isn't that an enormously empowering concept?' Seraph said in a gentle voice. 'As would be choosing a loving relationship with *yourself first,* and *then* another. Just a suggestion.'

'I see where this is going,' she said with defeat in her voice. 'Thank you, Seraph, but I could do with some time to digest all of this. *Please.*'

'Okay, but before you do that, tell me what you *really* want, Isadora?'

'I want to be happy, I really do,' she said with sadness.

'The way you have been choosing your life I would actually suggest you start with *wanting to want* to be happy, and go from there.'

'That bad, huh?'

'Perfect actually, because now you know how you really think, you can choose to change it. Awareness is always the key.'

'So I just choose what I want, right? Just choose, say *Happiness*, for example?'

'Indeed. Choose it in your thoughts, words and deeds,' Seraph said.

'That's it?'

'That and having a clear idea about how *what you want* looks and *feels*.'

'That sounds surprisingly simple.'

'Just a small catch...'

'Go figure.' Isadora rolled her eyes skyward.

'You will require your *Heart*. It is the only compass that will get you there.'

'Well that's just perfect, because I happen to have lost mine somewhere along the way.'

'Well you're not alone. It's currently an epidemic on earth,' Seraph chuckled.

'Fancy losing my heart, though…like it just walked right out on me one day…and then it was gone. I lost my heart, and God lost my file. I'm a little buggered really.'

'I have three things to say in response to that, and then it's time for me to go.'

'Fire away.' Isadora yawned, feeling sleepy again.

'One. Your heart didn't walk out. I would rather suggest you walked out on it.'

'I'll consider that.'

'Two. God certainly did not lose your file. That is a preposterous notion…it's like a drop of water in the ocean trying to convince itself that it is not part of the ocean. Prime Creator can not lose that which it is.'

'Okay,' she replied, subdued. 'What's Three?'

'Three. This is the funniest conversation I've had in quite some time,' Seraph said. 'Goodnight, dear Isadora.'

The angel chuckled as its vanishing light caused the room to return to darkness.

Did I miss something? All I said was God lost my file. What was so funny?

And Isadora fell back to sleep feeling somewhat puzzled.

Chapter Twenty-One

'Have you had sex with this guy, Izzy?'

Julie stirred her second cup of coffee before looking up from the swirling frothy milk surface long enough to shoot a penetrating look directly into Isadora's eyes. A whole week had flown by since they had met at Julie's travel agency to arrange their trip and they had just finished lunch at a Baker Street café.

'What sort of a question is that, Julz?!'

'Just a normal one, I thought.'

'I've only been on three dates with him.'

'So what? *Half* a date is enough for sex.'

Isadora laughed. 'For you maybe.'

'Sue me. I'm a hot-blooded woman. I'm not apologizing for that.'

'I would never ask you to, Julz. If it works for you, do it.'

'Honestly, I don't think it does work for me really. It never seems to amount to a proper relationship.'

'I wonder why.' Isadora shook her head.

'Damn fun, though. So…have you had sex with him?'

'God, Julz. That's private.'

'Oh come on! You kissed, yes?'

'Yes.'

'A lot, right?' Julie said with persistence.

'Ahuh.'

'Good kissing?'

'Ahuh.'

'Ooh damn, you're like a high security vault. Now what's to hide from your old friend?'

'Nothing. Look, I haven't had sex with him, okay.'

'Good, because if you do, please make sure you use protection,' Julie winked. 'Safe sex is always the best policy.'

'Okay. Can we move on from this subject now, please?'

'Sure, but you can't fool me. You're a dark horse, Izzy Bright.'

'You assume what you like. He's actually really nice. We've been on a few dates and he's been a total gentleman. That's it, period!'

'A total gentleman, huh! As if such a thing exists.'

'You're a cynic. He hasn't tried to get into my pants, Julz. Okay?'

Julie heard Isadora's tone soften protectively and recognized the unmistakable look of a smitten woman, which for some reason began to make her feel concerned. 'A few dates? So where has he taken you?'

'Dinner at a Thai restaurant, a walk in Regent's Park and lunch, a movie the other night, and...' Isadora paused.

'And what?'

'And dinner this evening...at his place.'

'And you don't think he's going to want to jump your bones in his private lair?'

'If he does, I'm a big girl now, Julz. I'll handle it.' Isadora fired her a look.

'Point taken. I shall back up my truck and mind my own business. Apologies, Izzy.'

'I know you mean well.'

'Of course I do.' She felt concern expand to a nagging sensation in her gut. 'But don't you think it will be hard saying goodbye in a few days time? I mean, it sounds like a very romantic connection and I get the feeling you're very taken with him.' She watched Isadora's reaction carefully.

'I am,' she hesitated. 'I like him a lot. He's different from the others...better.'

'Better? Darling, they always seem that way in a passionate new beginning. Try not to fall too deep too soon. Remember my theory of *Fast in, Fast out*.'

Julie had coined the phrase after noticing that men who raced a hundred miles towards a woman in the early onset of romance typically bolted just as fast the moment they had her. It was the classic *'U-turn phenomena'* as she liked to describe it. Although Julie had seldom succumbed to it, having been a rapid early learner. However, she had witnessed it on multiple occasions in other women's lives. Telltale signs were always evident, including the deep sense of shock and loss at him suddenly vanishing like a ghost. But Julie knew that was always the point – he had never been there entirely to begin with. Her ten percent withheld theory had served her well, until she happened to drop the ball with George.

Foolish me. The unbelievable bastard.

'You're like fine porcelain, remember, Izzy...and that's a compliment.'

'Thank you, but I would say I'm more like *broken* porcelain, actually.'

'You still haven't told me what happened with Hayden?'

'It's in the past, and the past is over. There's only *Now*.'

Julie watched Isadora squirm slightly in her chair and remained unconvinced. 'So he was a total prick then?'

'Maybe.'

'Yep, sounds like a total prick. Let's not mince our words with New Age expressions about being in the *Now,* Izzy. That might work for an enlightened Buddha, but pain is pain. *Now* comes *after* you feel and express that.' She nudged her gently. 'Let's forget Hayden. So you dig this guy Josh and you've got this blasted open return ticket. I can still change that for you this afternoon, you know?'

She watched Isadora shuffle her coffee cup nervously around the table.

'No don't do that,' she said, a little too quickly.

Julie sighed heavily. 'Well, if he really likes you he'll be here whenever you get back. But I still don't understand what you're doing considering traveling the Middle East on your own. You're one stubborn woman aren't you,' she said, watching Isadora scrape her chair back hastily and prepare to leave.

'I'm really not sure if stubborn is what I would call me these days, Julz. I'd better fly. I have to get ready for my date.'

'Well, I would be the last woman on earth to stop you from that. Shoo. Have fun.'

'I will.' Isadora smiled softly.

'Now, I'll be expecting a full report about this dinner date. You know that.'

'Maybe half a report. See you Sunday night.'

'Packed and ready, Egypt here we come,' Julie said, standing up and giving Isadora a big hug.

She watched her friend's overly slim body exit the café and felt the same disturbing sensation in her gut.

Something's up. I can feel it.

When Julie got a nagging feeling she knew it was usually on the money. Her Piscean intuition was seldom wrong.

She sighed again as her footsteps guided her back to the Travel Agency. Something was telling her to keep a close eye on Isadora. Egypt might not be quite the simple fun holiday she had planned on.

Chapter Twenty-Two

Isadora left the dinner table and settled into the comfortable black sofa as she watched Josh walk back into the kitchen with an empty bottle of wine. They had eaten a wonderful dish of lasagna that he had clearly spent some time preparing, along with a fresh green salad. She was impressed with his culinary skills. It may have been the effect of several glasses of alcohol over dinner, but he was now looking a little like the dessert to her.

Their previous few dates had ended with hours of passionate kissing, the thought of which caused a liquid warmth sensation to spread throughout her body. She had barely heard a word from Seraph all week, and although the angel had implied she shouldn't jump in too heavily with Josh, it had become increasingly difficult for her not to. So she had conveniently elected to ignore their earlier conversation and any suggestions.

What's the harm in it, I deserve this. A gorgeous man giving me attention.

She watched him disappear for a moment into the kitchen before glancing down to appraise her casual look of fitted jeans and a pretty green shirt that accentuated her eye color.

Yes, good enough, she decided.

Josh lived in East Finchley, not far from her. But he'd insisted on picking her up rather than have her ride the underground two stops.

'Unthinkable.' Was all he'd simply said.

His home was a basement apartment on a tree-lined street. Upon entering she had noticed how warm and tidy it was, along with its masculine tone of dark colors, solid furnishings and simplicity without home clutter.

Once inside she quickly made a beeline for his bookshelf. Isadora had been an avid reader since she was a child, having favored a peaceful existence. She had used books as an escape to avoid the zoo of her extended family and had later discovered people's bookshelves to be a revelation to her about aspects of their character. Josh was no exception with his neatly sectioned books divided into engineering, architecture and design, Hopi and Native American people and traditions, Shamanism, self-development, nutrition…and finally a section on Egypt that jumped out at her. She had set aside a book about Ancient Egypt and was now enjoying rifling through it.

'There's some great stuff in there about Egyptian archeology and the Pyramids and how they were built,' Josh said, returning with a freshly opened bottle of red wine and setting it down on the glass surfaced coffee table before sitting down closely beside her.

He smells so good.

'Actually, that's a subject I've done a lot of research about. I thought how they were built is still considered a bit of a mystery?'

'I guess that depends on who is telling the story,' he smiled. 'I can say from an engineering perspective that the Great Pyramid is a masterful and precision piece of work. Personally I can't fathom how it was constructed back in a time of supposed primitive technology.'

'Don't get me started on that subject.'

'Why's that?'

'I will never stop talking,' she smiled. 'It's fascinating.'

Fascinating, like his lips…

'Certainly intriguing,' he said putting down his glass of wine. 'And captivating, like you.'

Isadora registered zero internal resistance as he leaned over, gently pulling her face close as his lips melted onto hers in a searching kiss. Gradually removing the book from her hand he dropped it to the floor. Her heart was racing as she felt his passion intensify and his tongue probe her own. Her entire body fired up in a second and she returned the kiss with the same heat, staying locked in the embrace for some time and loving his now familiar mouth on hers.

He ran his hands through her hair and pulled her more deeply into him, hungry and tender at the same time as his tongue explored hers and she felt his body weight pressing her back into the sofa. She wanted him with every ounce of her being and knew she couldn't control herself and where the night was headed.

I want this. I want him.

He broke away from her for a second. 'God, I can't control myself with you.'

There was an electrical current of energy pulsating throughout the entire length of her body as her eyes locked with his. 'Then don't.'

It was all the permission he needed as she allowed him to gently take her hand and guide her off the sofa towards the bedroom, lit only by the soft light filtering in from the living room.

He pressed her back onto his bed and his hands slid under her shirt, undoing her bra before gliding over her breasts and causing her nipples to harden. Warmth flooded up from between her legs as he kissed and tasted her neck. She was losing herself, losing control, feeling her energy beginning to merge with his. When suddenly, from somewhere beyond her physical yearning, she felt the most curious intuition that ran counter to everything her body was telling her.

Maybe it was Julie's concerned comment about her being like fine porcelain, or Seraph's words challenging her not to be swept away and to consider what she really wanted. Or possibly, she was becoming fully aware of the critical condition her life had been recently revived from. Whatever the cause, Isadora wasn't sure. But a strangely self-protective feeling began to force its way up from deep within her, causing a potent intuition to radiate from her core like a sonar beep that she couldn't ignore.

She froze for a number of seconds as her inner knowing became stronger.

Something isn't right about this. I shouldn't be here.

Chapter Twenty-Three

Josh felt the moment it all changed. It occurred like the tiniest split-second ripple on the surface of still water, but it was glaringly obvious to him like a distressed animal caught in a trap. It was the moment where typically in all his usual sensitivity, he would have, should have and could have stopped. Only, he chose not to.

It was true he had been uncharacteristically frustrated and tense that day. He had fended off three more annoying phone calls, one just prior to picking up Isadora that evening. His theory about life being a *ten* and his ability to detach from complicated emotions had been tested to the limit earlier in the day, as was typical when Madelaine was attempting to orbit him with a view to landing.

So perhaps it was his instinct to squash any threatening memories of her that cancelled out his natural sensitivity and had affected him so much that evening, or possibly the build up of sexual tension from his last few dates with Isadora. But he didn't really care. The fact was, he wanted her. And he wanted sex.

With his unusual level of attunement to women, he knew something had just occurred that had caused a sexual hesitation in Isadora, but at the point it happened he had also just discovered how wet she was. Given he was rock hard and as turned on as hell, he was faced with a choice that normally would have caused him to pause and check in with her that she was okay, particularly as he knew how vulnerable she currently was. Normally he would have stopped and thought of her first. Normally. But on this night his inner tension drove him completely.

I need this.

Ignoring her hesitancy he pressed his hardness against her and drove his tongue passionately into her mouth as she lay beneath him on the bed. Drawing her shirt off her shoulder his lips moved down to the soft arc of her breasts, and as his mouth closed over one of her nipples he felt her concede fully to her aroused state. He had her. His hand found its way to her soft wetness and began to explore her.

Jesus, she feels so good.

Her body pressed back fiercely into his as her soft moans of pleasure intensified his state of arousal. As her hand slid inside his jeans and began to feel his hardness, a searing ripple of pleasure passed through him.

Christ...

As their clothing peeled off they were skin upon skin. When there was no place left for him to explore and he had brought her to an ecstatic height, he slipped deeply inside her. Nothing else mattered but this timeless place of pure wet pleasure, their bodies moving in rhythmical perfection, their sounds communicating how much they both loved it.

She climaxed with intensity when his own state of total arousal was near peak. It was only then that his orgasm liberated him. He lay physically spent and mentally at peace, drifting in silence for a time. His feelings for her were powerful and with the stillness of his mind he felt them fully as he lay holding her tightly. But his conscience prickled as he held her silent slim frame in his arms, and after their breathing had settled, he finally spoke.

'I'm sorry if things moved too fast for you.' His voice was soft. 'I didn't intend to...leap ahead with you like that.'

It was a distorted version of the truth.

'I'm happy, Josh.'

He could make out her face in the dim light and flinched inwardly with surprise at his feeling of guilt. His Hopi sensitivity and intuition could be a curse at times.

'You're so beautiful,' he whispered into her ear and meant it.

After some time he heard her breathing shift into a deeper state and his thoughts drifted to his father whom he was sure would never have crossed lines like that with his mother. He was so devoted to her and his family and was as unselfish a man as one could find. Josh knew it was a key ingredient in the success of his parents marriage, that and his mother's ability to respect and embrace his father's goodness. As a result, he had been privileged with a very happy childhood. He felt several particles of shame mysteriously float up from within, causing him to reflect a moment on the lowest point in his relationship history, when he had almost struck Madelaine out of sheer frustration.

God, why now? Why was she pursuing him? He thought about the last phone message he had received from her. She was her usual sultry confident self and typically authoritarian about her need to see him. He grimaced inwardly, feeling the reach of her tentacles and knowing he could only ignore her for so long with her level of determination. But he also knew he was done with her and the two of them were beyond over. He would call her in the morning and tell her to back off, that he had met somebody else, someone very special. That would make her disappear.

He moved closer to Isadora, spooning his body more tightly around hers, causing her to stir.

'I really don't want you to go on this trip,' he whispered.

'No?' She said sleepily.

'Purely selfish reasons, sorry. I know it is important to you, but I wanted you to know,' he paused. 'It would be easier if you had a timeline and were back in several weeks like your friend Julie.'

'I understand, but it's a little complicated, Josh,' she said with softness in her voice. 'I didn't expect to meet you, and it makes it hard for me too.'

'I'm glad to hear that,' he hesitated, uncertain about dropping his guard. 'You know I'll wait for you.'

The silence was disturbingly long. 'Really?'

'Absolutely. Are you nuts.' He squeezed her tightly.

But the strange gnawing sensation in his gut bothered him again as his thoughts returned reluctantly to Madelaine and her persistent contact. He would call her in the morning and get it out of the way.

He felt the soft motion of Isadora's breathing as he held her and fell into an unsettled sleep.

Chapter Twenty-Four

She had one day remaining to finish packing and clear up her belongings. Brigitte had kindly agreed to store some boxes in one of the rooms downstairs and Isadora had almost completed the job by late afternoon on Saturday.

He should have called by now.

She had already left a message with Josh and didn't want to leave another. He was supposed to have contacted her early afternoon to arrange to pick her up for dinner, but time had marched on. By eight-thirty in the evening, having left several more messages to check he was okay, she concluded uneasily that for whatever reason he wasn't coming. In the morning when he'd dropped her off they were both very loved-up and the only two people on the planet. His actions and words to date had indicated genuine interest in her. And now – silence.

Let's face it though, I've been way off base before.

She could feel her fragile sense of trust beginning to be heavily tested. She had given herself so totally and completely to him last night…and early in the morning. He had not only penetrated her body but also the deepest part of herself, and in such a primal way.

By nine-thirty she was completely in a tailspin and her mind had taken up residence for the night, something akin to having the most hellish relative come to visit. No matter what positive thought she attempted to throw at the onslaught of habitual pessimism, a doubly negative one would be fired back.

Jesus, was he just using me for sex?

By eleven that night she had exhausted herself in the mental battle of good versus evil and clambered into bed feeling emotionally flattened and uncertain. Having called on Seraph a number of times in a bid to receive answers and for help with her headspace, she realized that for some reason she had been deserted on that level too.

Hardly surprising, given that I ignored your guidance, Seraph.

She was now finding it difficult to believe she had actually witnessed the appearance of angels. Had she imagined everything? After eventually falling asleep she tossed and turned in a restless state, frequently waking to hear an unfamiliar voice in her head whispering the words to her over and over.

'You are the key itself, Isadora.'

She woke bleary-eyed at ten and after a few seconds reached for her phone. Blank screen. No messages, no anything. Surely this was just a bad joke, after all that crap with Tom and Hayden and the queue of others…now Joshua, too? It was all going horribly pear-shaped again.

By the time she had woken herself up, showered and triple-checked her bags for Egypt, it was close to two in the afternoon. She was scheduled to fly out the next day and felt a pressing need to see Josh before she departed. But there was still no response to her calls.

I can't just sit here twiddling my thumbs all day.

By late afternoon her intuition was giving her a shove and she made a decision to go to his place in East Finchley and see if she could find him. She had plenty of time to get there and back before catching a cab to Julie's place. Grabbing her thermal jacket from the top of a packed box she set off with renewed inspiration and determination. It felt easier to be on the move and taking action, so by the time she reached the underground station she couldn't believe she hadn't thought to travel to his place earlier. She had written his address down to send postcards so she knew where to go, but now it was getting dark.

Why did I leave this so late? Anything could have happened to him.

***

By the time Isadora reached his street she had been walking so fast she was almost out of breath. At the sight of his vehicle parked out front on the road a feeling of dread began to form inside her. Nearing the front of his home she slowed her pace and drew to a halt, suddenly uncertain what she was doing there at all. Slowly descending the steps, she peered into the lit living room through the tall basement window. Confusion hurtled screaming towards her as she observed Josh sitting closely on his sofa with a woman. She froze on the step like a deer caught in headlights. Her heart pounded in her chest. She couldn't see his face but the way the woman was looking adoringly into his eyes caused the feeling of dread to increase exponentially. A sick sensation spewed up from the pit of her stomach.

Maybe it's one of his sisters.

Even as she had the thought, she knew it was the kind of hope-laden drivel that was the equivalent of grabbing onto an oil-soaked pole and trying to climb North. The woman was looking adoringly into Josh's eyes in a way that clearly cancelled out the sister possibility, and his hand stroking some very long dark strands of hair tenderly off her face added the effect of darts being thrown at her chest.

Perhaps Isadora made a sudden movement that drew attention, she could never be sure. But the series of events that unfolded after those few horrifying seconds occurred with a shocking speed and surrealism. At the precise moment the full hideous impact of the scene knocked her breathing and logical functions out, the dark-haired woman caught sight of her standing on the steps.

Isadora, frozen like a cadaver to this point, began to back slowly up the stairs grasping onto the railing for support. As she reached the pavement she heard the door open below.

'Isadora?' Josh's voice pierced her body like a high-pitched note hitting a crystal glass. His foot was already on the bottom step as she looked at him, confused and uncertain.

'Josh…I don't understand. Why haven't you contacted me? Who is she?'

'Isadora, I…' He appeared shocked and somewhat anguished when suddenly a voice she didn't recognize spoke from behind him.

'She's Madelaine. His fiancé,' the woman said somewhat defiantly with crossed arms. 'Is this her?' She directed the words to Josh with a smirk on her face as if she had just noticed a cockroach on a wall.

It could have been the fading light but the woman appeared to Isadora for a moment like a hideous gargoyle etched into his front door.

'Christ, Madelaine. Just stop. Stay out of this.' A note of contempt appeared in his voice but Isadora couldn't absorb anymore. It was beyond Groundhog Day and her insides had already climbed to Defcon Two.

She stammered, unsure of him, of her world. 'Your fiancé? Is this true?'

'Look, Isadora, I don't know what to say right now.'

'It's simple, Josh. Just tell me that isn't the truth.' An icy coldness began to form inside her that had become a slowly developed response to lies and betrayal. It normally took her months or weeks to arrive at this place, and only after processing lots of information and self-deprecating emotion. However, years of experience and the now critical mass of bullshit in her lifetime seemed to accelerate her arrival here on this extra special occasion. She felt a strange form of detachment occur, much like her out-of-body experience in the car.

'It's complicated,' he said, extending his hand toward her and tentatively climbing a step as if he were approaching a person carrying a loaded gun.

'Complicated? Complicated?!'

'I'm so sorry, Isadora. There are some things I need to explain. I want to...' But she cut him off with force.

'To explain?!' Explain *WHEN* exactly?!' An energy was beginning to form in her body as she spun mercilessly out of control. 'Or is this a ten too, Josh?! Is this a bloody ten?! Tell me, tell me it's a Ten!' She spat the words out as if they were venom.

He looked at her with a helplessness that in any other situation would have caused her to rush to him. However on this occasion she felt like shoving a boot in his chest and kicking him back to the bottom of the stairs. And she had never felt that sort of aggression in herself before.

He was silent.

'You can't, can you...' The anger was swelling inside her '..because it's not a bloody *ten*, is it?! Is it!!' You're a coward. You're a lying gutless deceptive coward!' She spoke with a cold ferocity, watching him flinch as if she had plunged a knife into his chest.

'God, I'm sorry, let me...' He was walking up the rest of the stairs toward her, but she couldn't bear to hear anymore.

'Don't step ONE...DAMNED...BIT...closer. Just go, and be with her.' The words came out like blocks of cold steel as she caught a glimpse of the other woman wearing a contemptuous half smile.

'Josh, darling. She's right. Or do you want me to tell her, sweetheart?' Madelaine's tone was sickly and controlling at the same time.

'Stop it right now, Maddie,' his voice was low and threatening.

Isadora suddenly froze and everything went deathly still inside her at the sound of him speaking the woman's name with such familiarity. There was more that was unspoken, and as horrific as things already were, she needed to hear it.

'Tell me what?' Tell me what? Tell me, Josh.'

'I'm pregnant with his baby. There you go, that's done.' Madelaine's words were matter-of-fact, much like giving a maid instructions for cleaning her house.

Isadora's breathing became short and rapid and everything fell away except that one inescapable ghastly moment. She didn't see Josh flinch as if he'd been poked with an electric cattle prod. She felt her legs wanting to buckle and a spinning sensation inside her becoming more rapid. All she knew now was that she needed to get away from here, from this place, from that cruel twisted woman, but mostly from the man before her whom she suddenly realized she didn't know at all.

'All that shit about *soul loss*, Josh...Jesus, at least I had a soul to lose,' she whispered, her voice trailing off.

Taking a last horrified look at him through tear-filled eyes, Isadora turned blindly in the direction of the underground station and ran.

'Isadora, Isadora, wait!' He yelled after her.

But she blocked out his voice and ran as she had never run before, like a wounded hunted animal. And she did not look back.

Chapter Twenty-Five

She arrived at Golders Green station into the darkness of night, dazed and in extreme shock. Isadora felt as if she were blowing up like a balloon about to burst. She had to go somewhere. Be utterly alone. Something powerful was happening inside her body that she could not control. Her chest felt numb but below that, bubbles of liquid lava stirred in her gut. She found herself walking towards the wooded heath, devoid of human activity on the cold winter's night. The walls around the rumbling toxic wasteland inside her were caving in. She became aware of an immense pressure of energy desperately wanting to spill out from within her.

Although it was dark, Isadora was not thinking logically. She felt an urgent need to be deep in nature as a primitive state took over and she staggered panicky onto the tree and bush-laden heath. The air was damp and becoming icier as her feet trod across the sodden grass. Close to hyperventilating, she watched the frosted steam of her breath in a hypnotic state and heard a strange sharp ringing in her ears. Scenes of Josh flashed into her mind. A great weight pressed down upon her and her feelings began to push up like a massive seismic activity.

An intense and powerful energy began to pulsate through her, sending waves of liquid heat up her spine. She felt so electrically charged she could power up a city grid.

God help me.

The energy was overwhelming and began to take her over completely as she found herself surrendering helplessly to it. She was stationery now, amongst the shadowy woods. She could not feel God with her, or the angels. Isadora felt utterly desolate and alone.

A rumbling burning sensation in her belly was occurring more ominously now as a sound formed within her. Like a primitive wild animal she instinctively allowed it. It was growling, low and deep, crawling up from her womb, growing louder and louder as it moved towards her throat. She felt like a panther preparing to spring on its prey and couldn't stop the sound, nor did she want to. There was a need so deep within her now to allow it all, to express something her intellect could not interpret or convey.

She dropped suddenly to a crouch near the ground, her fingers reaching into the cold wet soil like claws gripping the earth. Down on her haunches, knees spread wide in a warrior-like stance, the growling became fiercer, deeper and louder, rattling in her stomach like a spring uncoiling. It was forming a long hum that vibrated potently within her and had a life of its own.

Despite the sensation of being in a trance, Isadora became aware that she was not alone. Unseen eyes watched her in the woods and they were many, gathering by the second. Like distant tribal ancestors joining her in a sacred rite and urging her on. They were chanting in the background, invisible yet powerfully present.

The noise both outside and within her became increasingly and exponentially louder, until finally, like a rocket being launched from inside her, a sound fired up from her deepest self. It was a growl that lengthened into a roar, then a fierce scream, flying full force from her womb.

It was rage. A rage so consuming it was as if her whole being was ejecting every stored hurt in her body from her entire lifetime, and lifetimes before. All the deceptions, betrayals, judgments, abandonments, and the unending sense of shame. Everything she had endured, everything she had carried, everything she had suppressed and denied feeling. All the parts of herself she had condemned and imprisoned, the worthlessness and helplessness, and every retreat to victimization. And the wounding to her innocence; an innocence that was gone - the precious grace of her childhood sucked up by a vacuum of earthly pain.

The sound flew out of her again with violence. There was hatred in it now; a desire for vengeance and destruction, all consuming. Everything unlived, unfelt and unspoken, screamed out of her with a force that kept her locked in her haunches and threatened to rip her body apart. The second bloodcurdling scream was long, an intense potency in it, a power she could not comprehend. She was overwhelmed with pain for what she had denied and withheld from herself - her birthright. Her own incomprehensible spirit and the freedom of expression that it came with; her voice and the dominion over her own psychic terrain. Shattering all the shackles with her own sound, she roared - unbridled, primal…free.

The third wave occurred just as powerfully, but it was different for her now. Isadora felt herself embracing it, fearless, surrendering to the energy flowing uninhibited through her. Her fingers lifted out of the soil, like claws rising to the heavens. She felt the power in her legs and thighs as she rose up from her haunches, fully upright like a warrior. Her head was thrown back, arms bent wide, as the primal roar rose from within her again. She engaged the energy fully now, welcoming it, as if all the painful ghosts of her past were standing before her and she was defiant, resolute and invincible. The trees of the forest were shadowy, the unknown eyes with them. All seemed to stand to attention with an understanding and reverence for the life force vibrating profoundly from within her.

It was as if roots were reaching down from her feet and connecting her all the way into the soul of the earth; as if the Great

Mother herself was listening intently, with the compassion of one who knew; of one who had suffered too. In that second, Isadora experienced an acute awareness that there was no separation between her and the world, this precious planet she stood upon. They were the same, their bodies ever connected in some mysterious union. There was nothing but devotional love and service emanating from beneath her, an all pervading love and the inexplicable truth that in Isadora's own capacity to feel everything, she was known and cared for completely by this great host she stood upon.

As time suspended, she began to feel as though she was standing in a pool of pulsating liquid energy. It was magnetizing around her, starting to vibrate and creep up into the cells of her body through the souls of her feet. She felt as if she was plugged into a socket as a current moved fluidly in waves up through her body. As the energy culminated in the area of her heart, moved out through the crown of her head, cycled outside her and back toward the ground, she felt washed with a divine and unconditional love. Overwhelmed with the experience and realization, a sob wrenched from her heart and flew out of her mouth. Feeling suddenly very weak she reached for the nearest tree to support her, and turning her body, collapsed against it. Sensing the same tangible energy flowing out from beneath its bark she slid down to rest on the earth, utterly exhausted.

The unseen eyes began retreating from this sacred place of passage, floating gracefully off into the ether like a group of fans departing a long-anticipated concert. Chants softly echoed into the night sky until the sound was entirely gone. Her eyelids hung heavy as she now found herself in a place of breathtaking expansiveness and stillness. Nothing else mattered anymore. She was not alone on this planet and never could be. She was part of it. Her life force and her heart beat in time with the great earth beneath and everything around her. All of the natural world was connected and she connected with it all.

You are the key itself. A voice whispered around her.

Sitting alone in the cold and the dark, and before losing consciousness entirely, Isadora realized that she did belong both on and to the world. Her life as she knew it would never be the same again.

Her energy utterly spent, she became vaguely aware of a soft light forming before her as she drifted into exhausted unconsciousness.

Chapter Twenty Six

Julie was deeply concerned as she looked over at her sleeping friend and leaned across to adjust the blanket more tightly around her. How the hell they had actually made it this far was a miracle. She sat back heavily in her seat and decided to pray for a moment. She had never been particularly religious or one prone to asking for help from intangible sources, but she did believe in a greater power and even angels. And this was one of those occasions where it was time to call on whatever miracles and assistance were available.

She softly closed her eyes.

Dear God, I know I'm probably not your most well-behaved soul, and sometimes I'm a bit brazen, my language can be dreadful...and I'm occasionally oversexed. But I thought I would check in with you to kindly ask for some help...if I still have some credit available that is. My friend, Izzy, needs your help, God. She's a sensitive soul that has taken a lot of knocks in life, and she's just had another. I think she could really do with a big hand like yours...not that I'm suggesting you have big hands. I'm not quite sure what to ask for specifically, but she's a very good person with a beautiful heart, and if you could please help her and make her life easier and happier I'd greatly appreciate it. Thank you, God. Amen.

PS: I know vengeance is said to be your territory and I shouldn't ask, but if you have a spare lightening bolt you could throw at

George, I'd be ever so grateful.

Sitting for some time afterward in an almost meditative state, she was just beginning to fall asleep when the plane experienced turbulence and began bumping about in the air. As the *fasten seatbelt* sign went on she noticed, to her left, that Isadora was beginning to stir.

Stay asleep, Izzy. Please.

Julie watched Isadora carefully as she began to move, at first lifting her head as if it were a heavy object balanced on a twig. She slowly opened her eyes as if they had been glued shut with syrup, registering discomfort as daylight blasted into the back of each retina.

'Izzy, Izzy...are you okay?' Julie's voice was filled with concern.

'Julz?' Isadora mumbled, her voice croaky from dehydration. 'Julz?' Reaching out she felt the warmth of Julie's hand take hold of hers.

'Yes it's me, sweetheart.'

'Where am I?'

'Currently? About thirty five thousand feet, somewhere over the Mediterranean. We're getting closer to Egypt.'

'Egypt? Oh God, that's right, Egypt. How did I get on the plane?'

'Don't you remember, darling?'

'Not much.'

'Oh,' Julie paused. 'Well, you showed up on my doorstep late last night looking like death-warmed-up and quite mute. I couldn't get anything out of you except a few words about Josh and a woman,' she hesitated, watching Isadora flinch. 'Oh, and somebody called Seraph - or an odd name like that – whom you said helped you and got you to my place. Do you remember any of this, Izzy?'

'Only vaguely.'

'I was so worried about you. I almost called off the trip, but you insisted we were going. You said you absolutely had to get to Egypt, and some other stuff about a big light appearing that didn't make any sense at all. Then you crashed straight out on the sofa. I gave you a sleeping tablet at the airport because we talked about that earlier for your motion sickness.'

'Yes we did. Thank you, Julz. My mouth feels like cardboard. Is there any water?'

'Of course. Here you go,' Julie said, unscrewing the top and handing her the bottle of water she had set aside.

Isadora gulped down half of it.

I should ask her, but I'm not sure if it's a good time, Julie thought.

'Izzy?'

'Yes?' Isadora looked at Julie through her sunken and tired green eyes. They looked lackluster in color with dark rings engraved like tattoos against the backdrop of her pale skin.

'I know it's probably too soon, or possibly too much for you to talk about right now, but what exactly happened...with Josh I mean?'

A pained expression washed over Isadora's face that was as revealing as it was saddening to Julie.

'We had this great night together Friday, and then he didn't call me over the weekend like he said he would. So I showed up at his place. I probably shouldn't have gone there, Julz, I know…but I did unfortunately. Anyway, there was a woman there with him,' she stopped.

'Go on, Izzy.'

'It was his fiancé, Madelaine.'

'Oh, good Lord, you're kidding me.'

'She said she was carrying his baby…' Isadora said with a vacant expression.

'Oh God, that's terrible for you. No wonder you were such a wreck.' Julie said, flinching inwardly as she recalled the moment she had found out that George was having a baby to another woman.

'Well, it's not like I wasn't warned in some way.'

'That's ridiculous, Izzy. You weren't to know that. Don't you dare blame yourself.'

'I guess not. Anyway, I ran, Julz. I just ran. I couldn't contain my…rage.'

'I'm not surprised. And if I ever see him I won't be containing my rage! Bloody lying using monster, I could break his balls.' As Julie finished talking she heard a rattle behind her causing her ears to prick up like a dog hearing a high pitched whistle from its master.

Drinks trolley, hallelujah!

As the flight attendant moved the trolley cart up beside their row Julie, still clutching Isadora's hand, motioned to the woman. 'Could we have some water, thanks.' She pointed to the bottles on the top of the cart with her free hand. 'And some red wine, too.' She mouthed the last words.

As the woman reached forward with several of the standard inflight baby bottles of wine and clear plastic cups, Julie shook her head as if in disagreement. 'We'll be needing a lot more than that, thank you,' she nodded encouragingly at the attendant as she placed more bottles on her tray table.

Turning back towards the sad far-off expression on Isadora's face, Julie made a decisive and firm decision. 'Look my friend, if this guy can be such an absolute arse then he is clearly not worth wasting too much emotional time over. Okay? I know that may sound like some flowery crap out of an Agony Aunt column or something, and I understand you're hurting and it's going to take some time, but let's face it, we've both been here before and we know the fastest way through this.'

Isadora looked back at her for a moment like a forlorn sheep ready to be shepherded with total hope and trust. 'What way is that, Julz?'

And Julie knew the fork in the road had arrived and which path to take.

'Booze, my friend. Booze.'

Chapter Twenty-Seven

Perhaps it was the red wine coursing through her veins, or all the crying on Julie's shoulder that made the thought of Joshua Hunter shrink to a more manageable load. With each glass of wine he seemed to disappear further into the background like thick plumes of vapor trailing behind the aircraft. Of course, Julie's fabulous sense of humor did wonders for Isadora too, although her friend did seem to get progressively confused and confusing by the time she'd knocked back her sixth glass of wine.

'They're bloody tiny plastic cups, don't you think, Iz,' she slurred.

Isadora didn't fully agree.

'And stuff Josh!' she said bashing a now empty cup down forcibly on her tray table and splitting it open as passengers in the adjacent row looked on in quiet amusement.

'He shouldn't have got that damn hussy knocked up when he's already married to some other woman. It's wrong I say, bloody wrong!'

'I think you must be confusing the story somehow, Julz,' Isadora said, struggling to keep up with the dialogue Julie seemed to be having with herself, or possibly the back of the passenger seat in front of her. 'Josh isn't married to anyone.'

'Well he's a fricking idiot,' she mumbled. 'He should be damn well married. To me! Dumb crazy man, Izzy,' she slurred again. 'It's wrong I say, bloody wrong.' She repeated herself a number of times before eventually closing her eyes and nodding off, head thrown back and mouth wide open.

Isadora stared at her, confused and perplexed for a minute before her own wine-soaked brain forgot entirely what she was thinking about. She quietly stacked the baby wine bottles in neat lines on her tray table, registering in a vague haze that she had never before seen Julie lose quite as much of her class or cool when she drank. Sure she could swear like a hardened criminal, but it seemed to Isadora that it was more than her drama with Josh that had driven her friend to drink.

What the hell is going on with Julie?

It was her last thought before she too fell into a wine-induced sleep.

***

Isadora and Julie stood in the passport entry queue in Cairo airport.

'Whose stupid idea was it to drink on the plane, Izzy?' Julie said, pressing her sunglasses into her face as if indenting them would block extra light.

'Ah, that would be yours, Julz,' Isadora replied dryly as she observed the length of their queue in dehydrated despair.

'You know, I think I would prefer to blame Joshua-bloody-Hunter-Gatherer-of-women, actually.'

'Do not mention his name, Julz,' Isadora lifted Julie's sunglasses onto her head, causing her to reel backwards.

'Christ, Izzy. Death by blinding,' she said waving her hands in front of her eyes.

It may have been the red wine still very present in Isadora's system, or the sight of Julie's bloodshot bleary eyes staring back at her, but she was suddenly overcome with an enormous sense of humor. She fell into peels of laughter, causing Julie to do the same and attracting all manner of stares.

Eventually they stopped laughing. 'Okay, Julz. We exorcised him on the plane. From now on his name is banned,' Isadora said firmly.

'Banned, banned, and more banned, Izzy. Couldn't agree more.'

'Hallelujah sister.'

Julie pointed her finger skyward with a mock serious expression. 'And let us not wallow in the valley of despair. I say to you today my friend…that I have a dream! I have a dream today. I have a dream that you are free at last, free at last, free at last!'

'Jesus, Julz, how the heck do you memorize Martin Luther King lines like that?'

'Inspired by my latest ex,' she grimaced.

'I see.'

'Ahuh.'

'And his name would be?'

Julie hesitated. 'George.'

Isadora saw the look of sadness hidden deep in her friend's eyes. 'God bless Martin Luther King,' she added quietly.

'Profound man, and very versatile. Yes, God bless him, Izzy.'

Chapter Twenty-Eight

The pleasantly warm air and hustle and bustle at Cairo airport only hinted at the chaos that lay beyond in the city of almost twenty million occupants. Julie was surprised to know what a relatively young city it was – having really only taken off after 969AD. Isadora, on the other hand, armed with years of research, felt as though she'd been handed a key to a long-lost vault.

It was nearby at the spectacular Giza Necropolis that the real history of the land had been laid down many thousands of years earlier. And she was about to gaze first hand upon the fascinating structures. As she'd told Josh, she would finally fulfill a childhood promise to herself. As a seven-year old she'd poured over an encyclopedia, marveling at pictures of the seven Ancient Wonders of the World. The pyramids were the last remaining wonder of them all and now the promise of a young girl was rushing back to her mind and heart. She could barely contain her enthusiasm, much to the relief of Julie, thrilled to see her friend's spirits lifting. Who cared about a hangover!

'Um ad-Dunya.' Isadora muttered.

'What's that, Izzy?'

'Mother of the World,' Isadora smiled at Julie. 'That's how Cairo is known here.'

'We're in nurturing hands then,' Julie said.

'Yes, we can hope.'

From the moment the warm dusty air filled Isadora's nostrils, she was hooked. Despite travel weariness, alcohol and residual sleeping tablet effects, not to mention emotional exhaustion from the previous twenty-four hours, Isadora felt heaviness lifting from her shoulders as the bedlam of Cairo captured her full attention.

In an effort to show respect and avoid any undue attention, both women had worn clothing that covered their bodies fully. Now with light-colored scarves wrapped loosely over their heads they wandered toward the taxi drivers who were separating them from the terminal exit. A number swarmed on them like locusts. Thank goodness their hotel had supplied an amiable driver for a courtesy pick-up. There he was, holding a sign with their names on it. Introducing himself politely in reasonable English, Akram guided them towards his waiting vehicle.

As they headed into the bustling and colorful streets of Cairo, Isadora was struck at once by the sense of light all around her, both in the glare of sunshine and in the sand and concrete color of the buildings. Despite Cairo being built up over the centuries, the wonder of the open sky with its stretch of blue painted on the vast canvas above was a huge delight. In London she had gradually forgotten to bother to look upward. Not only did towering buildings block much of the skyline, but the ceiling of the world above the city was all too frequently grey. For a moment she shuddered at the recollection before returning her full attention to the dazzling Egyptian sky.

Akram drove towards the downtown area where their accommodation was situated. His steering appeared a little dubious to Isadora as they hurtled along busy town streets, bumping and jostling all over the van. The driving style was apparently necessary as a form of human dodge-ball though, as locals in long Egyptian clothes randomly crossed the roads in front of them.

'This is crazy,' Isadora leaned over to whisper in Julie's ear. 'I feel like we're in one of those manic action movies where innocent pedestrians get taken out in car chase scenes.'

'Apparently this is the done way to cross the streets here,' Julie whispered back, smiling.

Isadora screwed her face up at the thought.

Akram continued to drive the vehicle down a single very long road as Julie scrutinized a map of Cairo.

'Salah Salem,' she declared triumphantly pulling her face out of the guidebook.

'What?'

'Salah Salem. It's the name of this road.'

Akram smiled into the rearview mirror. 'Yes, yes. Salah Salem. I take you downtown to best hotel,' he said, causing Isadora and Julie to look at each other with knowing smiles. After all, didn't every driver know *the* best hotel, cafe, restaurant or shop, to ferry weary travelers too.

Turning the van right at the next intersection and heading in the direction of the central downtown area, Akram weaved his way through the small streets with an undetermined mix of madness and expertise before finally pulling up in front of a building.

Their hotel was a French-run establishment situated five or six blocks from the Midan Tahrir, a large frenetic roundabout in the heart of downtown Cairo. Upon arrival, the women noticed their accommodation had an Egyptian-European flair in terms of furnishings, and a distinct stamp of French style. They both immediately warmed to their new short-term abode as they were directed upstairs to their bright modern room. Julie walked straight to the open balcony doors that looked out across some of Cairo city.

'Wow, Izzy. Come and check this out.'

Isadora approached the balcony, at first noticing a dusty haze hanging over the city. From their vantage point they viewed a sea of sandy buildings as far as their eyes could see. The late afternoon light was fading and a pink sky was forming off in the distance. At that very moment, standing together perched up high on the balcony, the haunting sound of the *Call to Prayer* echoed across the city rooftops. Despite the man's voice being broadcast through minaret loudspeakers across the city, the beauty and sacredness of the prayer almost took Isadora's breath away. She felt an incredible feeling of freedom and deep peace inside.

It was at that moment she determined she would avoid all conversation and thought about Josh. It may have happened yesterday, but yesterday was another world away and magic existed in this new land.

Here, she could forget her past and begin again.

Chapter Twenty-Nine

In the very early morning the *Call to Prayer* stirred Isadora from a deep sleep. A light appeared to be shining in through the balcony doors. They had closed them before going to bed because the temperature was a little cooler in the night at this time of year. Although, to Isadora, it felt as warm as the tropics. She couldn't conceive how cold it would be in London. Yawning, she stretched out, feeling the smoothness of the fresh cotton sheets.

I need to close the curtains. She blinked.

'Isadora.'

It was the voice of Seraph inside her head and she suddenly realized what the bright light was as she sat up on one elbow.

'Seraph, what are you doing here?' she communicated telepathically. 'Julz might wake up. You can't let her see you,' she looked anxiously for a moment at the bed a few feet from hers. In the light the angel was emitting, she could see Julie fast asleep with her mouth half open and breathing deeply. Seraph, who was now radiating a calming blue color, continued their telepathic conversation.

'She will not wake.'

'Well, if you say so.'

'I do.'

'What happened to me, Seraph? All that stuff in the woods, and I can hardly remember getting to Julie's,' Isadora said, recalling the memories like they belonged to somebody else's life.

'There was release and clearance of much old negative energy from your cellular body and new pathways of energy were activated. You did very well and will begin to feel different...lighter. We are most pleased.'

'I did very well? I just about froze to death, passed out by a tree from what I can recall.'

'But you didn't. You were never in danger, Isadora. The only danger would have been not to clear all that negative stuck energy from your body and being.'

She reflected a moment. 'I think I understand. Thank you...for keeping me warm, and for saving me.'

'No thanks required. All in loving service.'

'What did you do?'

'Bathed you in warm light until you arrived at Brigitte's, and kept your body heated.'

She sighed. 'I can hardly remember.'

'Yes, we did that too. Sometimes it is best that way.'

'You knew about Josh and you tried to warn me.'

'All is perfect, Dear One. All is perfect. You will know this one day.'

'You sound just like Josh.'

'Where do you think he got his theory?'

Isadora paused to register. 'Of course, from the great downloadable Angel advice in the sky.'

'That's good, Isadora. Very amusing.'

'Anyway, I'm glad I'm in Egypt, Seraph. It feels good.'

'So are we.'

'And what have you got planned for me here, I wonder?'

'That's rather dependent upon your choices.'

'And that's all you're going to tell me, right?'

'I'm just a guide, my friend. Not living your life for you.'

'You're so good.' Isadora shook her head.

'Indeed. One of the qualifications for being an angel.'

'And still a comedian.'

'Lightly. Remember, Isadora…Angels take themselves lightly.'

'Ahuh,' Isadora gave up.

'Good, at last you are ready to listen,' Seraph said reading her thoughts. 'Know this, I will be with you often as you travel this land, in unseen ways. Remember this always. Enjoy your time here. The path is laid before you, the choices you take ever perfect. Trust.'

Isadora's eyelids were feeling heavy as she noticed Seraph turning a vibrant purple indigo color. She lay back on her pillow, suddenly very sleepy.

'Trust,' she repeated in her mind.

'Yes. Trust, Isadora. All is Okay. Many blessings to you.'

Seraph disappeared again and so did she, deep into the dimension of sleep.

***

Bright daylight woke her again. It was pouring in through the open balcony doors. The soft white curtains were drawn open and motionless on a windless morning before a pristine blue-sky backdrop. It took Isadora about three seconds to remember where she was before excitement began pulsing through her veins. Egypt, blessed Egypt…and today she would see her beloved pyramids. She sat up in her bed with a start. Julie was seated opposite at a mirror attached to an ornately carved wooden dresser.

'Ah, Sleeping Beauty wakes.' Her head was wrapped turban style in a perfect white Egyptian bath towel as she applied her eye makeup. 'I was just thinking about waking you, Izzy. Did you sleep okay?'

'Yes wonderful. How about you?' Isadora reached casually for the glass of water by her bed, gratefully downing large mouthfuls whilst scrutinizing Julie's reaction. Was there any hint of her being aware of Seraph's visit in the night?

'Absolutely, like a baby after all that alcohol on the flight. Except for a vague memory of the Call to Prayer. Amazing isn't it, five times a day, every day. But it's so beautiful, it makes me think of Angels…like they're all around me.'

Water sprayed instantly out of Isadora's mouth.

'You okay, Izzy?' Julie raised her brow.

'I'm fine.' Isadora wiped her mouth and put the glass down.

'Really?'

'Just went down the wrong shute. Angels, nice thought. Sounds like you believe in them?'

'I do, actually.' Julie paused. 'You know, this might sound weird, Izzy, but I once had a car accident and I was standing near my smashed car in despair when I saw a mini park up across the road with the plate registration *ALL IS OK*. I swear to God my angel had arranged for that car to pull in right after my accident.'

'Wow, that's pretty cool, Julz. Someone must be looking after you.' Isadora recalled curiously that Seraph had spoken those exact words to her in the night.

'I know, I really do believe that. I've never forgotten that car plate. I repeat that line to myself a lot when things ever get tough. *All is okay*. It reminds me that a bigger picture exists that I can't always see or understand, and someone or something is taking care of me.'

Isadora was very quiet as she stared down at her bed covers. 'Amazing, Julz,' she said quietly.

'Izzy? Are you okay?'

'Yes of course.' Isadora snapped back to attention. 'I was just thinking how useful it is to have angels show up at car accidents. Hey, what time is it?'

'Seven-fifteen.'

'I'd better jump into the shower. We must get to the pyramids before it gets too warm out there.'

'Not before breakfast, Izzy. I hear the crepes here are something to die for.'

'Say no more,' Isadora said, springing out of bed and padding her way upon the cool tiled floor towards the bathroom.

The truth was, in that moment she was feeling very humbled. And she suddenly understood that it was no coincidence that her traveling companion was Julie.

Chapter Thirty

The crepes were indeed as legendary as their reputation suggested. They had ventured up to the rooftop terrace to breakfast outdoors with magnificent views of Cairo city. It was a memorable sight for them both.

'Wish you were a man,' Julie sighed, pushing her plate away as she finished her last mouthful of crepe.

'Oh? Why is that?' Isadora raised her eyebrows.

'Because this would be the most perfectly bloody romantic breakfast I have ever had.'

Isadora chuckled. 'I'm far from being a man, more the casualty of them. They're completely off my menu.'

'So you wouldn't be tempted by some seductive native or mysterious traveler whisking you off on a steamy Arabian night or something?'

'Nope. Steamy nights are off my menu too. Besides, you told me no Sheiks, remember.'

Julie watched Isadora survey the Cairo skyline, relieved to notice that she was looking more relaxed.

'True. You know Izzy, it's none of my business, and you don't need to answer if you don't want to because we said we would never mention his dreaded name, but...you did have sex with Josh, didn't you? Forgive me if we covered this on the plane, but I was rather hammered if you recall. I can't remember.'

Julie watched Isadora's face remain fixed on an unseen horizon as if weighing something up.

'I can't imagine you would forget a conversation about sex with even ten bottles of wine inside you, Julz.'

'Cheeky this morning, aren't we.'

'A touch.'

'So?'

'So what do you think? Spot the stupid woman.' Isadora's expression changed to sadness.

'Oh.' Julie was quiet for a number of seconds.

Damn. Hope she's not pregnant too. Disaster.

'Nothing stupid about you at all, Izzy. So you can drop that self-flagellating crap with me right now. I don't want a bar of it.'

God, her face is plummeting to the ground. Tears imminent.

'And was he any good?' Julie quickly continued, maintaining a serious face with a glint of mischief in her eyes as Isadora began to smile.

'Ah, so he was! Busted!'

Isadora began to giggle.

'You still need to answer my question.' Julie began to giggle too.

'Yes!'

'Yes, what? Yes, was he a rampant stallion?'

Isadora stopped giggling. 'You know, it was strange.'

'What, the sex? Was he kinky or something?'

'No. I just had this moment where I knew it was wrong. I knew I shouldn't be there.'

'I get that a lot too.'

Isadora smiled. 'And then I ignored that, and sexually it was like being on this rooftop, with this view...and these divine crepes to top it all off. Pretty damn sensational.'

'Oh.' Julie was quiet for another long moment. 'Bugger. Right then, best we get to those pyramids fast. Come on.' She stood up, taking Isadora by the hand and guiding her to the stairs. 'You know, I was rather hoping for more intimate detail. But breathtaking and like crepes will just have to do,' she said, turning to look at Isadora.

'But when you say *'crepes'*, are you referring to the crepe itself, or the maple syrup?'

'Julz!'

'I'm just checking.'

They laughed.

'You're killing me, Julz.'

'I hope not! But for the record, crepe-like sex does not remove the fact that he is an asshole and his name is banned again.' She winked.

***

They grabbed their daypacks from their room and headed outside to join Akram, waiting to take them to Giza.

'Lovely ladies, you see the great pyramids today, yes?' He beamed as he beckoned them inside the vehicle. They were dressed once more with pastel colored scarves covering their heads. Isadora's was soft pink, and Julie had her blonde hair tied up beneath a lime green cotton scarf. Mindful of ventilation in the heat, both were wearing light linen trousers and long sleeved flowing cotton tops, purchased before leaving London.

It was mid-morning by the time the van bumped its way out to the site of the ancient necropolis, dodging pedestrians along the way. Isadora was surprised to find the Pyramids, nestled on their sandy plateau, were also right beside the sprawling and busy suburb of Giza. It seemed somehow bizarre to her that such magnificently old structures were now so embedded amongst modern city chaos.

As the van pulled in beside the last buildings on the fringe of a

THE BRIGHT NEW DAWN

sandy landscape they sighted the magical peaks of two pyramids, towering above suburbia. The vision had been amazing even from a distance. Isadora felt her heart pounding and could hardly contain her excitement as they disembarked from the van. Half a dozen enthusiastic touts honed in on them like flies to a cowpat, hell-bent on selling them a camel, horse, or donkey ride to their grand destination.

'Ladies. Lovely ladies, I give you best camels for best price,' said one.

'Take my wonderful thoroughbred horses for bargain price, lovely ladies,' said another.

Julie, ever assertive, took over completely.

'Who can offer the best deal?' Instantly she was surrounded, leaving Isadora to watch her friend's lime green scarf bobbing in the air amongst the mob of persistent men. She couldn't help but admire Julie, looking like a blonde Audrey Hepburn with the large dark sunglasses, scarf, and immaculate pink glossy lipstick. She always carried an air of command and class about her, despite some of the questionable language that occasionally spewed forth from her mouth. Julie was a melting pot of the modern feminist movement, class and earthiness, with striking femininity thrown into the mix. Capable of turning from iron-clad steel to an alluring yet fluffy cloudlike substance, and from femme fatale to wise mystic in the time it took to say *Goddess,* Isadora found herself wishing she had a little more backbone like her friend.

'Bargain, absolute bargain. Forty bloody Euros for both of us. Hope you've got your riding breeches on, girlfriend,' Julie exclaimed returning to Isadora's side with a broad smile.

'Will do my best. So what's our transport?'

'The ultimate riding experience of course, darling,' she paused. 'Okay. I lied. Not *the* ultimate riding experience.'

'God, Julz.' Isadora feigned disapproval.

'Okay, okay. Camel of course, Izzy.'

'As only one does in Cairo.'

'Absolutely, darling. Now where has Bahir gone?' Julie's gaze followed the group of men dispersing. 'Bahir? Bahir.'

'Yes lady.' A smiling Egyptian man spun around. 'Please follow me,' he directed.

They traipsed across thirty meters of sand before Bahir stopped them both, asking them to wait. Five minutes later he reappeared, leading two very tall camels with saddles and bright colorful saddle-blankets. Isadora thought they looked rather bored with the whole ordeal and felt a little sorry for the animals when Bahir made them get down on their knees.

'Our chariots await,' Julie said, making a beeline to the nearest of the two and managing to clamber into the saddle with relative ease.

Isadora's camel threw her a very disinterested look before she gripped onto the saddle pommel and launched herself up onto its back.

'Like a bloody pro, Izzy!'

'I was thinking the same about you. Wow, don't they smell charming,' she said screwing her nose up.

Julie giggled, her expression changing to worry as Bahir encouraged her camel onto its feet.

'Oh, gracious!' she exclaimed.

Her camel was standing up front legs first and Julie tipped completely backward in her saddle, legs flying upwards, as she barely managed to stay aboard. As the camel's back legs came up she lurched face forward before finally regaining an elegant composure.

'Good Lord, Izzy, it's like riding a toy-boy!'

Isadora laughed her head off until she saw Bahir approach her camel and became suddenly very alert. He gave the camel a good smack on its rear quarters and she felt the animal heave upwards.

Having observed Julie tip backward and forward, Isadora counter-balanced perfectly, leaning forward right into her saddle and digging her legs into its sides until she felt the camel's weight shift. She immediately altered her posture.

'Quite the expert,' Julie quipped.

'Riding lessons,' Isadora winked back.

'Marvelous, darling,' Julie responded in a plum-like accent. 'Righto, Tonto. Off you go.' She waved her hand forward, causing Isadora to burst into laughter again.

'Feet, Julz. Use your feet.'

'Of course, Izzy.'

The camels began to amble forward and the two women wobbled from side to side until they adjusted to the rhythm of the movement. Bahir volunteered to ride with them, but both women opted for the adventure on their own, with his assurance the camels were completely tame and went to the pyramids and back on auto-pilot.

It was near mid morning and the temperature was already climbing. Isadora felt the rolling motion of the camel moving beneath her as she stared off across the sandy horizon. Far off in the distance the pointed peak of the Great Pyramid appeared. The mirage-like haze created the appearance of movement and only heightened the magical image as the camels plodded slowly toward their destination. Eventually arriving at the crest of a sand plateau that had been sweeping gently upwards, their view became more expansive as the three pyramids became fully in view.

'Can you believe this, Izzy? They're just so incredible.'

'Amazing, absolutely amazing. Awe-inspiring.'

Julie halted her camel, digging around in her daypack for her digital camera. 'I have to get a photo.'

The camels paused obediently as the two women looked out across a vast stretch of sand towards the majestic sight of the three pyramids.

'Astounding. You wonder how they really put these things together,' Julie said, taking photographs.

Isadora was in deep thought as she dragged the scarf off her head, dabbing it against her forehead and shaking out her long dark hair.

'You know, they barely have the technology in this day and age to create structures like this on earth, so what does that say about the civilization that existed back then, Julz. I mean, it was supposedly four and a half thousand years ago. How did they cut those huge rocks and move them?'

'I have absolutely no idea at all my friend, but those men must have had some damn fine bodies with a daily workout like that.' Julie smiled.

Isadora rolled her eyes towards the expanse of blue sky. 'Does your mind ever venture above your waist, Julz? I mean, aren't you just the tiniest bit curious?'

'Ah...' Julie paused for effect. 'Nope.'

'Julz, you can't be that ignorant,' Isadora said with despair.

'I'm kidding. Of course I'm curious, Izzy.'

They were interrupted by the sound of voices growing louder as several horses cantered up behind them.

'Geez, would you look at that.'

Isadora could make out the slight drawl of an Australian man's accent.

'Fantastic. Look at the size of them.' A second man responded with a softer accent.

The horses were slowing and drew to a walk, angling their way past the camels. They moved slowly and were at least six meters to the right as both women turned to see two pairs of eyes looking back at them beneath outback style hats.

'Morning, ladies.' The man with the stronger accent nodded his head towards them. 'Splendid day for a stunning view,' he said boldly, grinning at Julie. His tee-shirt was cut off at the shoulders, highlighting his well-toned biceps and tanned skin, and he was wearing sandy colored combat trousers.

'Yes, superb.' Julie beamed back at him, the pitch in her voice becoming higher as her posture shifted more upright on the camel.

The horses continued to move slowly past them and Isadora watched with curiosity as her glance fell upon the other rider. She noticed his eyes were bright blue and the corners of his lips were curled up in an easy kind of smile. He stared back at her a moment longer than she felt comfortable with.

'Ladies,' he said, nodding his head politely as they continued past, giving their horses a slight kick to nudge them back into a canter. Before long they were breaking into a gallop, whooping with delight as they charged off at speed, drawing further and further away.

Isadora watched as they rode off into the distance. 'When you said superb, Julz, I take it you were referring to the Pyramids?'

'Of course not! Did you see that man's arms?'

'No. I must have missed that whilst taking in the remarkable scenery ahead.'

'Oh rubbish, you just about fell off your ruddy camel. Come on, Izzy. I think Cairo just got world-class interesting.' Julie threw her a wink before nudging her animal back to life. 'Tonto, follow those horses!'

Isadora shook her head in mock disapproval, laughing as the camels ambled off slowly down the long stretch of sand.

Before them, one of the world's great mysteries loomed closer.

Chapter Thirty-One

They left their camels with Arab touts that Bahir had carefully recommended and began their explorations near the base of the pyramids by foot. It was late morning and dozens of tourists were flocking around the site like ants descending upon a giant mound of food. Isadora found the sheer size of the structures up close more breathtaking than she could have imagined, despite having looked at countless pictures and having read avidly about the Giza Pyramids. Julie dropped her comedy act and appeared deep in reflective thought as they stood at the foot of the Great Pyramid of Khufu, straining their necks upward in silence for several minutes.

'My God, it's an incredible engineering feat.' Julie broke the silence.

'Yes it is. One of the planet's greatest unsolved mysteries.'

'The guidebook says this is the oldest pyramid in Giza, dated at 2600BC. That's over 4,500 years ago. Look at the size of the blocks, Izzy. They're huge,' Julie said, approaching the chest-high base blocks. 'And joking aside, it really is hard to conceive how they could have moved them. They must weigh a ton.'

'Anything up to thirty tons, apparently. And there are about six million tons in total...just in this one alone - the Great Pyramid; Khufu, or Cheops as it's also known. It's the largest structure ever built by man.' Isadora's eyes were glued to the pyramid as years of research flowed out of her.

'Really?'

'Yes, really. The small blocks alone are anything between two and six tons. And the entire structure is 203 *steps* high, or forty-eight stories. It was the tallest manmade structure ever built until the Eiffel Tower.'

'Wow, isn't that incredible. So how the hell did they move the blocks here at all, let alone so perfectly into place? I mean, could a group of men actually lift these things?' Julie patted one of the blocks.

'Not without enormous effort.' A deep voice interjected confidently from behind them.

They spun around to see one of the men they had previously sighted on horseback, with his friend trailing not far behind.

'It would take an incredible amount of man power to shift one of these blocks, and to eventually get them up that high...' He gestured to the top of the pyramid. 'I reckon a crane would struggle with a job like this.'

'Actually, there are only a small number of cranes in the world that could cope with this scale.' His easy-going blue-eyed friend joined in. 'Some of these limestone blocks are up to thirty ton in weight, and I don't recall that cranes were in existence back then.' He smiled as he joined the small group.

Isadora noticed his reference to thirty ton and wondered if he had been listening in on their conversation.

'Well they got here somehow,' Julie added, throwing a slightly seductive glance at the man wearing the cut-off tee-shirt.

'Some sort of system of planks and pulleys, I guess,' he replied, giving Julie a lengthy stare.

'Mate, think about how long it would take to build a structure as huge as this, with planks and pulleys,' his friend said with an incredulous expression.

'Maybe fifty years or so. Let's face it, time is what they did have.'

'You think?' His friend continued. 'Back then many of them would be lucky to live past the age of thirty. Some sources estimated it would have taken one hundred and fifty years to construct this with manual labor – and that's with a huge team of men shifting at least twenty-five blocks a day. With tremendous accuracy of placement I might add, and in a way that still hasn't been conclusively shown.'

'Still, it could be and was done,' the taller of the two men said, returning his gaze back to Julie.

'Pretty damn mysteriously, if you ask me,' his friend responded, peering up at the pinnacle of the Pyramid.

Julie, who had been listening to the banter between the two men and watching the taller one with particular interest, took the opportunity to interject. 'I'm Julie...Julz, by the way,' she said, shaking hands gracefully with both men. 'And this is my good friend, Isadora.'

'Hello,' she added simply.

'I'm Dan, and this is my friend, Rob,' he gestured toward the slightly shorter of the two men. 'We're both from Australia originally.'

'Yes, your accent was a bit of a giveaway,' Julie said smiling.

'Mine is, but your accent is a bit mixed up, mate.' Dan looked at his friend with a grin. 'You've spent too much time in the States.'

'Well, the Australian accent wasn't working with the ladies,' Rob winked, patting Dan good-naturedly on the shoulder.

'We're New Zealanders, but we've both been in London for many years,' Julie added.

'Yes, you can tell by your accents,' Dan said.

'Well, it's nice to meet you both.' Rob smiled warmly at the two women.

Dan seemed a little Neanderthal to Isadora and was no doubt a bit of a sports jock, especially with his physique. Yet he had a commanding tone and an air of formality about him. Rob, although very polite, seemed more easygoing. Underneath the brim of his cowboy style hat she could make out soft brown freckles and lightly tanned skin. He was good looking in a non-classical way and his relaxed smile and friendly manner attracted her the most. She noticed he too had a strong-looking physique and muscular shoulders, accentuated by his fitted khaki tee shirt, yet he was slightly smaller and leaner in stature than the more athletic Dan. But they were both big men, much taller than her and Julie.

'And what brings you here, besides these fascinating Pyramids?' Julie asked.

'I have two weeks leave from a securities job in Iraq, and Rob here has just finished a six month spell there stitching the boys' body parts back together,' Dan said.

'Really?' Julie's eyes lit up. 'Sounds like a terribly dangerous place to be.'

'Sometimes, for sure. It's certainly not the safest part of the world.'

'So why go there?'

'Very good money in securities contracts. I wish it was for less shallow reasons, but that's about it. Rob here is the idealist, saving blown up soldiers...now that's a noble cause.'

'Oh, enough of that mate. These ladies are busy enjoying this ancient pyramid and trying to figure out how it got here,' Rob said. 'Which could prove a little futile given that some of the most learned brains on the planet are at odds on the subject.'

'How so?' Julie asked.

'Well there's debate about them in general because some of the archeological explanations don't quite add up. For example, the Great Pyramid here is supposedly dated at about 2500BC and is credited to Pharaoh Khufu, or Cheops as he was also known. Although some accounts of records indicate that Khufu himself said he actually only carried out repair work on the *existing* pyramids. He built three small pyramids for himself and his family. Apparently they're over there, to the East.' Rob waved his hand indicating the direction. 'One of the pyramids contains evidence of being the tomb of his wife.'

He continued with the small group, now transfixed. 'Over there you can see the Sphinx. Now people generally assume the Pyramids and the Sphinx to be about the same age, and maybe they are, but not 2500BC. The Sphinx itself shows evidence to support a much older existence. This is indicated by the amount of water erosion that has occurred at its base.'

'Water, in a desert?' Julie said confused.

'Yes. This desert was once a lush savannah, but the last rains date back to around 10,000BC. Which leads some to date the Sphinx much earlier, before the rains ended...about 10,500BC. There are hints of a much earlier civilization in existence around that time. One that was potentially very advanced too, more advanced than later civilizations.'

They all listened with interest.

'Fascinating!' Julie said.

'I had no idea you were such a scholar of archeology on top of your surgical skills. I take back my comments. I thought this was just a clever construction of stones somehow piled expertly in the desert,' Dan said.

'Well it's that, too.' Rob winked at his friend.

Isadora, who had been listening with interest, suddenly joined the dialogue. 'It's true, though. You know, Pyramids supposedly constructed both before *and after* these ones actually show a *less sophisticated* technology, which is odd really. You'd think the technology would advance through time. But it didn't.'

'Yes, it's like they just sprang up around 2500BC, totally out of technological context for that period,' Rob added. 'Maybe they exhausted themselves building this one, but isn't it a bit odd the Egyptians didn't continue on to build more like this in later years, with similar precision building and geometry, even on a much smaller scale? It's a curious thing.'

'Yes it is,' Isadora said. 'The Japanese actually tried to reconstruct a small scale pyramid like this back in the 1980's with modern technology and eventually abandoned the project. The problems they encountered defeated them. So what does that say? And look at the joins here between the blocks.' Isadora pointed to the base of the Great Pyramid. 'They were cut with incredible accuracy. Their civilization was much more advanced than many people realize, even to this day,' she continued, pointing high up to the middle of the pyramid. 'Forty-three giant granite beams were used in the Kings Chamber, some of them weighing up to seventy tons. Forget about the sheer size of them and how they got them there - that alone is an incredible feat. But they were cut with an accuracy that some experts say would have needed a faster drill than just about anything that exists today.'

'That's amazing, Izzy. I had no idea.' Julie looked stunned.

'Strewth, how do you explain that one, Indiana?' Dan nudged Rob.

'Well, they sure as heck didn't create them just with a chisel, I can tell you that.' Rob looked across at Isadora with a nice smile and continued. 'Like I said, it's a source of debate. But the builders seem to have had access to some sort of powerful force for that time period, somewhat like we have electricity in our age. There are many theories. Some suggest the use of high frequency sound and ultrasonic tools, but who knows. Maybe they had a completely different form of technology that our current level of evolution simply hasn't tapped into in the same way...or at all.'

'That's absolutely true,' Isadora said. 'Some of their craftsmanship remains unparalleled. There are other anomalies too. I once read that vases were uncovered dated from around 4,000BC, with very narrow necks that could barely fit a finger into them. Stone carvers to this day can apparently hardly match them, even with a long drill. So what does that say about their civilization? That they were a primitive people but just happened to carry highly advanced drill equipment on them? That doesn't add up to me at all.'

'Me neither.' Julie said looking perplexed.

'I'm completely stumped. You both seem very knowledgeable on this subject.' Dan glanced from Rob to Isadora.

'One thing is for certain, guys,' Rob said. There's a hell of a lot more to these Pyramids than we know, or may ever know in our lifetime.'

Isadora looked into Rob's blue eyes. She had been trying to figure out the feeling she'd been getting about him from the moment they met. Now she suddenly knew what it was.

Familiarity.

Chapter Thirty-Two

Later that night, Isadora was sweating profusely as she dreamed. It was vivid, in full color and alarmingly real. She was walking in a desert, the sun was high and the heat was burning through her white cotton trousers and blouse. Her clothing was sticking to her, outlining the shape of her body. Ahead of her and high up on a great rolling sand dune stood a tall regal woman with deeply olive skin and long jet-black hair. Her long flowing white robe moved in the breeze. Even at a distance, Isadora could make out a deep knowing look in her large and intensely blue almond-shaped eyes.

The woman wanted to tell her something and motioned her to move closer. Isadora felt transfixed, unable to escape her impact. She was mesmerized, drawn to her despite wanting to run as fast as she could in the opposite direction. She didn't want to know what the woman had to say. Something warned her that once she heard the words she could not turn back; her world would never be the same. Yet there was nowhere else to turn. Just endless desert and a searing heat that was burning her skin.

The stranger reached out to her, arms open and outstretched. Symbols were tattooed in black into both of her palms. She revealed them to Isadora as if they were supposed to mean something to her, as if she should understand.

'I have waited for you. For this time.' She spoke telepathically, just as Seraph did. 'Kneel.'

But Isadora couldn't kneel. She was uncertain, burning in the desert.

'Isadora!' Julie's voice suddenly called to her from across the sand.

'Kneel.' The desert woman instructed again.

She felt like she was melting but still she couldn't kneel. She was filled with uncertainty.

'Isadora, come back,' Julie implored from somewhere across the desert, until she felt her friend's hand grabbing her sweat-soaked cotton clothing. Taking another look at the woman in white she watched her blue eyes boring into hers, as if branding her. Then they became soft and filled with radiant love and deep compassion. Isadora felt known completely. Suddenly she felt fearless about drawing closer to the mysterious woman.

'Remember.' Her whispered voice was all around her, blowing across the desert like grains of sand.

'Remember what?'

'Remember why you returned.' The sand swirled all around the woman as she began disappearing. Isadora remained frozen and burning at the same time as a tornado of sand particles began to consume her.

'Isadora!'

She felt Julie's hand on her arm as she spun around to look at her. The turbulent desert had vanished to be replaced by an equally disturbing erratic light.

'Isadora, wake up. It's me, Julie. You're okay, you're safe.'

'Julz?' Isadora felt groggy as her eyelids flickered. 'Julz, where am I?'

Julie was peering at her, filled with concern.

'In our hotel, in Cairo. You've been having some sort of nightmare, and sweating badly. You're soaking wet.'

'Oh.' Isadora blinked several times, beginning to recall. 'You hardly ever call me by my full name, Julz.'

'I do when I'm worried about you. Are you okay? It must have been a bad dream?'

'I didn't really understand it.' Isadora was still confused by the lingering images.

Julie stood up, searching the room for something. 'Honey, here's the big news of the day. Few people understand their dreams.' She spotted something on top of the dresser and walked over to pick it up before disappearing into the bathroom briefly and returning to Isadora's side. 'You have to write stuff down before you forget,' she said, handing Isadora a hotel pen and pad before sitting down and dabbing her friend's forehead with the damp hand towel she had prepared. 'You need a shower. You're soaked, and the men are meeting us here at seven-thirty, remember?'

'That's right.' Isadora recalled saying goodbye to Dan and Rob before they left Giza the previous day.

'And Dan's military so they'll be bang on time, I'd bet my best underwear on it.'

'Of course you would.'

'It was probably those ruddy phone calls that caused your nightmare.'

'Phone calls?' Isadora said, still dazed.

'Yes, Izzy. Did that dream knock out some of your brain cells? Joshua Bloody Hunter.'

'Oh…yes. I'd almost forgotten.'

'So you should. He's made his bed and now he has to lie in it.'

'Well I expect it's all perfect, Julz.' Isadora said as if in a trance.

Julie looked at her with an expression of semi-disgust. 'It's not perfect, Izzy! I don't know how you can say such a thing! He's a selfish man. And after we had such a wonderful day at the Pyramids.'

'Yes we did.' Isadora smiled, ignoring her previous remark.

'What did he say in his messages anyway?'

'I didn't listen much to the first one and deleted the last two. He wanted me to contact him and he sounded distressed.'

'Oh, poor him. He can cry on that horrid woman's shoulder. Don't you dare feel sorry for him, Izzy!'

'I don't feel sorry for him.'

'Good, because the man is a horror story and he needs to leave you alone!'

'It's not entirely his fault.'

'Of course it's his fault, Izzy. Don't defend him. What are you saying?' Julie sat down on the bed exasperated and looked into Isadora's eyes.

'I'm not defending him at all. Actually, what I've been noticing Julz is that I have a longstanding and deep pattern of attracting men that don't treat me well, are uncommitted, unavailable in some way, or they just plain reject me.'

Julie was quiet a moment before stroking some of Isadora's loose hair gently behind her ears for her. 'Well, you certainly have had your share of idiots. Why do you think that is?'

Isadora paused. 'Because that's what I've been choosing.'

'Rubbish, Izzy. Like you choose men with stickers on their head saying I will not honor you. I will eventually lie, cheat on you, treat you like crap, abandon you…and leave you with a broken-arse heart?'

'Not consciously, Julz. But unconsciously that's exactly what I've been doing. I allow the crap, that's what I do. It's not like I don't get clues. I ignore all my intuition from the beginning, even when it screams truth at me. And I keep choosing dysfunction. I create it, I allow it…and I continue it. I'm responsible.'

'But why, Izzy? If that were the case, why would you do that?'

Isadora felt an echo of the sadness she had felt on the train in

London, on the massage table, and as she had run from Josh's house. A single tear rolled down her cheek.

'Because in a very deep part of myself I have believed that's what I'm worth.'

Tears welled up in Julie's eyes as she heard the words. 'But that is *so not* the truth of who you are, Izzy. You're such a beautiful and amazing woman,' she whispered, wiping the tear from Isadora's face and then the ones rolling down her own.

'I haven't felt that way in life, Julz. Not really.'

Julie saw the look of shame written all over Isadora's face as she spoke. 'Well how are we going to change that for you, Izzy?' she said softly.

'I don't think it's *we* who can change it, Julz. This is my journey to take.'

'Yes, but I can support you and you can accept and receive that…can't you?'

Isadora's eyes stung with tears at Julie's words. 'Thank you, yes I can. You're a wonderful friend.'

'I know,' she winked. 'So how are *you* going to change it?'

Isadora thought deeply for a moment.

'I'm not going to change it. I'm going to *choose* it, as every moment going forward unfolds.'

'Choose what?'

'Choose *exactly* what I *want*.'

'There you go.' Julie smiled. 'That's my girl.'

Chapter Thirty-Three

Robert Andersen sat in the taxi out front of the hotel feeling the heat of the day already beginning to form. He was wondering how the local women, heavily dressed and veiled, coped with the heat in Cairo. Although he hadn't seen many - they seemed quite a scarce fixture in the city. Not that he was used to seeing women lately. Mainly men. Bloodied, blown up, and broken.

It was almost seven-thirty and the two women were due to meet them any minute. He looked across at his athletic friend Dan, rifling through the Egypt guidebook they shared, and recalled the day they had met. Rob had just completed back-to-back surgeries on a makeshift hospital base in Iraq when Dan had showed up. He entered his life pretty dramatically, carrying in one of his wounded mates from a Hummer. The poor bastard had taken a large amount of shrapnel and was bleeding out severely. He had lost a leg, the sight in one eye, and his speech and memory would be badly affected, likely for the rest of his life. But Rob had managed to save him.

Dan had traveled many miles backwards and forwards over the weeks that followed, continuing to check up on his mate as he lay in critical condition. The two men had become friends during that time, with the common bond of being Australian drawing them together. He knew Dan had taken an immediate shine to the blonde,

Julie. Rob couldn't blame him, the woman was a looker. And after six months in the desert surrounded by men and carnage, the sight of a beautiful woman was enough to make a man pine for the feeling of her soft skin and body. More so with her in arm's reach. Julie was a hot and sexy woman and she had flirted openly with Dan the whole time. A man would have to be deaf, dumb, and blind not to notice.

Brains did it for Rob. Looks were a bonus, but for him there had to be a meeting of minds and a special feeling. It was a hell of a combination and he seldom encountered it, but that was what he ultimately wanted in a woman and a partnership. His friend Jessica had that rare combination and he was looking forward to seeing her back in Perth when he returned home at the end of the Egyptian holiday.

Julie's friend Isadora had smarts, that was for certain. He'd never before encountered anybody with a similar knowledge and interest in the pyramids. She was also a very pretty brunette and far more appealing to him than the flamboyant Julie. And she had those amazing green eyes that he'd been finding hard to avoid. Although quiet, she was a stand-out. He was highly astute when it came to assessing people, suspecting her to be deeply sensitive as well as intelligent. It would make her quite a complex creature for the average man, who generally liked to keep things very simple. But he was not an average man. He'd not been raised to be average nor had an average life. He knew the best fruit was always at the edge of the tree in the hardest places to reach. It was the kind of mindset and quality that had made him a gifted surgeon.

'The girls are here,' Dan said, opening the taxi door.

Rob looked out the window to see the two women coming out of the hotel carrying daypacks and chatting happily. Isadora had her hair loose but tied back softly under a light blue scarf which made the green of her eyes stand out more. He hadn't noticed before how long her hair was, but he was noticing now.

Stop staring man.

He had to snap out of it before they reached the vehicle.

Chapter Thirty-Four

Their taxi pulled in directly at the entrance to the Pyramids located on the Giza side of the site. It wasn't quite as exotic as yesterday's approach on camel via the desert, but it was difficult not to be captivated again by the magic of the scene before them.

'So, Indiana, what's in store for us this morning?' Dan said, nudging Rob as the small group assembled once again at the foot of the Great Pyramid.

'King's Chamber, buddy.'

'Sounds intriguing. Have you got any more gems for us about the Pyramid this morning, Indy?' Dan said, throwing Julie a wink.

Isadora saw the exchange and was surprised to notice Julie appear to blush.

Oh God, I think she's love-struck again. Just like that.

'Okay. Firstly, this really is like some sort of giant puzzle,' Rob said, extending his right arm in a circle as if sweeping it around the entire Great Pyramid exterior. 'No other pyramid is like it – not even close. It contains a baffling system of rooms, corridors, and tunnels.'

'Cool,' said Julie.

'For thousands of years a legend existed that the entire structure was little more than a granary for corn. That is until the twentieth century, when entirely new speculations were made. These have been abstract, scientific, archeological and mystical.'

'So what's it really for then?' Dan looked confidently at Rob.

'Geez mate, if I knew the answer to that I wouldn't be a surgeon now, would I?' Rob quipped. 'Let's go get our tickets and take a look. Perhaps we can figure it out where others have failed.'

The ticket office for the entrance to the Great Pyramid and its chambers was on its north-eastern side. Only one hundred tickets were on sale in the morning and the same amount in the afternoon, so they had arrived early. Within twenty minutes they had their tickets and were back at the base of the north face of Khufu.

As Isadora looked up she observed the two entranceways part way up the pyramid. She pointed to the more noticeable entranceway higher up.

'That was the Original Entrance. At some point it was sealed and because it blended so well with the surrounding casing it became invisible. It wasn't located until the ninth century when a treasure seeker 'Mamum' rediscovered the chambers. They bored a hole into the side, right there.' She pointed to what appeared to be a hole at least eight blocks below the original entrance. 'Eventually they found a passageway into the lower part of the pyramid and when they followed the passage back up they found the original entrance. It was said to be so well hinged that a single man could push it open from the inside, yet from the outside it was near impossible to find, or to open.'

'You've been doing your research, Isadora.' Rob looked at her with curiosity.

'I've always found the pyramids fascinating.'

'Yes, you often talked about them at school, Izzy.' Julie said with a smile.

Rob hesitated. 'Funny, I did too.'

'So which entrance do we go into?' Julie said.

'The forced entrance.'

'That hole? Then what?' Julie looked worried.

'Then we make our way up to the King's Chamber via the Grand Gallery,' Rob said. 'It will be a bit of a climb, but it has to be done. I've been looking forward to this for years,' he said smiling at Isadora.

'Then lets get in there, Indy. Ladies, after you,' Dan said.

And they all set off for the entrance.

***

The Ascending Passageway was close to a one hundred and thirty foot climb on a steep angle deep into the heart of the pyramid. With the tunnel a little over a meter in height they had to literally crawl up the steps, which were more like wooden grips in the ground. Rob was at the front setting a surprisingly good pace. Isadora was excited about finally being inside the pyramid and followed him closely, whilst Julie and Dan fell in behind. The climb was steep, and despite having a degree of fitness, Isadora found her breathing quickening. The walls and space around her were very narrow, the passage height was low and poorly lit, and for a few seconds an overwhelming fear began to unsettle her. She paused on a step halfway up to calm her mind. Hearing her stop, Rob turned to check on her.

'Are you okay?'

'I think so. My mind just started to spin out for a moment.'

'Understandable. You wouldn't be the first to be challenged by the confined space in here,' he said softly.

'Not to mention the thought of being buried under a pile of very heavy blocks,' Isadora joked.

'Why don't you try to focus on your breathing? Think of somewhere nice and relaxing to take your mind off things.'

'Up until now I considered Egypt nice and relaxing.'

'Fair point.' He grinned back at her. 'Well, how about thinking about how exciting it will be to see inside the King's Chamber.'

'Now you're talking.'

He waited patiently a few moments. 'Are you good then?'

'I'm good, thanks. Let's go,' she responded, grateful for his calming effect.

Below them, Julie and Dan sounded as if they were falling back further. Isadora could hear them talking but couldn't make out their words when suddenly Dan yelled up to them in the poorly lit tunnel. 'Hey guys, Julie's struggling a bit with the closed space. She's feeling a bit claustrophobic, so we're going to head back out.'

Both Rob and Isadora paused on the steps peering back down at the two heads they could just make out below.

'Julz, are you okay?' Isadora yelled down with concern.

'Yes, I'm fine, Izzy. I'm just not handling this confined space at all. It's freaking me out. I'm going back outside.'

'I'll come with you,' Isadora said quickly.

'No, it's okay. You carry on. I'd feel terrible for the rest of my life if I knew I was the reason you didn't make it to the King's Chamber,' Julie shouted back up the passage.

'It's okay, guys. I'll go with Julie.' Dan's voice boomed up.

'Are you sure?'

'Yes, no problem at all. Go on, you two have been waiting for this all your lives, but not me. So get yourselves up there. We'll see you afterward,' Dan said.

Before Isadora could protest further she saw them both reversing back down the narrow passage.

'Come on, we'll keep moving. They'll be fine,' Rob said, noticing the look of concern on her face. 'Don't worry about Julie, Dan will take good care of her. He's a good bloke,' he said with an encouraging smile.

Isadora searched his face for a moment. She felt oddly vulnerable at the thought of being split up from Julie.

I'm not sure I can trust him. Seraph, what do I do?

Perhaps the angel couldn't hear her inside the pyramid - she received no response.

Damn.

Her desire to see inside the King's Chamber was too great.

Rob looked down at her with a fathomless expression in his eyes before turning to continue his ascent.

Probably thinks I'm a chicken.

She just needed to guts it out and in another seventy or so steps she would make it to the Grand Gallery.

***

Isadora's heart was pounding rapidly by the time they reached the top of the Ascending Passageway. She was still feeling anxiety, despite her efforts to take her mind off her claustrophobia. The climb had been steep and the passage was small, dusty, and dimly lit. Rob was only several paces ahead and partly hunched over to avoid hitting his head against the limestone above. Isadora was sure he was going much slower than he was able just so she could keep up. He continued to turn and check on her. As both her body and mind faltered, Rob began to disappear in front of her, scrambling through the end of the passage.

'Oh wow!' she heard him declare as he reached the joint structure that marked the ending of the passage leading into the Grand Gallery.

'Come on, Isadora,' he reached out to her. 'Take my hand.'

Feeling tired from the climb and poor air she grasped it with relief, feeling his strong grip and strength as he helped pull her through the aperture and up into a full standing position.

'Wow, I see what you mean,' Isadora said, straightening her body fully after the long crouched climb and fixing her gaze on the view before her. 'Now that is one impressive bit of design and engineering.'

They were now standing in an area of significant space. Stretching a length of almost fifty meters before them and rising steeply upwards with a ceiling height in excess of eight meters, was the Grand Gallery. Both stood awestruck at its base, staring up into the eerie silence.

'Look at the granite blocks. How big they are and how smoothly the joints are sealed between them,' Rob said.

'Yes, it's sheer brilliance,' Isadora responded. 'See how the ceiling is corbelled so it narrows in the shape of the pyramid as it goes up.' She indicated above as she closely observed each block projecting a few inches from the next. 'This was no hit and miss technique. It's an architectural masterpiece.'

'It sure is,' Rob said. 'What's really interesting is that the corbelled ceiling feature suddenly appeared as a relatively new building technique at the time of this pyramid and was executed at a very sophisticated level. Then two generations later it wasn't used anymore. I find that quite odd.'

'It is odd. You would think they'd have continued with that level of sophistication, not regressed,' she said. 'You've been doing your research too, I see.'

'My mother was always fascinated with the Giza pyramids. I grew up hearing lots of stories about them. She was always convinced they were much older than the Khufu date of 2500BC and had a number of interesting theories about them. My father never agreed. It was always a source of friction between them. But then, he never really liked her thinking for herself. He was a surgeon too, with a very rigid and scientific approach to things…and he was pretty dominating.'

'Oh, that's tough,' Isadora said quietly.

'For my mother, yes. He liked to convince her she was going crazy. And he didn't like her questioning *supposed facts*.' Rob was scrutinizing the ceiling as he spoke but his gaze eventually made its way back to Isadora as he trailed off.

'So are your parents still together, Rob?'

'No, they split up when I was young. My father left us and I've barely crossed paths with him since then.' She saw him grit his teeth. 'I guess I pursued medicine in an effort to have a connection with him; to follow in his footsteps. A bit clichéd, I know. Not that I want to be like him in any way other than his surgical talent,' Rob said drawing a hand through his hair.

For a moment he struck her as slightly vulnerable, the blue of his eyes searching her face in a way that she couldn't interpret.

'What was he like?' she persisted.

'Pig-headed. A bully. And sometimes he would hit her,' Rob said matter-of-factly.

'God, that's terrible. I'm sorry.'

'Thanks, but it was a long time ago and she's recovered. I'm glad they split up.'

'So what's your mother like?'

'Great.' His expression softened. 'She's a counselor now. Very wise, and really gifted with people.' He paused, looking suddenly uncomfortable. 'Hey, I reckon we should tackle this next climb. We're halfway there. What do you think?'

'Sounds great.' She said watching him turn and take the first stair.

But her mind lingered on their conversation, and she was clear that he'd changed the subject a little too quickly.

Chapter Thirty-Five

By the time they had almost reached the top of the Grand Gallery she was experiencing an unusual sensation throughout her whole body. Isadora couldn't place what the feeling was or exactly why it was occurring, but it was like a vibration, becoming more intense the higher she climbed. Upon reaching the uppermost level of the Gallery, they stopped momentarily to look back down the steep incline they had just ascended.

'Incredible to think this was engineered inside the pyramid,' she said.

'Yes it is. But let's face it, the whole pyramid is a bit of a miracle. And the King's Chamber, now that's something else. Are you ready for it?'

'Of course I am. I didn't climb all this way with claustrophobia, anxiety attacks and near oxygen starvation, just to eat the cake and miss out on the icing.' She winked at him, surprised at her own spontaneity.

'You're a cheeky one,' he grinned. 'Come on, let's go.'

They waited for several tourists to exit the chamber before tackling the small entrance tunnel leading to their destination. It was narrow and rectangular and although Isadora found it was almost easier to crawl along on her hands and knees, she managed to maintain a squat position. She was grateful to be following Rob who seemed totally confident in his approach, every now and then turning back to check on her. He seemed as agile as a monkey, but there was no mistaking the solid strength of his legs as he moved through the small passage.

Within a minute they had emerged into the King's Chamber, where Isadora, now able to stand fully, stretched her legs and took a deep breath to try and get more air. The Chamber itself was very dimly lit, but it was still easy to distinguish the pink-red color of the granite that it had been entirely constructed out of.

'The ceiling is high,' Rob said, looking up surprised.

Isadora noticed it was about six meters or so in height and the entire space appeared to be built in the shape of a rectangle. But what caught her immediate attention near the far end of the chamber was a large and very solid looking granite sarcophagus.

For a minute they both stood transfixed, taking in their surroundings. Isadora noticed the strange vibrations in her body were becoming even more intense. She could have been hearing things, but it also sounded as though there was a low dull ringing in her ears.

'These granite blocks are huge,' she exclaimed.

'Quarried in Aswan as I understand it. Hard to fathom how they transported them hundreds of miles all the way from the south of Egypt and then managed to manoeuver them into place up here,' Rob said quietly.

'I know. It's incredible. And besides the granite ceiling it has four more raised and stacked roofs above. And they were created by massive granite beams,' Isadora continued. 'Combined they have an enormous tonnage, yet they didn't need to be present in the engineering of the pyramid. They're actually freestanding inside two huge limestone walls.'

'Yes, I read about that. They're entirely separate from the rest of the construction. Interesting, huh,' he raised his eyebrows. 'And not to mention the shafts.' He indicated to two small openings either side of the chamber that were roughly half a foot square in size. 'They went to huge effort to build those in. The longest one is up to two hundred feet in length, and despite them bending at points they maintain the same line.'

'To the star constellation of Orion back around 2500BC, right? Isadora said.

My blasted ears, she thought.

'Seems that way. They were pretty particular about everything, so there was absolutely no accident about the exit points of those shafts. It was very probable there was some connection to the constellation of Orion.' Rob noticed her patting the sides of her head. 'Hey, are you okay?'

'Sure. Just a bit of ringing in my ears, probably from the climb up.' Isadora dismissed the issue. 'Yes, the shafts are interesting all right. And look at the sarcophagus, it's just spectacular. I've heard it proposed that they might have drilled that in here out of a *single* block of granite.'

'Drills back in that time period...you really think?' he raised an eyebrow.

'It's left-field, I know. But they cut the granite somehow.'

'Well, I certainly doubt it was with a chisel,' he chuckled.

She looked across at the seven-foot six-inch long sarcophagus sitting near the end of the Chamber. 'They clearly wouldn't have been able to get that through such a small entrance either.'

'The stone would have to be sitting in here before they added the ceiling, I guess. You know, they never found any king's remains in here. Treasure hunters may long ago have emptied the tomb and removed the lid somehow, but it doesn't make sense...,' Rob said moving towards the granite coffer.

'What doesn't?'

'That the Egyptians of any period would ever bury anyone above the earth, especially a king. Their religion and ritual always placed the king's body *below* the earth, and they did this in every other tomb or pyramid. I mean, perhaps Khufu had a big ego and demanded it done differently for some reason, but I think it's still debatable he actually built the Great Pyramid at all.'

'You think?'

'Who knows really. But there was a radiocarbon-dating project in 1984 that placed some of the materials used at up to twelve hundred years prior to the supposed building period.'

'That's a big chunk of time passing. That has to blow a theory.'

'No, surprisingly it didn't. That evidence was largely disregarded and dismissed by the classical archeological fraternity,' he smiled at her. 'There have been other expeditions and projects that indicate anomalies, but nothing much ever comes out about them. Any results in the past have somehow never quite made it to the general public's awareness in a way that has any impact.'

'Funny, isn't it.' She smiled back.

'You may recall in the early nineties there was discovery of a door down the end of one of the Queen's Chamber shafts by a camera-mounted robot. Do you remember?'

Isadora nodded in acknowledgement.

'It made international headlines and was hailed as a major breakthrough, but then within days was played down, disregarded, and it took another ten years to get a camera-mounted robot back in there again.'

'Yes, it was a very long time to wait to pursue an amazing discovery. And they eventually drilled through that limestone block and found another door just beyond it, right?'

'Yes they did. And more hieroglyphs. But that was over ten years ago and now another decade has passed, yet again,' Rob said.

'So why is the world waiting so long?'

'I guess applications need to be submitted and accepted. And multiple committees need to approve everything.' He shook his head in exasperation.

'That does seem crazy. The Great Pyramid is surely a global legacy. You would think the only thing that mattered would be the truth and the pursuit of that as quickly as possible.'

'Yes, in an idealistic world maybe. But in our current phase of evolution you need at least one hundred reams of paper, as many meetings, and a thousand bureaucratic opinions to move anything along a fraction.' He smiled. 'At least they're slowly allowing the return of excavations and archaeological research here again.'

'Yes, that's great.'

'You want to know what I think?'

'What?' Isadora leaned on the Chamber wall for support.

'I really don't believe this Pyramid was constructed as a tomb at all.'

'Oh, really?' She was feeling quite faint and her eyes were becoming blurry as the low humming in her ears continued.

'Yes.' The chamber is particularly responsive to very low sound frequencies and they have carried out tests in here. Granite is a quartz bearing rock, known for the way it vibrates. They were clearly a highly intelligent bunch of people and built it using granite very purposefully. I find it very hard to believe they would go to all that extra effort to place an incredibly heavy type of stone in here, which would have been monumentally hard to cut and move. You'd have to have a damn good reason other than an ostentatious and grandiose design for a dead king. I think my mother has been right all these years. This entire structure was never intended as a king's tomb, it was used for something else. Something far more important, and with a much greater purpose.'

But Isadora wasn't listening. Her back was sliding down one of the polished granite walls as she blacked out and lost consciousness completely.

Chapter Thirty-Six

'Isadora?!'

Her sudden collapse in the King's Chamber startled Rob. Despite maintaining his usual cool that he applied with severely wounded soldiers in Iraq, he felt some fear at seeing her passed out in a vulnerable crumpled heap on the granite floor. It wasn't the first time that being in her presence had made him feel things he wasn't comfortable with. Earlier that day, when they had been standing at the base of the Grand Gallery talking, he'd felt as if he had known her for a long time. And he'd revealed way too much about things buried long ago. In an effort to get back to feeling normal he had hastily ended the conversation and continued the climb.

As she regained consciousness, Isadora complained of a humming sound in her ears. She was very disoriented, staring across the chamber as if she had seen a ghost. He was concerned about oxygen as she'd mentioned breathing trouble on the way up, so he wanted to get her out of the pyramid as fast as he could. In the end he half dragged and carried her down the steep incline, despite her occasional protest.

'We're almost there, Isadora,' he said, holding an arm around her as he observed daylight flowing in through the entrance ahead.

'Great,' she said faintly.

As they exited, bright sunlight caused her to blink and wobble on her feet slightly and Rob drew a protective arm more tightly around her waist to steady her.

'Take your time, you're still weak. Here, sit down,' he said, helping her lean back gently against a pyramid block and assisting her to slide down into a sitting position. 'You need to adjust to the light and heat out here.'

'I guess it would be a waste of time arguing with a surgeon,' she said, looking up with a smile.

'That's right,' he winked at her, turning to look for Dan who was somewhere amongst the tourists ambling around at the base of the pyramid.

I need a hand getting her down.

Scouring the ground level off to the left and about thirty feet away from the base blocks he spotted a pink scarf and the unmistakable blonde locks of Julie, smiling and laughing with Dan.

He cupped his hands together and yelled out, following up with a shrill whistle that caused a number of heads to turn and look up at them. But not Dan's.

Come on mate, look up.

'Dan!' He yelled again, this time with better effect, causing his friend to turn. Rob began waving, frantically gesturing for him to climb up. In a split-second Dan had moved from a state of casual laughter to one that was focused and highly alert. He was a trained elite at responding to danger and emergency. Before Julie could wipe the smile off her face from the joke they were sharing, he'd launched into a sprint and was up on the first block of the Pyramid, leaving her entirely confused as to what had just taken place.

***

'What happened?' Dan panted as he made it up to the entrance. 'Jesus, Isadora. Are you okay? he said, observing her sitting looking very pale.

She glanced up at him. 'I'm fine, Dan. Thank you.'

'You don't look that flash to me.'

'She blacked out completely up in the King's Chamber. She's weak and we need to get her down to ground level.'

Dan required no further explanation. 'No problem. We'll have you down in a jiff, Isadora,' he said bending right down to gently slide his arm behind her back, whilst Rob did the same on her other side.

Julie looked up at the scene with a fright.

Oh God, Izzy? She thought, jogging towards them.

What on earth has happened now?!

Reaching the base blocks, Julie wiped tiny beads of perspiration from her forehead as she watched the two men assist Isadora slowly down. It was now late morning and the sun was throwing intense heat onto the desert surface as they made their way to ground level. There was little shade so Rob placed his hat upon Isadora's head as they sat her down on the ground.

'It suits you,' he said handing her a flask of water. 'Here, drink up.'

'Honestly guys, please don't fuss. I'm fine,' Isadora said.

'Izzy, what happened?' Julie sat down beside her.

'I just felt a little faint in the King's Chamber. Probably just a little claustrophobia and poor air conditions. I'm fine, Julz. Honestly.'

'That wasn't quite the exit I was expecting, Izzy. I was anticipating you springing out of the Pyramid in sheer excitement at the unveiling of some great universal mystery.'

'If only you knew,' Isadora laughed nervously.

'I think the universal mystery caused her to pass out,' Rob said.

'What? You passed out completely?' Julie looked at Isadora with concern. 'You scaring me is getting to be far too much of a habit lately, Izzy.'

Rob raised his eyebrows at the comment.

'I need to stand,' Isadora said beginning to slowly rise from the ground, leaning against the Pyramid as she did so. 'I'm good, guys. No drama now. Just give me a minute and we can go visit the Sphinx.'

'I don't think so, Isadora,' Rob said, looking at her with concern.

'With respect, Rob, I didn't wait half my life and travel all this way around the world to rest up in a hotel room when I'm a stone's throw from the bloody Sphinx,' she said, dusting herself off with uncharacteristic irritation.

'Fair point, Isadora. Nicely put,' Dan said.

Julie smiled with approval at his comment. 'Okay, Izzy. I agree. You're far too much of an Egypt nut-head to bail out now.'

'Let's go see the tiger,' Dan said. 'Then I could use a beer. This heat is criminal. Mate?' He looked at Rob who had been watching Isadora quietly.

'Okay. But you stay hydrated the whole time, Isadora.'

'Doctor's orders, Izzy,' Julie winked at her.

'I'll stay hydrated,' Isadora said tapping the flask. 'Now lets get out of here.' She walked off without looking back.

In truth, she couldn't wait to get some distance from the pyramid and the King's Chamber, as what she'd seen and heard in there had disturbed her very much.

***

It was about the moment that Rob had been postulating about the purpose of the Great Pyramid in the Kings Chamber, and right before Isadora had slid down the wall and blacked out, that she had appeared to her again - the woman from her dream. She was flanked either side by tall dignified looking Nubian men and women in long white flowing robes, all staring at her.

It was as if Isadora had suddenly catapulted into a different reality or dimension. She felt frozen, aware of her body and Rob's voice drifting off in the background until he had eventually disappeared completely. She was alone with the seven strangers as they stood before her, fanning out into a semi-circle behind the dark-haired blue-eyed woman.

The deep humming tone in the pyramid had become palpable. She was aware of it vibrating intensely through her whole body, although it seemed to be coming from all around her in the Chamber. She felt the source of the vibration below her as if it were being funneled up through her feet.

'I have awaited your return,' the woman with the large blue almond-shaped eyes spoke to her telepathically. 'Remember.'

The last word seemed to be communicated inside her head simultaneously from all of them. Despite her fear at potentially being somehow suspended in an alternate dimensional experience, she was trying very hard to make sense of everything.

'Remember what?' She communicated back telepathically.

'Remember who you are. Remember why you came here,' the woman said taking a step closer, her eyes boring into Isadora's.

What the hell is happening to me. I don't understand any of this.

Why were these strange people appearing to her? Her mind was frantically grasping for logic, for a way she could grip onto the reality of the life she knew.

How did I get here?

The vibration in her body was most powerful in the center of her chest, and these people - these unusual compelling people - were actually standing before her.

'We have awaited your return. It is beginning.'

'What is? Her vision was blurring. 'What is beginning?' The vibration intensified in her body as she felt her back slipping against the cold granite behind her.

What is beginning? What is? I need to know.

'Recalibration.'

The vision before her was beginning to dissolve and Isadora locked eyes with the woman before she disappeared entirely.

'Recalibration? I don't understand. What do you want with me?'

'You must Awaken now,' the woman whispered softly.

It was the last thing Isadora recalled before circles of expanding darkness closed in over her eyes and her body slid to the cold granite floor.

Chapter Thirty-Seven

'So what exactly *did* happen to the limestone casing that once covered the Great Pyramid? It must have looked even more spectacular then,' Julie said as they walked away from the pyramids towards the Sphinx.

'Without a doubt,' Isadora responded. She was beginning to shake off her King's Chamber experience and was feeling a lot better. 'The limestone was apparently white and highly polished, and it was said to appear like light itself.'

'That would have looked so great.'

'Yes, the casing joints were fitted together with an unknown mortar mix and had an accuracy that made them virtually naked to the human eye, apparently one fiftieth of an inch. It would have looked absolutely amazing.'

'You can't even comprehend that!' Dan exclaimed. 'It would've looked fantastic alright. Like a single sheet of cover on each side.'

'Dazzling, like a gigantic sparkling stone in the desert,' said Rob, full of enthusiasm. 'You have to consider that the pyramid base covers thirteen acres of land, which is a huge structure, and that entire area is level to within a half inch. That's a phenomenal surveying feat. It would be almost impossible to match that today, with modern technology.'

'Wow. Thirteen acres almost completely level?! Who were these people?' Julie said.

'I know. It's crazy, isn't it. The entire pyramid contained enough cubic volume of stone to construct a large number of churches, cathedrals and chapels. It's a staggering size. The glimmer it emitted from its surface at the time the casing was fully on was probably visible a long way off the earth. Mindboggling to comprehend, and such a damn shame it has gone,' Rob said.

'What happened to it, Indy?'

'I understand that a great earthquake occurred around 1220AD that destroyed much of Cairo. They removed most of the limestone casing to rebuild a lot of the city's public buildings.'

'Are you kidding me? There was really that much limestone?' Dan said with amazement. 'I mean, there must have been a huge amount for them to use, and I'm sure a lot dislodged from the quake, but hell, surely that was a bit short-sighted to remove it all.' He shook his head in disbelief.

'There were twenty-two acres of coverage, apparently. In fact, the Grand Mosque in Cairo is built almost entirely from the casing of the pyramid,' Isadora said.

'Strewth!' Dan looked impressed.

'Wow!' Julie added

'It was said to be covered in hieroglyphics.'

'What? The limestone casing? Twenty-two acres of it?'

'By some accounts.'

'So what happened? Did they retain the hieroglyphics somehow? Dan asked.

'No, they didn't. The builders removed them, for the new buildings,' Isadora said softly. 'There would have been potentially thousands of pages of inscriptions and now they're all gone.'

'What a damn shame,' Dan said. 'I bet if that were the case, the hieroglyphics could have answered a few very big questions.'

'Yes. I reckon they could have, my friend. I reckon they could have,' Rob added thoughtfully. He was looking at the Pyramid, but inwardly his mind was elsewhere. He didn't understand fully why, and he needed to figure it out, but Isadora was stirring up strong feelings in him that he wasn't used to, or comfortable with. From the moment she had fainted in the King's Chamber he had felt very protective towards her despite the two of them having only just met.

'Now we'll never know. Humanity will probably never know, and it's a great shame,' Isadora said quietly as she fixed her gaze ahead on a famous and captivating carved structure.

The Great Sphinx lay directly before them.

***

'Such an interesting combination,' Julie said as they assembled front and center of the Sphinx. 'Man and beast.'

'Yes it is,' Isadora said, noticing the ringing in her ears had unfortunately returned.

'It's certainly big. Indy, what are the dimensions on tiger here?' Dan said.

'Well, she's over two hundred feet in length, about seventy feet high and almost forty feet across. But the real beauty of her is that she's carved out of a single block of stone.'

'Well how the hell did they manage that? Now don't tell me they whipped out their chisels.'

'I'm strongly suspecting more than chisels,' Rob winked at Dan. 'In all seriousness though, nobody knows what tools they used to carve it, even in this day and age.'

'Heck, another mystery...the place is full of them. And you said that the Sphinx is probably a lot older than some classical archeological estimations because of evidence of the effects of water, yes?'

'That's right. An American Professor verified that the pattern of erosion on the limestone body is consistent with the effects of rainwater beating down upon it from above. We're not talking a little bit of rain either, we're talking hundreds or thousands of years of it. And as I mentioned yesterday, it's estimated that level of rain hasn't occurred here since this was savannah land. Which would place her closer to 10,000BC or earlier.'

'So, do you think it's a girl lion, despite the bloke's face?' Dan said cheekily.

'Lioness,' Julie batted her eyelids and almost purred at Dan, whose jaw dropped for a second.

'I'm not so sure the face we see now is actually the original. There have been a lot of renovations made to the Sphinx over time. It has been buried in sand and rediscovered many times, and I gather some of the Pharaohs have had a crack at rebranding her. It's possible it was once a female face, and the odd scholar has suggested possibly even an African-American woman. But for me, I guess I just associate cats more with the feminine for some reason. Who knows,' Rob said.

'Archeologists and historians have found many pictures of the Sphinx drawn with wings, the body of a lion and ox, and the face of man…' Isadora added.

Damn. My blasted ears are ringing loudly again, she thought.

'Well, its creators must have been pretty darn confused.'

'I sincerely doubt that its creators were confused, Dan,' Isadora responded. 'I suspect that it was more the *regression of civilization* that has created any confusion.'

'Half man, half beast. That about sums us up,' Julie chipped in, 'Although the Sphinx should be the body of a man with the head of an animal if it had anything to do with our current time period.'

'I thought the theory was that our brains are located south of our belts?' Dan grinned as he stared back at her.

'That's also true,' Julie looked down at his shorts for entirely too long. 'If you think about it, the Sphinx is depicted as an animal with human intelligence, and I could accept that. But frankly, humankind seems to be operating these days more like they have an animal brain running around in a human body, so I'm with Izzy about the regression of our civilization.'

'I'm not going to argue with two women, so the smart thing to do is to change the subject,' Dan smiled. 'Mate, get me out of this.'

'I can try.' Rob grinned.

'You said there's strong evidence our big cat here is much older than many think?'

'Yep.'

'Well, that does seem to suggest that an advanced civilization existed much further back than known previously, given that they created this masterpiece. So that must have been a huge archeological breakthrough?'

'Well not for everyone, Dan. The implications are pretty significant if the date of the Sphinx's creation is pre 10,000BC. I mean, that would defy the orthodox history of mankind...you know, the linear development of cave man to our current highly evolved species...' Rob's voice held contempt. '...that kill each other senselessly and needlessly. I mean, an earlier civilization couldn't possibly have been more evolved than we are now.'

Isadora noticed the note of sarcasm he finished on.

'So yes, there would be big implications with a revised timeline to the theory of evolution and human development.'

'Well I guess that would be an obstacle for some. Nothing like buggering up eons of conditioned thought and the idea that we are the exalted human race,' Dan joked.

Isadora smiled at his comment. 'And on the subject of linear development, what about the pyramids. Khufu only alluded to renovating them after all.'

'I think regardless of when they were built and by whom, there's still the point that pyramids built both *before and after* these Giza ones were markedly less evolved in all sorts of ways. It's like in 2500BC they found a vault filled with incredible pyramid-building knowledge, and once they built them, sealed the vault again rapidly so that later generations didn't have a clue how to create them anywhere near as well,' Rob said.

'Okay, so regardless of whether the Giza Pyramids and the Sphinx were built around the same time or not, what's kitty-cat really doing?' Dan said. 'Guarding the gates; standing to attention? Purring madly at the heavens?'

'Apparently facing East. And if she was created pre-10,000BC as evidence suggests, then it transpires she was probably looking at another lion in the stars.'

'How so?' Julie asked.

'Well as we know, the Sphinx appears to have a lion's body. Every dawn during the Spring equinox around 10,500BC the sun rose in the sign of Leo. So that's what she was likely looking at back then...'

'Herself,' Dan laughed. 'A great lion in the stars. That would be an interesting coincidence.'

'Yes it would.'

'Pretty clever if that were the case,' Julie added. 'I mean, if they knew the star constellations that well back then, it could have been like a monument for its own time.'

'Indeed. You have to understand that the Egyptians, or whoever built this, had an incredible grasp of physics, geology, engineering, and astronomy. The accuracy of measurements around the entire Great Pyramid exterior indicate how incredible their knowledge was. They come within millimeters in many cases,' Rob said. 'It's phenomenal in a way that's challenging even for modern architects to align buildings to the North, South, East and West directions. No structure to this day has been constructed with such astonishing precision of alignment to the four cardinal directions as the Great Pyramid was.'

'That is impressive,' Julie said, gazing back at the pyramid site.

'Very impressive. So whatever their reason, whether it was the Spring Equinox or some other celestial event, the positioning of the Sphinx was in no way an accident. These guys didn't do things by chance. It was a very big and accurate deal alright.'

'The burning question remains, why were they left here at all, Rob?'

'These structures were all placed here for a specific reason and I sincerely don't believe it was simply to do with a dead Pharaoh. The oldest record of the Sphinx, inscribed on a granite stone dated at 1400BC, stated something about a *great magical power that existed in this place from the beginning of all time.* The Sphinx and the Pyramids are like a glaring symbol from a way of existence long extinguished from humanity. And personally, I think it's sorely missed.'

'You're pretty serious about all of this, Rob.' Dan looked at him with curiosity.

'Yes I am.' He responded quietly. 'I've seen what man does to man, and I've had my fill of it, mate. There has to be another way. I can't believe we were designed to kill each other like we do. Surely not.'

'I agree, Rob. We're destroying each other, and our world. We've become an appalling species in many ways,' Julie said. 'The people who built this would probably turn in their tombs if they knew how low we've stooped.'

Isadora, who had to this point been standing quietly listening to both the conversation and the increasing ringing in her ears, was feeling very peculiar again. As if she was about to black out once more. The Sphinx appeared to be shimmering like a mirage in the desert, and her friends had become strangely way off in the distance.

She wasn't even aware of the words that began to come out of her mouth.

'That's exactly why they did build all of this.'

They all turned to look at her as she continued. 'Because they knew it would last through the ages. Our forefathers knew this time would come.'

'What time, Izzy?' Julie said

'The time when humanity would wake up from their long dark sleep.'

'Wake up, to what? Izzy, are you okay?' Julie said, suddenly concerned about the far away gaze on Isadora's face.

'Wake up to who we really are. To our true nature and heritage as people on earth and what we've been entrusted with. They were left as a key; a key for this time. They were passed on as a mystery that stands testimony to the true intelligence of humankind. And until we correct our imbalances and return to that intelligence and life-honoring ways, their reason for being remains silent and obscured and the key to their existence as hidden as our own. So yes, they were created with absolute purpose, and are waiting.'

'You're not making any sense, Izzy. Waiting for what exactly?'

'They are waiting,' she whispered staring into space, 'for the Architects to return.'

Rob looked at her with surprise, and Julie stared at Dan with raised eyebrows. Isadora was gazing trancelike at a place they could not see, experiencing a feeling that rose from the deepest part of her. The words she spoke had come mysteriously from somewhere else, and not as she knew herself to be. Nor did they come from this time. And now, she realized, neither did she. Perhaps it was the curious experience in the King's Chamber that had unlocked her own personal vault, but suddenly Isadora knew precisely why she had been fascinated for so many years by the pyramids and the Sphinx. It was because she had existed in this very same place before.

THE BRIGHT NEW DAWN

But it had been long ago, at the time of their creation.

Chapter Thirty-Eight

'Bugger me, that was intense,' Dan said, taking a long sip on his cold beer. 'Is she always like that?'

Lately, a lot, Julie thought, worried.

'Not really,' she said casually, looking into his hazel brown eyes with a smile and noticing they had a slightly yellow hue. 'She's just been through a bit lately. Dated an idiot of a man. Actually several…in a row. I think it's been affecting her,' she said taking an excessively large and unladylike swig of her white wine as they sat at the bar in the air-conditioned luxury of the Hilton Hotel where the two men were staying.

'I see,' he said thoughtfully. 'A few of those about.'

'Yes there are.'

'Why do women stay with men like that?' He shook his head.

'Love.'

'Stupidity.'

'That's harsh.'

'Well it's not love if it hurts and they're treating you badly.'

'Sometimes it's more complicated than that, Dan.'

He took another long sip of his beer. 'Nope, it's not actually,' he said placing his glass down on the table and looking Julie square in the eyes. 'You just have to have the courage and self-worth to walk away when someone isn't treating you right.'

'It's not always easy to spot until it's too late,' she said noticing how broad and muscular his shoulders were in his tee-shirt.

He loved looking into her eyes. 'Sure it is.'

'How?'

'You women just launch your feelings into things without checking out the landscape fully first. You don't want to see the truth.'

'I think that happens with both sexes.'

He picked up his beer again. 'Yes it does.' He paused thoughtfully. 'But women have a higher casualty rate.'

'Well, we're wired a little differently.'

'You sure are. And what about you? Have you been toasted, fried and barbequed, by some idiot.'

'Of course I have,' Julie said softly, grateful for the dinner earlier that was now absorbing the alcohol she was throwing back.

'Hasn't stopped you?' he said, looking at her a little sheepishly over his glass.

'No. Thankfully the heart mends.'

'I guess.'

Julie saw the chink of vulnerability that registered through his eyes and was suddenly aware of some interesting information about him. 'I hope Isadora is okay,' she said placing a mental bookmark before changing the subject.

'She'll be fine. Just a big day in the heat. Rob's over there now, he'll look after her. He's a good man.'

'Yes he is. I should really finish this drink and get back to our hotel. See how she's doing.'

'She'll need to rest, Julz.'

She liked hearing him say her nickname. 'I guess so.'

'Besides, did you hear those two banging on about the pyramids and the mysteries of the universe,' he chuckled. 'They have plenty to talk about.'

'Yes, I expect they do,' Julie said, thinking about her friend tucked up in bed with a nice handsome surgeon tending her. 'You're right. I'm on holiday and I need to relax. She'll be fine.'

'So you'll stay a while?'

'Yes I will,' she said looking at him with renewed conviction as she took another mouthful of wine.

'Good,' he said watching her lips on the glass, 'I'm glad.'

***

'Isadora?'

It was Rob's voice again. For a moment she remembered coming to in the King's Chamber, thinking she might still be there, and then felt the comforting softness of a bed beneath her. She slowly opened her eyes, noticing the cream-colored lamp by Julie's bed was on and throwing soft light into the hotel room. She could see the sky beyond the open balcony door darkening and Rob sitting beside her bed. She wondered how long he had been watching her.

Although a smile formed on his lips she could see concern in his eyes. He was wearing a different shirt so she must have been sleeping a while.

'Rob?' The question in her voice asked a million more. She vaguely recalled them all leaving the Sphinx and traveling back to the hotel in a taxi van.

And he understood. 'You've been sleeping for hours, Isadora. I left Julie and Dan at our hotel after dinner to come over and check how you're doing,' he said. 'It's after eight. You've been out for over five hours.'

'So I missed the cocktails then?'

'No cocktails for you tonight,' he smiled at her sense of humor. 'But I did bring you up some dinner, if you're hungry.'

She saw a tray beside him on Julie's bed with a colorful array of salad, bread, falafel and dips, some fruit and a large glass of water. 'You've had quite a day.'

'Quite a week or two, really,' she said thoughtfully.

He was silent, dropping his gaze to the floor for a moment. 'I'm going to check your temperature before I let you eat that food. Okay?'

'Sure,' she said, suddenly feeling self-conscious and drawing the crisp white sheet up to cover the top of her breasts. She was wearing a black silk low-cut nightdress that Julie had helped her into before she had fallen into a deep exhausted sleep.

He flinched at her movement, unsure where to look, before leaning forward in his chair and gently placing his hand on her brow. His touch felt comforting to Isadora who was beginning to recognize that her exhaustion came from a much deeper place than the drama of events with Josh, the flight, and the King's Chamber experience. It was life itself. Years of strain and anxiety, draining and uncertain.

God, his hand feels good. So reassuring.

She felt his warmth flow into her as if he were filling her up, like gas pouring into an empty tank. Closing her eyes she relaxed as a deep peace washed over her.

Kindness. This man is kind.

'Well,' he said softly, 'I think you'll live.'

'That's great news, doctor,' she said. Their eyes locked for the briefest of moments and Isadora felt her heart beat a little faster. He was so familiar to her. It was strange.

'Do you remember what happened at the Sphinx, Isadora?'

'Not really. I was talking to you all and the heat must have gotten to me,' she lied.

'Do you remember what you were talking about?'

'Not really.'

'The *Architects returning*? Ring any bells?'

'No,' she lied again.

'Okay. I think you're suffering from some heat exhaustion. You should try and eat something,' he said, placing the meal in front of her before standing up. 'I'm going to leave you in peace, and then I think you should get straight back to sleep. You have a big train journey to Aswan later tomorrow.'

'Okay. Thank you for everything, Rob,' she said, unable to argue about her need for sleep despite enjoying his company. She would have liked to talk with him more about the pyramids, particularly what he had been talking about before she passed out in the Chamber.

'No problem. I'll see you tomorrow,' he hesitated for a moment, looking at her with the same unknown expression as he had in the Grand Gallery. 'Good night, Isadora,' he said walking to the door.

'Goodnight, Rob.'

But he didn't look back.

***

'Jesus,' Rob whispered under his breath, shutting his eyes as he leaned against the closed door outside Isadora's hotel room. 'Harden up, man.'

She was definitely beginning to have an effect on him, and so was this land. He had always wanted to come to Egypt. Years of hearing his mother talk about the pyramids and ancient civilizations had inspired him from an early age, so it was a foregone conclusion that he would eventually make his way here. But he never expected to meet someone who shared the same kind of passion for the mystery of the Pyramids, and with a similar knowledge about them. Beautiful too. Beautiful and fragile. He was going to have to control himself, otherwise he would mess her up, not-to-mention the perfect life plan that he'd spent months thinking about in that hellhole Iraq.

Over dinner Julie had shared in confidence with him that Isadora was recovering from a horrible time with a dishonorable man back in London. She hadn't gone into details and Rob was far from being an angry type of person, but hearing of Isadora's maltreatment made him feel like flattening the guy who had hurt her so badly. His instincts had become rapidly and surprisingly very protective toward her for reasons he couldn't fully fathom. He had to try and blank her from his mind though because he couldn't afford to get involved when he was headed back to Perth and Jessica. What he needed most now was rest. He'd been doing a lot of tough surgeries before arriving in Cairo and really needed to catch up on sleep. With any luck this evening he would get that, and hopefully without another strange dream like he'd had the night before.

Chapter Thirty-Nine

Joshua Hunter sat in his office absentmindedly looking out at the Thames River. He had four days of unshaved stubble gracing his face and a glass of scotch in his hand, actually his third, which was unheard of for him at two in the afternoon. He'd taken a call earlier that day that he couldn't absorb fully. All he could do was sit and wait. His confusion was complete, and with his mind splintered in multiple directions he was living through a personal nightmare.

What the hell do I do?

Isadora was gone. She hadn't returned any of his calls, no texts, no emails…no anything. Just leaving a very big vacuum, with Madelaine bouncing around inside it creating total havoc. It was a disaster. And he'd brought it all upon himself. He couldn't blame Isadora for showing up uninvited. She had stumbled unwittingly upon the truth and he should have had the decency to talk to her way before that happened. He was a coward. He'd handled things appallingly, badly hurting her and their connection beyond reason or probable repair.

What a crock my theory about life being a ten has turned out to be. She was right, this is not a ten. It's a bloody zero!

Reflecting back on recent events, he now knew conclusively that jumping into bed with Madelaine over six weeks ago was the biggest mistake out of many with her.

One night of lust and I'm saddled with the black widow.

How he couldn't have seen her clearly for who and what she really was from the start was beyond him now. She was as calculating as a human could be, but he had let the snake in the door again.

Wisdom is what happens when you've fucked up your life and there's nowhere left to go. Hindsight is a bitch.

Taking a last large swig of scotch, he planted the empty glass down firmly on his desk, catching sight of the framed photos that sat at one end. There were his parents, smiling and happy, and also an old black and white one of his Hopi Grandfather. Joshua had grown up hearing great stories about his Grandfather. His father had raised him to be proud of the sacredness and traditions of his Hopi ancestry. But today he felt a far cry from that, and only the deepest sense of shame.

Reaching over, he scooped up the photo and looked into the face of his Grandfather, staring back at him full of dignity.

Cheveyo...Spirit Warrior. What on earth were you thinking, old man?

He sat as if communicating through the photo to the spirit of his Grandfather. After a few minutes memories began to flow through Joshua's mind. His life had been charmed from the moment of his birth. Things had always come to him easily. His degree, places to live, work, girlfriends...and most especially girlfriends. He had never had to work or strive too hard to get women. They always came to him because he was good-looking, sensitive, and naturally attuned to them. So perhaps that was the reason why, although being a loving man, he never really applied or committed himself excessively.

He hadn't even tried that hard with Cynthia, and yet he'd loved her deeply. In the end, he had let her walk away with the justification that distance was between them and they were young. It was a tough insight to get, but Josh suddenly realized how complacent he had been with love throughout his life. He hadn't fought for things or people that mattered to him. He'd been a passenger. If he was honest with himself, it was why he had enjoyed the stimulus and drama of Madelaine. And in outgrowing her and his addictive patterning, he thought he'd become a stronger man. But not strong enough. He had let Isadora go with the same damaging level of weakness. In a rapid new self-assessment, Joshua realized that what he really lacked was backbone.

Placing the framed photo back gently on the desk and staring thoughtfully at it for some time, he wondered if his Grandfather had named him Spirit Warrior because he knew it was something he would be called to learn how to be. He had not yet honored his Hopi blood and it now seemed like life, and possibly his Grandfather too, were urging him to do so.

Maybe you know a lot more about me that I haven't figured out yet, old man.

He stared at the picture a moment longer, when suddenly the strangest feeling came over him, bringing with it an eerie clarity and certainty. Without hesitating another second he picked up the phone and called his Personal Assistant.

'Yes, Joshua?'

'Denise, I need you to organize a flight for me, right away.'

I know exactly what I need to do.

Chapter Forty

Isadora slept soundly again through much of the night. Her state of exhaustion was deep and she was finally able to surrender to it. Thankfully she didn't dream again and was also oblivious to Julie creeping back into the room later that night.

She woke up the next morning feeling ravenously hungry. It was early light outside, not long after six. Looking across at the other bed, Isadora could see her friend fast asleep, some blonde tousled hair poking out from above the sheets.

She was contemplating getting up for a much-needed shower when the atmosphere in the room changed and she recognized who was there instantly.

'Seraph?' Isadora said telepathically.

'Yes, Dear One.'

'I've been waiting to speak with you. I have some questions.'

'Of course you do.' The angel said lovingly.

'The woman in my dream, and in the pyramid. Who is she?'

'She is your guide.'

'I thought you were my guide?'

'We are both your guides, but I am tasked differently.'

'Really? In what way?'

'In the *Accident and Emergency* way.'

'Oh?' Isadora said confused.

'Critical condition, Dear One.'

'I see. And she is...what?'

'She *was* an ancient goddess, from a time long forgotten, and you have known each other before.'

Isadora began to see colors forming in the corner of the hotel room and recognized the outline of her friend appearing, a pink hue radiating from the angel's heart center.

'She holds knowledge and keys to universal truths, ones that are sadly long forgotten from this planet. Many millennia ago there was a great race of beings living in this world. They lived in peace and harmony with nature and its cycles, and with each other. Love, respect, and the interconnectedness of all life were founding principles upon which all their actions were based. They carried great knowledge of life, science, masonry, the stars, and advanced technologies unknown to the world at this time,' Seraph paused.

'Go on. Tell me more.'

'It was a time of great peace and love on earth and much ritual was carried out. She stood at the forefront of this time and has returned again and again in many guises.'

'So why appear to me?'

'You have been her loyal friend before.'

Isadora was speechless as Seraph continued.

'And she has much work to do here. Her energies are now required more than ever in this current phase of earth's evolution.'

'But she's not alive here and now?'

'No. She is not incarnate, nor will she ever be again. Her vibration and her service is now way beyond that of a mortal life. She has elected a mastery role beyond the density of earth plane, as have other wonderful beings that once graced this world and continue to serve it. Her vows of service remain, however, as does her energy on the planet. She continues to work and serve lovingly through those that know and remember her and the ancient ways.' A blue-green hue was forming in Seraph's center.

'So she has returned. But why to me?'

'To guide and direct you.'

'Guide me where exactly?'

'To retrieve knowledge and understanding of the ancient ways.'

'I see.' Isadora was thoughtful a moment. 'Look, I don't mean to sound disrespectful, but do I get a choice in any of this?'

'You always have choices, Isadora. You know this now. There is always free will and free choice wherever you are located in the Universe.'

'As my intellect understands it.'

'And as your heart knows. Have patience, Isadora.'

She remained quiet, uncertain of what to say, absorbing the impact of everything she had just been told.

Seraph continued. 'It might favor you to ask yourself what would bring you the most joy in this lifetime, not from comparisons of how others in this world choose to live their lives, but from how you know your heart and soul to be.'

'I'm not sure I know my soul that well, Seraph.'

'If you listen hard enough, you will. Understand this: self-fulfillment lies in the path of following your soul's urgings.'

'My soul's urgings…,' she said with exasperation, 'that doesn't seem fair somehow. It sounds like trying to fulfill the wishes of a very distant ancestor on a remote side of the family that I've never even met. I don't feel any connection with *my soul's urgings*, or what you're saying at all.

'You will.'

'If I choose it.'

'That's correct.'

'A choiceless choice.'

'Meaning?'

'It doesn't feel like I have any choice at all except to choose it.'

'It's *your* script, dear Isadora. You set the rules of your own game,' Seraph said.

'Yes, but what if I've changed now? What if what I want has changed and it has nothing to do with *my soul's urgings*. What if I want a *normal* life this time instead of God knows what.'

'I think you'll find that God does know what. And besides, who said the two are mutually exclusive?'

'It seems that way,' she said with exasperation.

'A mistaken thought. Besides, what's *normal...*,' Seraph chuckled.

Isadora looked across at Julie sleeping and sighed with despair. 'I don't know what to think of anything that you're saying right now. In honesty, I just feel punished for crimes that I'm not aware I committed.'

'Really?'

'Yes really. I mean, where's my damn simplicity in life, Seraph? Where's my partner, my love, my life with him? Is that so much to ask for - for any decent and talented *God* to create? I mean, is that such a stupendous stretch for the bloody Oceanic Everything!' Tears formed in her eyes. 'Unending shit in life, and now you tell me I have to go further, be stronger, dig deeper, know more…and I have a strange spirit-woman appearing to me telling me things I don't understand, and I'm passing out in front of friends, and I haven't a clue what's going on!'

'And?'

'And…I can't do this right now!' Isadora's eyes grew large with frustration. 'I can't. So please, just go. Just let me be,' she said suddenly withdrawing like a hedgehog inside a prickly shell.

'As you wish, Dear One.'

'And don't call me *Dear One*!' she said angrily. 'I'm not Dear anything, okay!'

'Understood. But let me tell you, self-pity does not suit you.'

'I don't bloody care.' Tears flowed down her face.

'Isadora,' the angel paused, 'you might wish to consider that it is in the path of your soul's urgings that you will find your true happiness...and your true mate.'

'What do you mean *my true mate*?' she sniffed, more alert.

'The one most in alignment with who you are and what you came here to do and be.'

'Well how in God's name do I find him, Seraph?' she said, dabbing her moist eyes with the sheet.

'You don't have to find him.'

'Why not?'

'Because, Isadora, when you are ready, he will come for you.'

Chapter Forty-One

As the train moved steadily South through the darkness toward Aswan, Isadora was feeling sleepier as the noise in the carriage from other travelers began to gradually die down. She glanced across at Julie in the seat opposite, sound asleep on Dan's shoulder. He was trying to stay awake, his head jerking up as fast as it fell forward. Isadora was certain he was remaining in the same fixed position so as not to disturb Julie's comfort. It was unexpectedly endearing of him, she decided. He was actually a very caring man. And after his chivalrous assistance at the Great Pyramid she had discarded her former impression. She had made an unfair judgment of him.

They had boarded the giant diesel train earlier that evening for the eleven hour and six hundred mile journey south from Cairo to Aswan. The interior of the locomotive was old and weary with fading curtains and worn upholstery, and because of a ticketing mix-up they had missed out on their booked sleeper carriages. Julie lost her cool and Dan had to step in to calm her down.

'Bloody hell, you'd think that something could just go according to plan. I worked so hard to make sure all our trip details were perfect,' Julie said, as they entered the tired looking carriage and found their seats. 'Inconceivable!' she finished with a tone of disgust as they sat down in the booth-like seats, facing each other.

'The seats will be fine, Julie. Sometimes life just doesn't go according to plan,' Dan added.

'Well it damn well goes to plan in my world!' Julie fumed some more.

'Just try to let it go, babe. At least we get to sit together,' he said, gently nudging her arm.

It was about this point Isadora realized that Julie's heady state the day before was entirely down to some sort of romantic interlude she had experienced with Dan, and this was clearly continuing. Julie softened immediately at his use of the word babe, squeezing his muscular arm as they sat down together. They giggled like a couple of school kids. Isadora had noticed the little touches and looks between the two of them earlier that day as they wandered around the Cairo museum. However she'd been so busy sleeping the past forty-eight hours, she had missed the two evening meals with the group and failed to spot the telltale signs. Her friend was completely besotted. As she focused on them sitting opposite her, now it was clearly evident. Lingering looks, hands grazing each other's thighs, occasional whispering into each other's ears, and the fact that they seemed oblivious to everything going on around them.

Only Julz could step straight off a plane and into the next great romance, Isadora thought with a smile as she closed her eyes, grateful for the chance to rest again.

***

By the time she reopened her eyes it was dark outside with a hint of moonlight lighting up the sky from behind sparse fluffy clouds. She wasn't sure how long she had dozed, but she could make out the Nile River across the carriage to her right, its surface glistening with moonlight as the train moved steadily through the desert night. Looking across at the opposite seat, she smiled at the sight of Julie still asleep on Dan's shoulder.

Rob, who had been sitting quietly next to her trying to read the guidebook under very dim light, looked up at her.

'Penny for your thoughts?' he smiled.

'Oh. I think I must have missed something,' she nodded toward the sleeping couple sitting across from her.

'Yes, while you've been resting up these two have been…acquainting themselves,' he said softly. 'Are you feeling better, Isadora? You seem to have been exhausted the past couple of days?'

'Yes, much better thanks. I've been unwinding a lot. I've needed to catch up on rest.'

'Ahuh,' he said, remaining silent for a moment and glancing down at the open book. 'We all need time like that sometimes.'

Isadora had been feeling increasingly comfortable in Rob's company, particularly after their afternoon at the Cairo museum where they had joked and laughed a lot together. She had wanted to ask him something since they met. Now was the chance.

'What's it like doing surgery, Rob? Saving someone's life?'

He closed the book and turned his body slightly to face her. She could just make out the clear blue of his eyes beneath the cap he was wearing, along with the soft dusting of freckles over his cheekbones.

'What's it *really* like? You honestly want to know?'

'Yes I do.'

'Well, I'd have to say it's one of the most humbling experiences I could have.'

'Humbling?'

'Yes. Very humbling.'

'How so?'

'Well I have this life in my hands, someone completely in my care. They want more time, another chance, even if they can't communicate that. And I have an opportunity to help make that happen for them. I'm in live tissue, the flesh and blood of a life, and

I know that if I do my job and if the wounds are repairable then the body in all its wisdom will do its utmost to heal…it's a truly remarkable organism,' he paused. 'And yet, there is some part in the process that's not my choice, where I know I'm largely helpless as to the outcome.'

'What do you mean?' Isadora watched him carefully.

'Honestly, I think some of it boils down to the spirit of the person. Their will or their inherent make-up, or maybe the amount of time they really need or are intended for on this earth…but it's quite a mystery. In some of my surgeries there has been a moment where the balance can swing either way and even though I know I've done my absolute best to save that life there's a place that lies utterly beyond my power or my comprehension. In those moments there's nothing I can do except keep their vitals going and wait. That's when I feel the most humbled.'

'About what exactly?' Isadora persisted.

He paused thoughtfully. 'The recognition that life, the choice for a person to be here or not, is not ultimately in my hands. Yes, I can apply all my knowledge and skills to stitch a person's body back together, but I can't stitch their soul. I can't tell you the amount of times I've had a young soldier on my table and someone that conceivably shouldn't live does, and someone else who has the ability to make it, doesn't. So I've learned to wait, and sometimes to even pray, while this unseen communication takes place between what I think is their soul and some other great force in life. In those few moments or days of communion between their spirit and the source of our existence, I really believe a choice is made.'

'A choice?'

'Yes, a choice to stay or to go. It's not my choice to make, nor is it in my power to control. I didn't create them, and although I may be a source of surgical skills and hope, I'm not God. So when they breathe again, or when their heart stops beating, in those seconds it's like holding witness to a powerful dialogue I'm not really a part of.'

'Wow.'

'Yeah, that's what is amazing - not that I may have saved a life, but that I got to be present to those profound moments where a soul chooses which direction it wants to go next.'

For a moment Isadora was not sure where to look. His words revealed such depth, but also reminded her of her own juncture in life as she had stood on the cliff in Ireland.

'That's a surprising response,' she said quietly, 'I thought it might be a little more…clinical.'

'Sorry to disappoint,' he said, looking a little sheepish.

'Please don't be sorry at all. That's entirely the kind of response I would have hoped to hear. If you don't mind me asking, are you a religious man?'

'I'm a very lapsed Catholic, actually. I'm not fixed about religion these days, although I can say that I believe in a greater force. A loving and benevolent creator or source of some sort.'

He smiled at her before looking down once more at the closed book on his lap. 'You know, I've never described saving a life quite like that to anyone before. It probably sounded kind of cheesy.' He grinned, and for the first time she noticed his sensual lips as his eyes held hers again in a way that unnerved her.

'It's not cheesy at all. I'm grateful for your honesty. Actually, I understand what you mean about a life being held in the balance.'

'Oh?' he said raising an eyebrow. 'You do?'

Isadora could have kicked herself as the words slipped out of her mouth. She was in danger of revealing far too much about herself as she had with Joshua. The feeling of rejection came hurtling back to her with a velocity far greater than the speed of the train. Her stomach lurched and the words in her throat froze instantly. She looked away from him toward the black void on the left side of the carriage and felt the rolling motion of the train beneath her merging with her old friend anxiety.

'Maybe another time and conversation. I'm feeling a little sleepy now. Thanks for such a great answer to my question, though.'

It was all she could think to say before resting her head back, closing her eyes, and shutting out the feelings inside her.

***

As dawn broke and the first rays of the hot desert sun threaded their way through the dusty windows of the train, Rob became aware of a weight upon his left shoulder. Somehow in the course of the night and with the gentle rocking motion of the diesel locomotive, Isadora had managed to end up sleeping on his shoulder. Her left forearm was wrapped across her body and her left hand rested lightly on his thigh. For a few seconds he felt his breathing stop at the feeling of her body so close to his. Turning his head gently to the left he saw she was fast asleep. He caught the faint sweet smell of her hair and found himself wanting to lower his head to nuzzle into it and feel its softness after many months of no physical contact with a woman. It had probably been a mistake to travel with Isadora, but what could he have done. Now that Dan was clearly besotted with Julie it left him having to spend more time with her.

He shut his eyes again, retreating to the comfort of darkness to think about his situation. Life seemed to have a funny way of turning everything on its head just when he knew where he was headed. After all, he'd never intended to take the six month contract in Iraq, but he had some military experience and it had fallen into his lap when he was doing some locum work and extra training in America. So on an idealistic whim, and with consideration for the surgical experience he would gain, he had taken it.

Hell, he should have made an excuse in Cairo and caught a plane straight back to Perth sooner. Yet something was increasingly compelling about his current trajectory.

Like a moth to a flame…I'm a damn fool.

Maybe it was the pyramids and his desire to explore them and other mysteries of Egypt, but he couldn't lie to himself either. It was this intriguing beautiful woman that he was finding the most irresistible. If they spent more time together perhaps he would figure out why he was so drawn to her.

Who am I kidding?

Getting to know her better would run the risk of making life more complicated for him, and he'd had enough time to consider the next stage of his life whilst in Iraq. Bloodied soldiers and the extent of their wounds from shrapnel and explosive devices had worn him down. He had known that getting disheartened was a possibility in the world of surgery, but nothing had prepared him for the constant succession of horrific physical injuries to the wounded soldiers on his table.

War was a sham and an utter waste of life. He had frequently questioned how on earth he'd ended up working in such a hellish nightmare, and had found himself pining for Perth and thinking about Jessica again. They had talked a lot on the phone and by the time his contract was up he firmly knew the direction he wanted to take. Until now. Now he was strangely captivated by two enigmas – the ancient site at Giza and the woman sleeping on his shoulder. He wasn't sure which was more confusing and mysterious, but lately it seemed he had been dreaming about both. Rob sighed heavily as he became aware even more strongly of Isadora's body against his. He opened his eyes again to look down at her. If he was strong he would be fine.

Glancing over at Dan, he was surprised to see Julie had woken up and was watching him.

'Morning,' he said softly.

'Good morning,' she whispered back, still appearing very sleepy as if she had just awoken.

But she wasn't sleepy at all. Julie was in fact wide awake and had been watching the man staring down at her friend with deep curiosity.

Chapter Forty-Two

The train, having stopped briefly in Luxor, now lurched back to life as it continued its journey South. Isadora felt the jolt of movement and began to stir from a restless sleep. She had been dreaming again, but this time the content had unpleasantly included Josh. The day prior she had quietly deleted several more voice messages from him without listening to them.

I just have to be strong and put him behind me now.

With her eyes still closed she became aware that she was in fact lying on Rob's shoulder and that the other three were all awake and talking. She cringed internally.

Brilliant, how do I get out of this one.

Lying on his shoulder for a few minutes more, Isadora considered how she could appear to wake up as unobtrusively as possible. With some deliberation, she finally made her decision. Faking a rousing yawn she rubbed her eyes and sat up.

'Wow, now there's a beautiful morning view to wake up to.' She stretched her arms upward, gazing out the window as they all followed her line of sight. The sun was sparkling on the water's surface and fishermen on the other side were casting their nets from the banks of the Nile into the river's shallows.

'Good morning sleepy,' Julie smiled, looking back at her. 'Surely you must have reached your REM quota by now.'

'You'd think so, wouldn't you. Did I just catch you discussing the Sphinx?'

'We thought that was the only thing that would wake you up,' Rob said.

She smiled back at him. 'So what were you saying about the Osirian Temple beside it?'

'Rob was just telling us that the temple must be about the same age as the Sphinx because the water erosion features are the same.'

'That's right. All the other temples and tombs appear to be weathered by wind and sand,' Isadora added, now wide awake. 'Rocks weathered by rain have a distinctive undulating appearance, like we saw at the Sphinx.'

'You know, the Osirian Temple was created by carving massive blocks of limestone off the body of the Sphinx,' Rob continued. 'Its body was originally encased in this limestone and the blocks they carved out and moved were about two hundred ton in weight each.'

'Is that right, Rob?!' Dan exclaimed. 'Surely they couldn't move blocks that size with manpower and a few pulleys. That just seems a ridiculous notion. And I thought the granite blocks in the Great Pyramid would be hard enough to move.'

'I know. It's crazy, but it's astounding how many people don't really stop to think about these things. I guess the bulk of humanity isn't trained so well to consider information for themselves. Anyway, you guys saw the blocks. You know how big they are,' Rob said.

'They were frigging huge,' Dan responded.

'And you saw how accurately those blocks were joined together as well,' Isadora added.

'Yes, they were near perfect. It's just mindboggling,' Julie said.

'It is. And moving the darn things would be a feat in itself, but maneuvering them in so tightly next to each other...geez, that's something else,' Dan said impressed.

'A number of decades ago in the States, some engineers were tasked to lift and move a two hundred ton boiler. They used one of the largest cranes in existence back then, and had a secondary crane to move it into place,' Rob went on, 'It took them six weeks to prepare for the lifting. I mean, ask yourselves how easy it would have been for a *less evolved* people to do this kind of thing with huge blocks of rock and none of the technology we have. And if you look at the size of the cranes today that can move thousands of tons in weight – they're a staggering size.'

'That certainly provides perspective, Rob,' Julie said. 'Seriously though, why don't people think about this stuff more, question it for themselves?'

'Hard to say really. The world's population is so full of poverty and poor education, or greed and materialism, that some gigantic blocks of carved rock in a desert aren't too much of a concern. For whatever reason, I guess people aren't curious enough to enquire. Let's face it, we live in the age of fast food, fast everything, and it's a dog-eat-dog world. So who cares if there was potentially an amazing and advanced ancient civilization that pre-dated us. It's just not deemed relevant to humanity's existence,' Rob responded.

'Relevant? Of course it is,' Isadora said. 'Humanity's very existence may depend upon this kind of knowledge.'

'How so?' Dan asked intrigued.

'Well, I think to accept that such an advanced civilization pre-dated our own would upend our current interpretation of history and create a greater freedom of thought about humanity's true identity. I'm talking about a shift in consciousness, ultimately. In all honesty, I think we are descendants of wise, intelligent, loving and benevolent ancient ancestors, not some ape-like primitive people. And if people really got that…they might lift their game.'

'Here, here,' Julie nodded in agreement. 'At least some of us aren't descendants of apes!'

'The knowledge and understanding of this ancient world restored to the earth could empower human beings to think for themselves in a new way about who they are. And potentially live more responsibly with peace.' Isadora paused. 'It just may not be quite so economically viable.'

'Yes, peace is a bitch. War is lucrative,' Rob added with sarcasm.

'Now that's a bit harsh, mate,' Dan said defensively. 'What are you saying about the need for armed forces in the world?'

'What I'm saying is that soldiers often put their lives on the line for an ideal, but the sad reality is that behind any war the motivation for it lacks integrity. Guys are out there fighting for *their country*. Really? Maybe they get a few heroic gestures thrown at them, but so what. When the hell of war is done and they get sent back home at the end of it all, they're frequently marginalized and misunderstood anyway. And on top of that they have to recover themselves from God knows what injuries and psychological pain. They return to a world totally disconnected from the reality of the one they have inhabited - and the one they've inhabited has in all likelihood been created out of a lie.'

'We need defense forces, Rob. There are some bad bastards in this world, and there's a lot of oppression of the innocent.'

'That's right Dan, there are some self-serving twisted bastards. But I can guarantee you, for every soldier's life I have held in my hands, an innocent civilian or child lay bleeding and dying in some painful hideously unjust death. And I can tell you, it's hard enough looking into a soldier's eyes and watching them die.'

Isadora and Julie listened respectfully in subdued silence.

Dan was tense. 'War is hard, Rob. It's a sacrifice. It's just how it is and how it's always been.'

'And why is that? Why the hell doesn't mankind evolve? Why such an unending need for power. And so much greed.' There was anger in Rob's voice. 'What's the majority of war for anyway…for God? Does God really need defending? Does our Creator demand that level of death and destruction in his name?'

'I think it's about freedom, brother.'

'Freedom?! Jesus, what's fighting for freedom mean if you're blind and in chains as you're doing it. There are no winners in war. I know that now.'

Dan was silent for a moment. 'It's a good thing your tour's up, mate. I think you've seen enough.'

'Yep,' Rob said crisply. 'I think I have.'

He looked out at the peaceful setting of the Nile as if seeking solace and barely spoke again for the remainder of the train journey.

Chapter Forty-Three

Aswan, or 'Assuan', was a modern city and one of the driest inhabited places on the planet. The last rainfall had been a thunderstorm some years earlier. The sky was continually blue and the temperatures very high, and nothing short of cotton was going to cut it for clothing in the dry desert air. The heat hit them like a vaporized tsunami wave as they stepped off the train onto the platform. It was close to noon.

'Phew, now that's like standing in front of an open oven door,' Julie declared, disembarking from the carriage.

'Let's hope the hotel has good air-con,' Dan added, wiping beads of already-forming sweat from his brow. 'What's our plan for the rest of the day? Have we got time to get to Lake Nasser? I could do with a swim,' he said, nudging Rob in a good-natured way and keeping things light after the seriousness of the train discussion. But neither man was the type to hold onto any grudges.

'That's quite a distance to go for a swim, Dan. You might want to try the hotel pool first,' Rob grinned.

'If anyone's keen, I'd love to check out the giant obelisk in the stone quarry later today,' Isadora said.

'Sounds good,' Julie responded decisively, 'and we should set off early tomorrow morning for Abu Simbel, Lake Nasser and the Temple of Philae.'

'Well, there's our plan then. Let's get to the hotel, see what we can organize for transport, and have a swim before we do anything else,' Dan said.

The two Australians had changed their hotels so they were staying at the same place as the women. Dan had seemed pretty determined before they left Cairo to relocate their accommodation, despite dropping a little luxury in the process. To Isadora it was now abundantly clear where his motivation lay. She could also lay bets on the fact that he was less interested in swimming than he was in seeing Julie in a bikini. She smiled knowingly at his comment, and Rob caught the expression on her face. He grinned as if reading her mind and she spontaneously smiled back, realizing as she did how good it was to see him looking happier again after the serious mood on the train journey.

'I hope you girls packed your bikinis,' he winked, throwing her unexpectedly off-guard as they set off down the busy platform toward a band of eager cab drivers.

Isadora blushed a little at the comment and hoped the others hadn't noticed. It was possible that Rob had just been flirting with her.

***

The pool atop their hotel, although simplistic in style, had a panoramic view of Aswan and out towards the Nile. They checked in, had a quick light lunch in the hotel restaurant, and arranged transport for the following day before making their way up to the rooftop. The water looked particularly inviting in the dry and burning heat of the afternoon sun.

The men strolled ahead of Isadora and Julie, with Dan moving straight to the pool, peeling off his tee-shirt as he did so, and revealing a jaw-dropping physique. He had broad and muscled shoulders and arms, a wide chest sloping down to a highly defined abdominal six-pack. His strong physique, stacked inside a tall frame with a deep tan acquired from an extended period of time in the Middle Eastern sun, only served to highlight his muscle definition. He was an object of great physical beauty, particularly against the backdrop of the white concrete hotel roof and the desert stretching out beyond.

Julie's eyes widened and froze in a cat-like stare as if sizing up an antelope on the African plains and preparing for the attack. She followed every inch of Dan's body movements as he threw his singlet on the chair and launched himself straight into the pool.

'Lust. I'm officially in lust, my friend,' she said, turning to Isadora with a glazed and devious expression in her eyes.

'And now you just need the pitchfork for the picture to be complete,' Isadora said dryly.

'Luke, the force is strong in this one,' Julie winked back at her.

'Well, off you go. He's waiting.' Isadora smiled.

She watched her friend strip down to her black bikini, revealing an equally beautiful and curvaceous body.

Dan wolf-whistled immediately. 'Wow, hot stuff! Get in here and warm up the water,' he exclaimed in his typically forthright Australian manner as Julie deliberated at the side of the pool before diving in.

Isadora watched the scene unfold as she sat down for a few minutes on a lounger chair, laying out a towel and removing her white cotton top.

Rob was across the other side of the pool by now. He was in long board shorts and had also removed his tee-shirt revealing another excellent physique. He had golden-tanned and freckled skin, and was solid and manly-looking in a way that made Isadora look at him much longer than she intended. She had become attracted to him if she was really honest with herself, but she dismissed the feeling quickly as she stood up to slip off her skirt, revealing a pretty turquoise bikini that wrapped around her statuesque frame and showed off her long toned legs.

'Come on, Izzy. The water's gorgeous,' Julie exclaimed.

'You are,' Dan growled back at Julie as he began chasing her around the pool.

'You game, Isadora?' Rob called out to her from across the pool before disappearing with a splash into the water.

With a body bordering on an orchid white color apart from her arms, Isadora hadn't seen any significant light in months so instead she decided to lie on the lounger for a while before taking her first summertime dip. 'I'm going to catch some sun first,' she called out before lowering her sunglasses over her eyes and relaxing back on the chair.

Isadora felt the cold very easily in life. As a child, she'd always been the family member huddling by the fire because she couldn't stand the freezing temperatures and the loss of sensation in her hands and feet. Instead she stayed indoors and frequently had her nose burrowed in books, which was where much of her fascination with Egypt and the Sphinx and Pyramids had developed. Where others sweltered in the heat, she was very much in her comfort zone. Her body and sometimes her brain, simply didn't function when she was cold, so she was relishing the dry hot conditions. They were good for her spirit, as was the warmth and good humor of her caring traveling companions.

Drifting rapidly into a warm relaxed state, every cell in her body hungrily vacuumed the life force energy radiating from the sun. She began to contemplate how astronomy had been actively practiced in Egyptian temples with astronomer-priests watching the skies and making regular observations. According to the myths of Isis and her beloved partner Osiris, the righteous dead became stars. She had read much about their union in all the literature on the Sphinx and the Pyramids.

Recalling now their legendary story as she knew it, Isis was sister and wife of Osiris, a popular ruler. He was tricked by his jealous and plotting brother Set into an untimely death and his body chopped into parts and scattered throughout Egypt. In her great love for him, Isis scoured the land and united all parts of Osiris except his unfound phallus which she fashioned out of gold before proceeding to breath life back into him. He was resurrected and then able to have a proper burial and ceremonies, becoming known as Lord of the Dead and the Afterlife.

In Egyptian culture the constellation of Orion had been long regarded as the home of the God Osiris, and in the heavens slightly below was the star Sirius belonging to his consort, Isis.

How romantic, Isadora thought.

The stars were sacred to the Egyptians because of their strong mythical association with Isis and Osiris and their deep love. Indeed, the Great Pyramid at Giza was designed with eight-inch square shafts running all the way out to exit towards the heavens. If one had been thin enough to lie in the southern shaft in the King's Chamber around 2500BC they would have viewed Orion's Belt from there every night. Conversely, a shaft from the Queen's Chamber, although sealed at the exterior end, was aligned with Sirius, the star of Isis.

Beyond that though, why had the Egyptians ever taken such a huge interest in the stars, Isadora wondered. She knew that in 3200BC Sirius had become the most important star to their civilization because it apparently rose at dawn at the beginning of the Egyptian New Year, and when the Nile waters began to rise. But the stars were clearly more than just seasonal indicators to their civilization. They must have worshipped Isis and Osiris enormously, she pondered. For whatever reason, they had chosen or known the connection of those deities to particular stars like Sirius, along with the middle star on the belt of Orion. And the Great Pyramid seemed quite devoted to them. Having seen the Giza complex now with her own eyes, it seemed much less of a tomb and more of a ritualistic building with a definitive purpose, like a temple.

She could still clearly recall the eyes of the mysterious and beautiful woman boring into her in the King's Chamber. But if she really did have a strong association with her, why was it so important she connect with that spirit now? And why did she need to be initiated into ancient ways by her?

In the background she became aware of the sound of her three traveling companions splashing about in the pool as she lay stretched out deep in thought. She felt the rippling of a breeze stirring around her like a light afternoon desert wind. A familiar voice spoke in her mind and she realized it wasn't a breeze at all.

'Isadora.' Seraph's voice interrupted her stream of thought.

'Yes, Seraph,' she communicated calmly, accustomed as she now was to the curious interjections by the angel.

'Remember your sunblock.'

'What? You're kidding me, right?'

'Not at all.'

'Is that all you wanted to tell me?'

'Yes it is, actually.'

'I thought perhaps you could explain why it's so important for me to be initiated into the ancient ways?'

'Not right now. Just remember your sunblock and enjoy your afternoon.'

Chapter Forty-Four

Isadora had been thinking how odd it was for an angel to tell her to apply sunblock and was just reaching for her sunscreen when she felt spots of water dripping onto her body. Startled, she looked up to see Rob standing over her, water drizzling somewhat sexily down his body.

He smiled at her as he stood drying himself off with a towel.

'Are you taking a dip, Izzy?' It was the first time he had called her by her nickname.

'In a little while.'

'Need a hand with the sunblock?' He gestured toward the bottle she was now holding.

She felt suddenly nervous. 'I'll be fine, thanks.'

'On your back. I mean, sunblock on your back.'

'I guess so,' she said, considering Seraph's unusual guidance. 'Thank you, that would be great.'

Rob sat down promptly on the lounger next to hers and reached for the bottle as Isadora rolled onto her stomach. She began nervously wondering what her backside looked like in her bikini bottoms, but had to admit to herself that she liked the idea he was about to touch her.

After making sure they were dry, he rubbed his hands rapidly together to warm them first.

'Quite the professional.'

'I have my moments, and my uses,' he said smiling at her and pouring some sunblock lotion into the palm of his hand.

She noticed how long his eyelashes looked when they were wet and how they highlighted the blue of his eyes, before turning her head away from him to instinctively hide her face. She wasn't quite prepared for the sensation of his hands on her skin and as he began to apply the sunscreen to her shoulders Isadora felt an immediate tingling response throughout her whole body, sending goose bumps all over her hips.

Please God, don't let him notice those.

His hands felt strong and decisive, a man's hands, yet with the flow of an artist making careful and beautiful brushstrokes on a canvas. Rather than hastily slapping the cream on, his movements were slow, almost sensual, and as thorough as she could expect a surgeon to be. He spent time on her shoulders and rubbed the sunblock down over the back of her arms and back up into her neck, giving her a gentle massage and causing a ripple of pleasure throughout her whole body.

He surprised her most by lifting the bikini strap on her back before continuing to sensually fan his hands down onto the sides of her ribcage and the small of her back. Perhaps it was how she had begun to feel at his touch, but his movements seemed to become very slow motion. She was starting to feel very hot in her body and she was sure it wasn't to do with the sun. There was an energy between them.

Despite her attempts not to, she was becoming turned on as his hands slid low near her bikini bottoms and he massaged more of the sunblock down into the top of her hips. The sensitivity and feeling in his touch was affecting her.

Retaining a hand on the small of her back and keeping a connection with her skin, Rob poured more of the sunscreen onto the back of her thighs and moved fluidly down her legs. It felt as if his hands were exploring her flesh and unveiling her, sending waves of pleasure into her pelvis.

She really didn't want him to stop at all and lay feeling somewhat aroused. But of course it had to end and upon finishing paying careful attention to her toes, he stopped.

'Well, I think that's you done,' he said, with what sounded like a hint of huskiness in his voice.

'Thank you. You're quite a talent,' she turned her head back to face him.

'All part of a surgeon's training.'

'Really?'

'No, I'm just kidding,' he laughed.

As they looked at each other, Isadora became more aware of the chemistry that was present between them. She suddenly felt exposed to him in a way she wasn't expecting. Rapidly searching for words to break the moment she said the first thing that popped into her head.

'Would you like to come and see the obelisk later today with me?'

'Love to.'

'It's supposed to be huge…I mean, taller than any other obelisk by a third.'

'Yes,' he paused, 'and if it had have been completed it would've weighed over thirteen hundred tons and been the largest piece of worked stone in history.'

'That's so impressive,' she responded. 'You wonder why they went to such lengths to create something that would have been ridiculously difficult to move.'

'Well they must have had some sort of confidence they could move it. You know, some people think that acoustic levitation may have been applied as a way of moving things in Egypt's past.'

'Acoustic levitation? I wasn't aware of that,' she said, feeling grateful for the chance to talk and cool down at the same time.

'Yes, Scientists know that sound can clearly affect matter, and the ancient Egyptians understood the principles of acoustics and incorporated them into their architecture. There are examples of broken obelisks that when struck still resonate like a giant tuning fork.'

'They make a sound?'

'Hell yes, very definitely.'

'Solid rock making a sound…interesting. It's one thing making an obelisk transmit sound, but levitating a giant object like that? It sounds like something out of a sci-fi movie.'

'It does, doesn't it,' Rob responded. 'Kind of implausible, yet scientists today can levitate tiny rocks using sound vibration with a very low frequency sound.'

'It's a bit of a leap from levitating tiny rocks to a giant obelisk, though.'

'True. But Egypt is still a land of great mystery, after all. They moved them somehow and maybe manpower was enough, but if some of the best cranes on the planet once struggled with a two hundred ton object, then I'm not sure a thirteen hundred ton obelisk would be that easy.' His eyes searched hers. 'It will be great to see it, though.'

'Yes, we should try and head off in the next hour or so,' Isadora said.

'Here,' Rob responded, taking off his cap and handing it to her. 'The sun is strong. Wear this. I'll go get another.'

'Thank you.'

But he was already up out of the lounger and heading back to his room. And Isadora was left feeling entirely flustered.

***

Julie had been cuddling up with Dan in the water, but with a radar for action more advanced than those found on navy ships, the scene beside the pool had not passed her by at all. It was turning out to be a most perfect holiday.

'Baby, you rock.' Dan was pressed to her tightly with his arms wrapped around her whispering into her ear as the water made gentle lapping waves against their bodies.

She smiled, leaning back to look into his eyes. 'I can tell,' she said seductively.

'You can, can you?' he said leaning in to kiss her.

'Ahuh.'

She felt his hardness pressing more against her as his lips found hers and she melted into him.

***

Closing the hotel room door behind him, Rob padded barefoot across to his bed and lay on it. He needed some time to cool off but not because of the sun. It was completely as a result of Isadora - of touching her body. He raised his arms up to rest his head in his hands and let his mind go where it needed. Christ, what was he thinking, volunteering to rub sunblock onto her body. He was trying to be strong and instead he had pretty much walked straight into a lioness's den. Only she wasn't a lioness. She was definitely feline, but she was more the kind of cat with a divine body and eyes who purred when you stroked her.

This country and being free of a warzone was affecting him. Not only was he having strange people and symbols appear to him in his dreams, he hadn't been with a woman for quite some time and now his testosterone was begging for attention. He had to maintain some control because what he really needed was to be with Jessica right now. He was just in transit, and that was it. Another week or so and he would be back up in Cairo and on a plane to Perth and the life he was planning to begin.

Only, his mind didn't want to think about future plans another world away. It wanted to think about Isadora and their connection, and how her body had felt beneath his hands. He began to drift mentally and allowed his mind to go back over those moments, remembering the feeling of her skin. She had such a beautiful body, great breasts, curves in exactly the right places and those long slender legs that went on forever. But more than that, she was a captivating woman full of feeling, intelligence and mystery. She really was a rare breed, and she had responded to him. He had felt her relax and surrender to his touch and had enough experience with women to know that she was enjoying herself. And he'd noticed the tiny goose bumps forming over the soft rise of her hips. In fact, his attention was so caught up in her that he hadn't even stopped to consider exactly how low his hands had swept near her bikini bottoms. He was feeling increasingly attracted to her and had an unusual compulsion to worship her body. His sensual touch hadn't seemed to bother her at all, more the opposite.

He felt powerfully drawn to her in ways he hadn't experienced before. The feelings he was experiencing unnerved him, particularly as he was used to having a lot of control as a surgeon. Yet it was also exciting. Despite the strange series of events the past few days he was beginning to feel more alive than he had in a very long time. His body clearly agreed as he looked down the bed at his now well-defined erection poking up against his damp and clinging board shorts. Reaching down, he touched himself as he began to feel his increased arousal. After months of control he couldn't hold back anymore. All he could think about was her eyes and her silky skin and body. He reached inside his board shorts feeling his hardness. He was going to have to do something about it before he could return to the rooftop. But not here. Dan might walk in.

Sitting up on the bed he took a deep breath and sighed heavily before standing up and walking into the bathroom. As he turned the shower tap on he told himself he should be thinking about Jessica. But stepping in under the water and feeling the sensation of it running over him, he knew that there would be only one woman embedded in his mind in his moments of pleasure.

And she was lying several floors above him.

Chapter Forty-Five

Aswan was simply stunning to Isadora. She'd fallen in love with the place the moment she stepped off the train. Perhaps it was the dry desert heat that she felt such a connection with, or possibly the sight of the sacred Nile River flanked with tall palms and dotted with feluccas romantically drifting on its meandering waters under a permanent blue sky. Yet the visual sights were really secondary to the feeling of a far deeper connection that was seated in her soul. It could only be likened with the sense of coming home. Her heart remembered the land with the feeling and certainty that she had been here before, and had also known great joy and great peace in that time. It was as if life-force energy was being breathed back into her spirit, and ancient ones were whispering to her across time to wake up from a long coma and remember herself.

She found herself recalling her conversation in the restaurant with Josh about *soul loss*. Was it possible she could have fragmented not only from parts of herself in earlier years, but also from possible previous lives? If that were the case, she certainly wanted to reconnect with any life she had lived in this place. She smiled at the thought.

'Izzy?' Rob was looking at her curiously. 'You look like you're a million miles away.'

The cab they were traveling in had just pulled up in front of the ancient granite quarry, home to the giant unfinished obelisk. Julie and Dan had decided not to join them, opting for time on their own instead, which was of no great surprise to Isadora.

'Lives,' she said, somewhat vaguely.

'Sorry?'

'Lives...I was a million lives away,' she said exiting the cab.

As Rob wandered around the vehicle and joined her, his eyes held the question before his lips spoke the words. 'Reincarnation. You reckon you've existed here before?'

'I'd say so.'

'Why's that?'

'Intuition. Familiarity. Knowing,' she smiled. 'It just feels like I've definitely been here before.'

'Funny.'

'Yes, I'm sure that sounds odd.'

'No. I mean I've had that feeling, too. I had it more at Giza and in the Great Pyramid, though.'

'You did?'

'Why so surprised?'

'I'm not sure. It doesn't quite fit with the surgeon thing somehow...a bit too unscientific and esoteric.'

He laughed. 'Well maybe that makes me a wishy-washy kind of surgeon then.'

'I doubt that very much.'

They both stopped at a booth to pay their entry fee as Rob turned to Isadora. 'You look great in blue, by the way. It brings out your eye color.'

It was an unexpected compliment that caused her to blush. She was wearing a long cotton light blue dress she had picked up in a market near her hotel. Comfortable sandals and her dark hair tied up underneath a soft white scarf completed her outfit.

'Thank you.' She smiled at him.

They continued into the quarry, looking at some of the strange granite markings along the way before arriving at the enormous obelisk. It was lying flat in a deep trench that had been cut away around its circumference, with its base still attached to the rock floor. They stood in silence, impressed at the sight before them.

'Well you can see why they abandoned the project,' Isadora said, looking thoughtfully at the large crack running down the obelisk.

'Yes. It's a great shame.'

'But even if they did complete it and it didn't have the flaw, I can't comprehend how they would have even lifted it, let alone move it. One theory is that it was intended for Karnak Temple, but that's a huge distance for an object over thirteen hundred tons in weight.'

'Like I said, their movement of large rocks is certainly a mystery,' Rob added quietly.

'Acoustic levitation...hmm...that's certainly an interesting thought.'

'Yes it is.'

'That's not a huge space around it to work from either, is it?'

'Not at all. There's pretty much no maneuvering space down there.'

'It's hard to conceive how they carved it at all. I mean, it's not as if granite is the easiest rock on the planet.'

'Exactly. And where are the work markings on it?' he said.

'I know, it's strange, but it doesn't look like pickaxes or stone hammers were used on this,' she responded, peering closely at the sides.

Rob was crouched down and examining the obelisk carefully. 'What it actually looks like are tracks of a shovel in the snow, and that's really odd because...'

'Because what, Rob?' Isadora said staring at the baffled expression on his face.

'Because it indicates the rock would have had to have been almost...well...soft...to leave markings like that.'

'Which leaves us with another very strange puzzle.'

'And unfortunately no way to solve it...at least perhaps in this lifetime,' he winked at her.

***

'I'm trying hard to understand how the Sphinx may have been built much earlier than the Pyramids yet they're so connected to each other.' Rob and Isadora were sitting in a cafe overlooking the Nile after their visit to the granite quarry and the obelisk.

'I know, I've been thinking about it too. It's actually almost like they were designed together in the same period to serve a purpose, but there's potentially thousands of years of time between them,' he said.

'Which tends to imply that the entire layout was planned together, or even partially constructed at some point...'

'Around the time of the creation of the Sphinx.' Rob finished the sentence for her.

'So maybe the builders of the Pyramids were never able to complete the complex at the time of the Sphinx. Or they were simply following and completing a plan across time at a much later date.'

'And that might potentially explain how the structures were so advanced in 2500BC and there were no later developments of the same kind and technology. It's really quite mystifying.'

'The layout at Giza seems very specific.' Isadora was reflective. 'I mean, what do you really think? If you were to throw out a theory, outrageous or otherwise, why do you think they were put there? And by whom?' She picked up her cup of very sweet tea taking a sip with a grimace.

'I agree with some of the less conventional researchers that there's a connection with the stars and the constellation of Orion. As you know, the shafts in the King's and Queen's Chambers aligned perfectly with Sirius and stars in Orion's Belt around 2500BC, therefore they must have known well in advance of building them where their orientation needed to be.'

'Yes, their layout does seem very specific to the belt of Orion.'

'And ties in with the myth of Isis and Osiris,' Rob said.

'You know, for years I've wondered who would have designed them.'

'And what do you think?'

'Honestly,' she said. 'What I really think is… Priests. Ancient Priests who somehow had access to deep mystical knowledge and wanted the site created in accord with that. I believe it was for the purpose of some great planetary, cosmic, or spiritual reason.'

He looked at her, slightly taken aback for a moment. 'Well, if that were the case then they must have found a way to pass on the knowledge for the Pyramid construction, or store it in some way. Like a time capsule or somewhere vault-like.'

'Something like that.'

'It has been said that records of the civilization of Atlantis would be found buried in a chamber somewhere under the front paws of the Sphinx.'

'That's right,' Isadora said. 'But they have never found anything to date that we have been told about. And speculation about Atlantis, its reality and geographical location, have been rife for years.'

'No, they haven't uncovered anything we've been made aware of. But according to myth and folklore at least, in that chamber lies a library housing old knowledge of the time prior to the great flood that likely wiped out that civilization.' Rob paused as if considering something.

'Wouldn't that be incredible if true. It would certainly shed a great deal of light on things if they could uncover it,' Isadora added.

'What do you really think, Izzy?'

'Honestly? I think the incredible engineering of the Great Pyramid certainly suggests a far greater purpose than a mere tomb, and I think the King's Chamber holds a key. There's a vibrational aspect to it, which may have been damaged or reduced over the millennia, but it was certainly significant. As you mentioned, granite is quartz-based and carries sound and vibration, and they certainly went to some effort to get those massive beams in there.'

'Yes they did.'

'And possibly, the pyramid in its entirety is a gigantic instrument of some sort...perhaps to do with detecting earth vibrations, earthquakes and such, or even more subtle energies.'

'Yes, it does have those curious ball and socket joints at its base corners, which implies a requirement for adjustment to movement, slight or otherwise. But aside from the quartz-bearing properties of granite, what makes you say the King's Chamber has a sound vibrational aspect to it? I get the feeling you know something more that I don't.'

Isadora hesitated, uncertain how much to reveal to him about her experience in the chamber. 'It's just something I read once that has stuck, I guess. Those granite beams in the King's Chamber are free standing in terms of the Pyramid structure itself. So there had to be a very purposeful reason for that. And I'm convinced the Sphinx is part of that entire complex by design, not by random chance.'

'Your views are interesting. You know, a French engineer suggested that the Sphinx may stand over a seven hundred meter tunnel that leads to the Great Pyramid.'

'Well if that did exist it would certainly indicate a designed connection, but for what reason?'

'It's a little odd, but I've been dreaming about this stuff all week,'

Rob said, staring off down the Nile.

'What do you mean? Dreaming about what?'

'Oh, at night I've been having these crazy dreams that have been affecting my sleep. I'm in this tunnel, and I know the tunnel connects between the Sphinx and the Pyramid.'

'That's amazing, not crazy. What are you doing in there?'

He locked his eyes onto hers as if the sparkling blue of them were looking for a place of trust.

'Well I'm on my way to a ceremony of some sort in the Great Pyramid.'

'Oh.' Isadora said with surprise.

'I told you. Crazy.'

'Not at all. Do you know what the ceremony is for?'

'I'm betting it's for something religious or spiritual.'

'Betting? Why's that?'

'Well,' he paused again, searching her eyes. 'Because I'm wearing long white robes and I have symbols on my arms and hands…'

Isadora's eyes grew larger as she stared at him, waiting for him to finish.

'And I'm pretty sure, Izzy, that in the dream, I'm a Priest.'

Chapter Forty-Six

The moon was waxing close to full as Isadora looked out the hotel window toward the flowing waters of the Nile, its surface twinkling with moonlight. Behind her, the room was bathed in the soft glow of lamplight and felt very still and peaceful. She was alone. Julie was out with Dan for the evening, which was becoming increasingly the norm as they merged like teenage lovebirds. Isadora genuinely enjoyed seeing them as a couple and was at this moment actually quite grateful for some solitary time to think.

She had shared dinner with the group and then exited politely and quickly. Her connection with Rob was becoming a little blurry around the edges and she needed to stay as independent and strong as possible for the next solo leg of her journey. She had noticed him looking at her a lot lately, although she could never quite read the expression on his face or gauge what he was thinking. Sometimes it appeared that he liked her. At other times it felt like he wanted to run from her as fast as he could. Then he'd revealed his dreams where he was a Priest - which after all the unusual experiences she'd been having was getting a little too weird and coincidental.

And then there was Josh, still nudging at her insides. She had focused her attention on Egypt and forcibly blocked him from her thoughts, yet the feeling of him would surface from time to time like a mist rising off a swamp. She hadn't explored her feelings about him fully and really didn't want to anymore. It was enough to have experienced the deepest sense of disappointment that he'd not even had the courtesy or respect to contact her when he said he would, or to be honest about where his life was actually at before events spiraled badly. Yes, he had phoned to leave messages for her in Egypt, but it was all too little too late. Deep down she hadn't really let him go, but that would happen in its own natural time. He had seemed so perfect before the soap opera events unfolded, and yet if she was really honest with herself, she hadn't looked before she leaped. She had liked what she saw and felt, yet she'd been vulnerable and far too open when they had met. Still, despite the mess to her insides she was no doubt supposed to cross paths with him on that fateful flight back to London. He had gifted her with insight and motivated her in a way she hadn't previously felt, so she had taken some good from it.

Unfortunately he was weak though...sadly.

As she perched on the ledge, looking out at the pristinely clear moonlit sky speckled with brightly twinkling stars, she breathed in the magic of the view. Isadora felt an incredible serenity in Egypt that was more to do with a deep feeling of remembrance. She had more and more questions lately about life. What she wanted most right now was to have some answers from Seraph. It seemed so long ago since the angel's arrival in her bedroom that night in Ireland. Their conversations had been intermittent at best, but Seraph hadn't contacted her so much lately. Surprisingly, she now found that a little unsettling. Despite their unusual relationship, she was missing her friend. Perhaps, she reflected, it was like a child being raised...gradually one would let them explore more on their own, hold their hand less and let them find their own way in the world.

She was still deep in thought when colors began to form on the walls beside her and turning to face the source of the light she was struck by an incandescent purple glow emitting from the angel's heart. Waves of light beamed out at her like a star and Isadora immediately felt a deeper sense of peace.

'It's good to see you, Seraph.'

'And you, Dear Isadora.'

'I've become very fond of our conversations.'

'As have I. I understand you have some questions for me.'

'Yes I do, thank you. The woman who appeared to me, my…other guide, she said something about *recalibration* beginning. What did she mean?'

'You felt the vibration in the King's Chamber, yes?'

'Yes I did, before she appeared and before I blacked out.'

'Recalibration is the shift that is occurring.'

'What is it?'

'It is a transformation of the frequency you vibrate at.'

'Seriously?'

'Yes, Isadora.'

'So how does that work?'

'If you were to take negativity and toxic stress, for example, the vibrational frequency of this is dense and low and creates havoc in the body-mind-spirit system.'

'Sounds logical,' said Isadora.

'Yes. And if you are carrying this negativity at a cellular level then this will *inhibit* an increase in your vibrational frequency.'

'Okay.'

'So you have been shedding low vibrational energy in the form of old dysfunction and trauma from your field and are being recalibrated to run at a higher frequency,' Seraph said.

'Releasing all the dense vibration…like back in London in the woods,' she affirmed. 'And at a higher frequency, what happens?'

'Your consciousness magnetizes situations and people of equally high or greater frequency to you at faster levels. Your life can become easier, healthier, more abundant and far more enjoyable.

And your higher frequency impacts your entire life, people, and the field of energetic interaction around you.'

'That sounds positive.'

'Yes. Positivity and creativity are also features of a higher vibrational frequency.'

'So, because I've been running at a lower vibrational frequency due to carrying old emotional baggage, I've been attracting at that lower level?'

'Yes, indeed.'

'So what actually happened in the King's Chamber?'

'As you know, the chamber consists of quartz bearing granite and can transmit at a very high frequency. It was activated inter-dimensionally by ancient priests while you were in there, and being around that vibration raised your own markedly. Your system thus received recalibration. Subsequently, it will be easier for your new guide to connect with you and for you to manifest at more sophisticated levels.'

'Well that sounds like good news.'

'Indeed, it is.'

'Yes, but why? What's the purpose of increasing my vibrational frequency ultimately.'

'Spiritual awareness.'

'That's it?'

Seraph chuckled. 'There's not much more to get beyond that, Isadora.'

'Really?'

'Truly. Besides, your other guide cannot access you at a dense vibrational frequency.'

'Why is that? You can.'

'I'm designed for that.'

'And she's not?'

'It would be something like getting a President or Prime Minister to wash your dishes.'

'Wow. She must be important.'

'We all have our importance. The body is as functional as its weakest cell,' Seraph said.

'Nice analogy. So why just me?'

'Actually, it's not just you.'

'Oh?'

'There are many being recalibrated at this time. The clearing of dense vibrational frequency is occurring everywhere, creating great upheaval and distress.'

'Why?'

'Because the time of change has come and the consciousness of humanity is being elevated.'

'Elevated for what, exactly?'

'For the transformation to a more advanced human spiritual consciousness, Dear One. For an infinitely better and new world. It is considered well overdue on earth.'

'Seriously? So most of humanity is being recalibrated to increase spiritual consciousness?'

'No, Isadora,' Seraph paused, 'actually, the planet in its entirety is.'

Chapter Forty-Seven

Despite it only being eight in the morning, the air was warming and the sky was its usual perfect blue. The group stood quietly assembled in the Nubian Desert before the massive rock temples at Abu Simbel. Behind them, fifty kilometers from the Sudanese border stood Lake Nasser, the massive man-made reservoir of water that drifted back into the distance as far as their eyes could see.

'This has got to be my Egyptian highlight,' Dan said, standing with his arm around Julie's shoulder, 'besides you of course, babe.' He gave her an affectionate kiss on the lips and squeezed her body into his as she looked up at him through sleepy eyes.

'Well it was certainly worth the early start,' Rob added.

They had left the hotel at four in the morning and traveled over three and a half hours through the night and a stunning sunrise to make the desert journey by minivan to Egypt's popular tourist site. The two huge temples located on the banks of the artificially created Lake Nasser had undergone a massive relocation operation in the early sixties. They had been rescued from being submerged by the extensive lake waters created by the construction of the Aswan High Dam.

'The relocation here to this artificially made cliff was an eight-year project to secure the temples as a heritage site,' Isadora said.

'Another remarkable engineering feat, only a modern one this time.' Rob held her eyes.

'It's amazing. To think this lay hidden in the sands for centuries,' said Isadora, looking up at the four colossal statues that were originally cut into the side of a real cliff face.

'Really, for centuries?' Julie said.

'Yes, they were built in 50BC by the great Pharaoh Ramses II and were eventually buried under sand for a very long time, until the early eighteen hundreds when a Swiss explorer found them.'

'That's a long time for structures so big to be lying hidden under sand,' Dan added. 'Why were they built?'

'The entire temple complex was dedicated to the Gods and to stand as a lasting monument to the Pharaoh himself. The smaller temple was built to honor the Goddess Hathor and his great love, Queen Nefertari.'

'Nice honoring of his woman. Sounds like a great man,' Julie said.

'He ruled for sixty-seven years at the height of Ancient Egypt's glory and he was certainly a powerful proud man. Look over there at the smaller Temple of Hathor. Nefertari's statue stands almost as high as Ramses.' Isadora pointed across to the second temple where they stared at the six tall statues depicting the Pharaoh and his queen that were carved into the sandstone cliff. 'Because of his need to maintain his superiority, it was extremely rare for any statue to appear at the same height as him.'

'Well he must have loved her a whole lot then,' said Julie.

'Yes, having her statue at a similar height to his own certainly was real testimony to his love and respect for her,' Rob said, glancing over at Isadora again for a second and catching her eye. She wondered if perhaps he was engaging her on the subject, so she continued.

'Queen Nefertari was the royal first wife to Ramses and held a position and status which had been unequalled by a woman in

Ancient Egypt. She accompanied the Pharaoh on important journeys and took part in religious and civil ceremonies. Her tomb, the Temple of Hathor, was one of the most beautiful ever discovered.'

'She must have been an amazing woman and lived an incredible life for that time,' Julie said. 'I wonder what made her so special to him.'

'Apparently she had real political acumen and was renowned for her beauty. She was even special enough to become deified, which was unheard of. There are scenes of her coronation by Isis and Hathor in her tomb in the Valley of the Queens,' Rob said.

'Your knowledge never ceases to surprise me, mate. I don't know much about Isis and have never even heard of Hathor before.' They had stopped near the entrance to Ramses temple and now stood dwarfed by the four colossal statues of the seated Pharaoh. Dan looked at Rob as if waiting for an answer.

'I research, Dan. Hathor was a goddess of the sun, moon and sky, and linked with Aphrodite and Venus...love and beauty. She was said to encourage singing, dancing and being joyful.'

'Nice. My kind of Goddess,' Julie said with a smile.

'Isis was central to the ancient Egyptian religion and rituals,' Rob continued. 'She was revered as the Supreme Creator Goddess and divine midwife, mother, and wife; consort to Osiris. She was also renowned as an alchemist.'

'An alchemist?'

'Yes, mate. Alchemy - the origins of basic inorganic chemistry, and medicine really.'

'Well you would know, Doc,' Dan winked.

'Alchemy can be referred to on both material and spiritual dimensions. Of course it's more commonly associated with turning base metals like lead into gold. Egyptian metal technology and mummification contain the origins of alchemy and its roots. But it's also very associated with spiritualism, philosophy, and personal transformation. For example, practices such as yoga have an alchemical component, where the mind and the spirit subtly evolves over time,' Rob explained.

'You've done a bit of yoga haven't you, Izzy?' Julie said.

'Yes I have.'

'I guess alchemy in some respects is about achieving wisdom. Although in the case of Isis I think it had more to do with transmuting the physical body into a state of immortality,' Rob finished.

'Yes, Isis was about immortality and the soul's journey after death, but also she was very much about love,' Isadora added.

'Love?' Dan raised an eyebrow.

'Yes, love. As a deity she was said to divinely help unite lovers and can be called on to this day for that purpose. Romantic love between couples was a cornerstone of the faith of Isis, and the faith of Isis was very widespread. It existed in every corner of the Roman Empire, even during the formative centuries of Christianity.'

'Perhaps Isis brought you to me,' Julie whispered sleepily up at Dan, which appeared to transform him into marshmallow on the spot.

'She was also strongly linked with sexuality as a deity. Sacred sexuality to be more specific.' Rob glanced across at Isadora with a soft smile.

'I'm liking this Isis,' Dan chipped in causing the other three to laugh.

'Yes, I understand sexuality and sensual expression were an important part of Ancient Egyptian life, from birth to death and rebirth, and they loved and celebrated life to the full,' Rob continued.

'And apparently men in the Ancient Egyptian era were not afraid of demonstrating their love either,' Isadora added.

'Well hallelujah to that.' Julie nudged Dan as the group made their way to the entrance of the impressive temple dedicated to the great Pharaoh. It cut into the sandstone hill and stood between the four thirty-three feet high seated statues of Ramses II.

As they entered the ancient temple, Isadora trailed behind the other three with her mind far from the Pharaoh and his impressive temple construction. Instead she was curious as to the increasing connection she seemed to be having with Rob. Their shared knowledge and coincidences were beginning to pile up, and as she gazed at the impressive temple walls covered with hieroglyphics she was thinking about his reference to sacred sexuality.

But it wasn't his words she was recalling. It was the intimate expression on his face as he had looked at her.

Chapter Forty-Eight

The 'Island of Philae' had also been a relocation project during the Lake Nasser development and was now sited on the nearby Island of Agilka. The Island and its expertly reconstructed temples and masonry was one of the most picturesque sights that Isadora had seen. Situated in amongst the flowing waters of the Nile and surrounded by shrubbery, it held a mystical and profoundly peaceful aura. It was possible it had retained this for much of the several thousand years of its existence, Isadora thought.

As she wandered outdoors through the Hall of Nectanebo, she felt herself slipping through time as if the world had not changed for two millennia. What must it have been like to live in a culture that worshipped Isis as the Ancient Egyptians had? She was curious as to the nature of the woman, this Goddess. Being on the Island of Philae felt completely like returning home to Isadora. It was as if some part of her had always been certain of setting foot again on its sacred soil. Being here brought her the deepest sense of peace.

Having stuck together all morning for their foray into the temples of Abu Simbel and the visit to the Aswan High Dam, Julie and Dan took the opportunity to disappear together in one of the most romantic sites in Egypt. If Isis was truly a Goddess of Love and attributed to uniting lovers, then this was surely a place that such a couple would fall in love, if they weren't already.

Strolling amongst the tall pillars she explored the detail of the beautifully carved hieroglyphics and floral designs in a state of quiet awe. Dressed in a pink cotton tunic over her flowing white cotton pants and with her hair tied back loosely with a hairband, Isadora radiated simple femininity. Her face, now deeply bronzed from the week of sun exposure, highlighted a vibrant light green sparkle in her eyes, and the deep rest she had been experiencing had softened her features.

Rob was trailing behind her in respectful silence and noticed she appeared to be in an almost meditative state. So he took his time before venturing to her side.

'This place was once a haven for the faithful and one of the last functioning outposts for Egyptian religion and the worship of Isis,' she said thoughtfully as he walked up beside her. 'It closed in 551AD when Christianity became dominant as the form of religion and worship.'

'It certainly does carry a timelessness and peace about it,' he responded thoughtfully, looking at her lips as he did so.

'Always the love story of Isis and Osiris. It's everywhere here.'

Rob was beginning to feel the same compelling desire for her that he'd felt when applying the sunblock to her skin by the pool. 'Yes it is very romantic.'

'Perfect place for lovers,' she said without thinking, and then felt a surge of nervous energy flow through her body. 'The Temple of Isis is just over there.' She indicated across the remains of the Hall. 'I can't wait to see it.'

He watched her pick up her pace as if she had small jets on her heels. Within a few seconds she had widened the gap and was fast disappearing around a temple column, her long pink cotton top fanning out behind her. Rob paused, as confused by her rapid exit as he was by the unfamiliar feelings he was experiencing.

Damn.

Egypt was turning out to be a much more complex mystery than he had bargained on.

***

Rounding the pillar with her heart beating rapidly in her chest, Isadora took a sharp inhalation as she captured her first sight of the wondrous Temple of Isis. Oriented South to North, the original and much smaller Temple had been built in 370BC by Nectanebo, the last king of the thirtieth dynasty of Egypt. It now consisted of a court, a vestibule, a number of antechambers, and an inner sanctum where the sacred image of Isis was kept. Centuries later the court and vestibule had been converted into a Christian church with Coptic crosses carved into the walls, much like a new company branding after a successful takeover bid.

She moved quickly, seeking greater distance from Rob as her feet glided like cat's paws in amongst the ten huge pillars of the Hypostyle Hall. Long ago they had been beautifully painted to symbolize the first plants, trees, and flowers of the earth. Now they were eroded. Yet they retained a timeless beauty, and the power and mystique of the period of Ancient Egyptian worship still hung almost tangibly in the air.

Isadora felt a flutter of air around her face as if a breeze were blowing up off the Nile and she heard an unmistakable whisper across the temple.

'Love is everything.' A female voice echoed all around her as she spun to locate its source.

As Isadora looked across the Hall a mirage-like form of the beautiful woman from her dream and inside the Pyramid suddenly appeared between two of the large pillars. However, this time her form was so three-dimensional that she looked like a real flesh and blood human standing before her.

'Love is all there is,' she said softly to Isadora, who froze on the spot as the woman's eyes bored deeply into her soul.

'Why are you here?'

'The wisdom of our age is returning.' Her whispered words were everywhere, filling the temple space.

'What do you mean, *our age*?'

'Our age, Isadora. The wisdom of the Ancients and the path of Sacred Love. You are remembering where you came from and who you are.'

'Remembering? Sacred love?'

'That which you know, that lies within you. That which is you, yet you have not trusted.'

'I don't understand.'

'You will. I am with you soon, my friend,' her voice whispered across the ancient temple once more. 'I have awaited your return. It is time for you to remember.' The woman began to slowly drift back behind one of the pillars, her flowing white robes billowing around her like heavenly clouds, until she had vanished completely.

'With me soon?' She looked at the now empty space before her.

God, now there's two of them, she thought with exasperation. *I was just getting used to Seraph.*

'Isadora?'

For the second time in minutes she froze, hearing Rob's voice behind her. She wondered exactly how long he had been standing there and whether it was possible he'd heard any of the dialogue.

'Are you okay? You raced off.'

Hearing his footsteps softly approach, her heart was beating loudly in her chest as she felt him place his hand sensitively on her shoulder. She was undeniably attracted to Rob. He was real. And she so needed to feel something real right now.

'Izzy?'

She was bobbing in a sea of confusion at the tenderness in his voice. The world of angels and ancient goddesses appearing before her was becoming all too much and as she turned to face him she was filled with feeling. He searched her eyes as if waiting for her to reveal and express herself. Moments passed in deep silence as the pair remained locked in a trancelike and energetic embrace that caused everything else to fade away. His blue eyes were holding her and she was falling into them. His lips were drawing closer to hers. When suddenly, as if pulled by an invisible string, Isadora felt jerked out of the dreamlike state. She was as startled as if someone had just thrown a glass of cold water in her face.

God what am I doing?

Breaking away abruptly, she stared at him wide-eyed in surprise as she tried to catch a full breath.

'God. I'm sorry, Rob.'

'Izzy, I...'

'This place is getting to me. I should go.' Dropping her gaze she moved swiftly around him, heading back in the direction she'd come.

'Isadora, wait. It's okay.'

'No, it's not okay!' she said, more fiercely than she intended.

He watched her almost break into a run as she disappeared rapidly behind a pillar, leaving him standing confused at the center of the temple. Completely puzzled, he turned and gazed inquisitively at the spot between the two pillars that Isadora had been facing.

Rob was wondering who the woman was that she appeared to have been having a conversation with.

Chapter Forty-Nine

'You were pretty quiet over dinner, Izzy. Something up?' Julie appeared out of the bathroom in a robe, padding barefoot towards her bed with a white cotton towel containing her blonde mane in a turban-like fashion. Isadora was stretched out on her bed in the soft lamplight watching a small lizard plastered to the wall, its bulbous eyes searching for any unsuspecting insect to have the great misfortune of crossing its path.

'Not at all.'

'It can't be sleep deprivation, my friend. You're now officially considered a giant in the world of slumber.'

'Funny, Julz.' She smiled back at her.

'I hope you're not bothered by me spending lots of time with Dan. It's been playing on my mind a little lately. I mean, what kind of friend am I? Dragging you all the way over to Egypt and running off with the first stranger I meet.'

'You're a great friend. I wouldn't be here if it weren't for you. And it's perfectly fine that you're spending time with Dan. I'm happy to see you happy.'

'Thanks, darling.'

'And let's face it, you don't get to meet macho handsome hulks like him every day, do you,' Isadora said.

'Well, not every day.' She smiled. 'I really am sorry I've

abandoned you lately though, Izzy. It's so typical of you to be understanding.'

'It's no problem, Julz. You do like him a lot, don't you?'

'Yes I do.' Julie said softly. 'You and Rob were quiet tonight. I thought you guys were getting on great. Did something happen at Philae?'

'Nothing untoward.'

Rubbish. Julie thought.

'I was kind of hoping you two might hit it off. You seem to have a lot in common and I thought maybe there was chemistry there too.'

'Look, I like Rob a lot, Julz. I do. It's just that...well, I'm getting over the last one, and I need to prepare myself mentally for traveling on my own after Luxor. So I really don't need any more complications with men.'

'Yes, but you wouldn't view him as a complication if you didn't have some feelings for him.'

'He's nice, Julz. Okay. But I want this time for me. It's what I need right now, not a man. I just want to be on my own. It's my choice.'

'I respect that, Izzy. But everyone needs somebody sooner or later. You don't have to prove you're so strong. There's nothing wrong with loving someone and letting yourself be loved. We're all vulnerable at the end of the day.' Julie spoke gently, hesitating before continuing. 'I can't help but get the feeling you've been running from love, my friend. You said you attracted these non-committal scenarios with men, but honestly, I really wonder if it's so you can keep avoiding something.'

'I'm not really sure, Julz. I think that's why I need some time on my own.'

'Do you think it has something to do with your mother's sudden departure when you were young? I mean, it's quite likely that has affected your sense of trust and security in relationships.'

'Perhaps.'

'Look, I know things happen for a reason, Izzy, but for what it's worth, it wasn't fair. You know that, don't you. It wasn't fair you were left so young. It was far too much to figure out at an early age.'

Isadora blinked back several unexpected tears and bit her lip. 'I guess.'

'Hey, why don't you just enjoy Rob and his company. He likes you. Besides, you never know where things might lead.'

'He's going back to Australia, Julz. And I'm…not quite sure where I'm headed right now, so I don't see that it could possibly lead anywhere.'

'I've been thinking about that, Izzy. Do you really think that it's a good idea to go traveling on your own around the Middle East? Seriously, you've been through a lot lately and I think having company might be better for you. We've been having such fun.' Julie sat down, perching on the bed beside Isadora.

'I'll be fine Julz, honestly. Like I said, it's something I just have to do - for me. I need this time. Besides, we're never truly on our own in life, are we.'

Julie looked at her with curiosity for a moment before replying. 'I guess we always have our angels. Perhaps you can borrow mine for your travels ahead. *All is okay*, remember?' she said smiling.

'Yes I do remember, and I believe that now. I believe I'm being watched over.'

'Well, there's still time to change your mind, and I can easily contact the London office when we're in Luxor and have your flight changed.'

'That's kind of you, but I sincerely don't see any change of plan occurring.'

'It's that guy, Josh, isn't it. He's really mucked you up.'

'No it's not actually. It has nothing to do with Josh anymore.'

Isadora paused as she searched Julie's face. 'Look, Julz, before this trip, even before Josh, I wasn't in a good place. My faith has been slashed to ribbons the past few years and I've needed to find a way to trust myself again. To find my own strength. And maybe you're right on the money about my mother. I have been avoiding something inside myself, I'm just not sure what it is. But I do know there's a new pathway ahead. I met someone not long ago who helped change my perspective. They made me believe something more about existence. They gave me hope.'

Oh God, was it Jesus? thought Julie.

'You're beginning to sound like you had a religious experience of some sort.'

Isadora sighed. 'What if I did, Julz? What if that's exactly what I did have. You know, what if you were given an incredible experience and a chance to follow an adventure in life, to find yourself and your faith again. What would you do? Would you pursue it?'

'I don't know. Probably, yes. Izzy, what happened to you?' Julie was concerned.

'Look it doesn't matter what happened. Let's just say that life happened. I'm asking you to trust me. I'm okay. And I'll be okay in my travels.'

Julie looked unconvinced. 'If you say so, Izzy. But I need you to know that if you change your mind, or your plans, I can help you. Or if you ever need someone to talk to about absolutely anything, or you need somewhere to stay when you're back in London, you know my door and my heart is always open.'

Isadora felt the lump forming in her throat. 'That means a lot to me. Thank you.' She reached over and the two hugged warmly.

Julie rose from the bed and wandering into the bathroom closed the door gently behind her. For a while she stood in front of the mirror searching her own eyes, deep in thought.

LOUISE BEKER

God, I sure hope you heard my prayer on the plane. Don't let me down now, I'm counting on you.

Chapter Fifty

By the time the sun had peaked high in the sky the next day, heating the vast expanse of desert surface, they were drifting idly in their felucca down the Nile on their journey north to Luxor. The banks of the river were dotted with fishermen casting nets and occasionally children gathered to wave or peer at the strangers with interest, always with bright open smiles on their faces.

As they shored up later in the day for a night sleeping out under a beautiful clear canvas of stars, everyone was hungry and ready for land. The moon was already rising high and full in the sky with its bright glow lighting the sandy beach where they were to sleep.

After a tasty Egyptian campfire meal prepared by their felucca captain and mate, Julie and Dan departed for a moonlit stroll leaving Isadora and Rob alone. He'd been uncharacteristically quiet and rather subdued around Isadora throughout the boat journey. The reality was, he really didn't want her to push him away any further. Mustering up courage, he smiled at her as they cozied into sleeping bags near the fire.

'Beautiful night, isn't it?'

'Yes, the full moon is perfect. We're very lucky.' Isadora returned his smile and felt her defenses soften as she thought about Julie's words the night before.

'Hey, let's see if we can find Orion's Belt and Sirius,' he said, inching his sleeping bag closer to her before lying back on the sand.

'The sky is certainly clear enough for it.' Isadora lay back flat on the ground beside him.

'Okay, let's see. We'll start with Sirius.' He pointed to a bright star in the sky. 'There it goes. What a beauty. Brightest star in our heavens and one of our nearest neighbors, the Star of Isis.'

'She's easy to spot alright, when you know where you're looking,' she said.

He searched a little longer before pointing back up at the sky. 'And there's Orion's Belt nearby, at the center of the constellation Orion the Hunter.'

'Where exactly?'

'Right there,' he said, taking her arm and guiding her finger to a point in the sky.

A shiver of pleasure ran through her at his touch. 'Oh, I see now,' she smiled.

'So the three stars of the belt are Mintaka, which means *the belt*, no surprises there; Alnitak, which means *the girdle;* and Alnilam, which means *string of pearls.*'

'Beautiful names.'

'Yes they are. They're all Arabic names. Alnilam, the one in the middle, is the largest of the three. It's thirteen hundred light years from earth, much further than the other two on either side which are more around eight hundred light years away in distance,' he said.

'Wow, it must be a massive star. It's still brighter than the two nearer ones.'

'Yes, it sure is. It's apparently ten thousand times more luminous than our sun.'

'Defies imagination really.'

'And of course, you know about the idea of the Giza pyramids being positioned and built to mirror Orion's Belt, yes?'

'I do. There's uncanny mathematics and astronomy behind it all.

It's often suggested the Pyramids were built to mirror those stars, with Menkaure, the smallest pyramid at Giza, set slightly offline of the other two - just like Mintaka is in the Belt,' she said peering up at the sky.

'I know. And let's not forget computer simulations that correlate the placement of the pyramids as an exact mirror of Orion's Belt above and below in the years around 10,450BC,' Rob said.

'The Age of Leo.'

'When our cat friend the great Sphinx was quite possibly created.'

'Yes, but then to go on and actually build the pyramids thousands of years later, and build in features like having a shaft point directly to stars in Orion's system while they were at it…they had to have been thinking way ahead of time and been very clear about where the stars would be. That just boggles the mind really, doesn't it.'

'It does,' Rob said, looking into her eyes in the firelight. 'It really seems like the architects started something so purposeful way back then, with a view to it being completed in the form of the pyramids at the time they were built. Imagine designing something with that much foresight and for whatever reason saying *right, we'll create and leave the plan and they can whack those pyramids up in eight thousand years or so.*'

She laughed.

'Seriously though, Izzy, they knew so much…so much more about our existence.'

'They really did seem to.'

His sense of wonder touched her heart as he continued. 'They seemed to understand so many things about earth's place in the cosmos, the constellations and the great astrological ages.'

She looked back at him, holding his eye contact.

He was quiet for a moment. 'And now we find ourselves lying here under that same sky almost thirteen thousand years after the

Age of Leo.'

'At the beginning of a whole new Age…The Age of Aquarius.'

'The Great Age of Enlightenment,' Rob said thoughtfully.

'Really? I guess we can hope for that. It has to be better than the Age of Ignorance we've been moving through.'

'It does have to be. We can hope that human beings stop doing the terrible things they do to each other,' he said quietly.

'Rob,' Isadora hesitated, uncertain of what words to choose, 'the war in Iraq must have been a terrible experience for you, truly. I'm sorry.'

'All war is terrible, Izzy. Look at the last century. Unending wars, and so much loss of life. Then add all the disease, poverty, starvation, obesity, depression, greed and corruption…and if the shit isn't happening *to us* we numb ourselves out with food, alcohol, television, drugs, pornography and the pursuit of money and materialism. Jesus, some human beings even kill their own children. Who are we as a species? Really, who are we…?' His voice trailed off.

Isadora remained silent.

'Surely we're not just this, Izzy. Where are we really from? What are our true origins?'

She paused. 'If I were to look to the designers of the Sphinx and the Pyramids of Giza, I would have to say somewhere out there, Rob,' she said, pointing to the darkened canvas of stars. 'That's where our true origins lie…and maybe where they are destined again.'

'There's certainly some form of vastly higher intelligence out there, Izzy. I just know it.' He sighed heavily.

'I think so, too.'

Rob gazed at the stars for some time before rolling slightly onto his side to face her. 'I'm glad I met you.'

She felt suddenly shy. All the complexity of life seemed stripped away and they were just like two innocent kids hanging out under the stars. 'I'm glad I met you too.'

He stared into her eyes as he leaned fractionally closer toward her. She could almost feel his breath on her face.

'There's something I've been wanting to do for some time,' he said.

'Really?' she whispered nervously, feeling the chemistry pulsate between them and unable to move.

'Yes,' he said in a low voice as he moved his face in close to hers and kissed her slowly and deeply.

Her body tingled all over as if a billion tiny power cells had just lit up inside her and she felt his arm close around her as he pulled her closer to him. His breath merged with her own as his tongue began to explore her deeply, tasting her. She felt lost and found all at the same time as she began to respond freely with passion, wrapping her arms around his strong back as he rolled more fully onto her.

Pulling away briefly, he stared into her eyes. 'So that's what I've been wanting to do,' he whispered.

'I'm glad you did,' she whispered back, looking back into his eyes and forgetting about any need for defenses.

Reaching across to her face, his hand stroked long strands of hair off her cheeks and over her ears. 'You're a far greater find than anything else I could have imagined in Egypt, Izzy.'

The words sent a wave of soft vulnerability through her as he kissed her again, until they eventually heard the voices of Julie and Dan returning.

And he held her protectively as they went to sleep.

Chapter Fifty-One

It was early afternoon when the felucca eventually drifted into Luxor. As they disembarked, a crowd of young children shouted 'Baksheesh, baksheesh,' begging for money as they flocked around the small group.

Julie, as ever in the know about these things, had been advised to bring bags of pens as an offering instead of money and began to happily distribute them, much to the children's delight.

'Nice thought, babe,' Dan said smiling at her after she had dispensed with several dozen of them.

'Thank you,' she said reaching up to kiss him. 'At least I don't have to worry what they spend their money on, but I should have brought paper too.'

'Come on,' he said, 'let's catch up with those two before we lose them.'

'They're getting on very well, aren't they,' Julie said, smiling with delight as she watched them strolling ahead holding hands.'

'Yes they are,' Dan paused. 'Bit of a surprise, to be fair.'

'Why? Don't you think they're compatible? They seem so perfect together and have so much in common.'

'Yes, but I really didn't think Rob would involve himself, especially after you said she'd been mucked around by a guy who hadn't got rid of his ex.'

'But it's good for Izzy. It's helping her forget. Besides, she could do with spending time with a nice man.'

'As long as she can handle the goodbye I guess that's okay,' he said.

'Well, it's a just a holiday thing, but you never know where things might lead.'

Dan stopped, surprising Julie as he spun her around and looked at her with seriousness. 'Sweetheart, we're different. I already know I want to see you again. And trust me, I'll be beating down your door in London very soon.'

Julie almost purred at his words. 'My beautiful handsome man,' she said planting a long kiss on him.

'Honey, they're not quite into public displays of affection in this part of the world,' he said, pulling back and noticing they were attracting a few disapproving looks from locals.

'Bloody westerners. You're right, it will keep,' Julie said, giving him a hug before breaking away. 'So you don't think Rob likes Izzy enough?'

'That's not the problem.'

'What is it, Dan?' she said, noticing he was looking uncomfortable all of a sudden. 'Dan, what is it? You have to tell me now.'

He looked up at Rob and Isadora as they mingled further into the market crowds ahead.

'I shouldn't say, but I don't really want to see your friend get messed up again.'

'Well what is it, Dan? Tell me.' She followed his gaze to Isadora noticing how happy she was looking with Rob holding her hand. Julie began to feel uneasy.

'Well, I think he has a woman waiting for him back in Perth,' he said tentatively.

'You're absolutely kidding me!' Julie felt her blood beginning to simmer.

'And I got the strong impression he's decided to head down the aisle with her when he gets back there.'

'This is a joke, right?'

'No. Sorry, darling.'

'I would call that seriously uncool!' she said, biting her lip with annoyance.

'Yeah. To be fair though, Julz, I think Iraq has knocked the poor bloke about a bit. I think he's a bit confused right now.'

'I don't give a continental damn about that, Dan. That's my friend he's toying with,' she said managing to cool her outer emotion.

'I think we should just let them be, babe. It's just a couple more days after all,' he said, nervously noticing her strong reaction.

Her eyes narrowed as she looked ahead at Rob again. 'Sure thing,' she said coolly.

But inwardly, Julie's blood was beginning to boil.

***

Isadora felt fabulous as she spent the rest of the afternoon with Rob wandering around the markets and Luxor Temple. They'd just completed their own tour of the wondrous Karnak Temple and were standing near the entrance talking animatedly.

'That was spectacular,' Rob said. 'Karnak is the largest ancient religious site in the world. And it sure has to be one of the best. The size and grandeur is just so amazing, isn't it?'

'Yes it is,' she smiled back at him. 'And the original plan for the Karnak temple potentially dates all the way back to about 3700BC.'

'Before the pyramids, huh.' He winked at her. 'There were some bright cookies in these parts too.'

'Yes, there were. I guess you know that a lot of temples at

Karnak seemed to have been systematically deconstructed and the stones used for the construction of temples elsewhere?'

'That's right…they moved them to do with the changes of the major astrological cycles. The precession of the Equinoxes.'

'I believe so. Although to be honest I don't really understand the Precession of the Equinoxes in terms of how that works out there.' Isadora waved her hand towards the sky. 'Astronomically, I mean.'

'Would you like me to have a go at explaining?'

'That would be great,' Isadora said with interest.

'Okay. Imagine the axis between the North and South Pole's of earth has a slight wobble.'

'Why the wobble?'

'Basically because of the gravitational pull between the sun and moon. Think of the movement of a spinning top as it slows down - that's what the wobble looks like.'

'Okay.'

'So the earth's north and south ends move a tiny fraction each year and, relative to fixed stars in the heavens, it causes the stars to rise twenty minutes later each year. Now, let me explain that a bit. What that means in terms of the poles is that if you take a pen at each end and let it flow with the movement at the axis, it would end up drawing a circle in the heavens at each end of the planet.'

'Alright.'

'Okay. So the annual twenty minute change caused by the tiny wobble adds up over the centuries. And basically, to come full circle it takes almost 26,000 years to complete a full cycle.'

'That's the bit I get confused about.'

'What, the circle coming to a full cycle?'

'Yes. Visually how that works out there.' She looked up at the sky.

Rob paused. 'Well, imagine the poles with pens at each end drawing a circle in the heavens that is created by the slight axial wobble, and it is coming full cycle. Here,' he said, crouching down to draw a picture in the sand.

'Ahuh, I think I'm getting it.'

'The thing to note is that *precession* actually relates to the apparent gradual *backwards* movement of the visible universe, as viewed from earth. So in terms of a visual example, if you put two cars side by side going around a circular lap and one is traveling forty miles an hour and the other one thirty eight miles an hour, the slower car would appear to move backwards to the faster car.' He stood up again.

'And the two cars aren't going the same pace because of the gravitational pull, so-to-speak?'

'That's right.'

'So how does that correspond to where change occurs over time in relation to where the stars appear at night?'

'If we look up at a star at midnight on, say New Year's Eve, and then return to exactly the same spot seventy-two years later, that star will appear to have moved one degree backwards in the sky. That's the same with the whole universal backdrop for that matter. Are you with me?' Rob asked.

'I think I'm getting somewhere.'

'Great. So the sun and stars don't actually move backward. They just *appear* to be in a different place because you have arrived *early* as far as the sun and stars are concerned. Think of the two cars.'

'I'm with you. You're saying that after however long the faster car, that being earth, would lap the other car and end up beside it again. But it would actually *appear* that the slow car, the universal backdrop, has gone backwards the full lap and that's why it ends up beside it again.'

'Yes, nice. In the case of the apparent backwards movement of the sun and stars as they appear to us, it doesn't amount to much movement in a year, but after 25,630 years it has completed a full

360 degrees, or one complete circle of the heavens, or one backwards car lap…and this long time period is called The Great Year.'

'Which is divided into the astrological ages, right?' Isadora said.

'Correct. With each transit of an astrological sign in the heavens, and its corresponding *Age,* lasting 2,160 years, or one *Great Age* of that 25,630 Great Year cycle.'

'So they had to keep moving the temples, because they noticed over time their star positions were wayward because of precession of the equinoxes?'

'I guess so. Bit of a big job every once in a while, though,' he said.

She laughed. 'Absolutely, but it must have been important enough for them to want to do it. I think it's incredible that they had such a knowledge of that movement…that they paid that much attention over time, and their rituals and worship were so intrinsically linked with the stars and the zodiac constellations and the precession movement.'

'Yes. It was incredible.'

'And so now here we are moving *backwards* out of the Age of Pisces, which we've been in for well over two thousand years, and into the Age of Aquarius at this juncture in the precession of the equinoxes.' Isadora said.

'You've got it.'

'And you called Aquarius the *Great Age of Enlightenment* last night. Why's that?'

'Aquarius as a sign is the Water Bearer, not because it's a water sign, but because it's the third and last of the astrological air signs. Air is always concerned with knowledge, relationships, people, communication…stuff like that,' Rob said.

'Okay.'

'So the Age of Aquarius pertains to *enlightenment* because

Aquarius is associated strongly with things like integrity, the power of the mind, advanced intuitive faculties, technological scientific advances, entrepreneurialism, higher levels of awareness, spirituality and consciousness...'

Spirituality and consciousness? she thought, looking taken aback for a moment.

He saw the expression change on her face. 'I probably sound like I need a padded cell, right?'

'Not at all. Carry on. I'm a captivated audience.'

'Okay. Then of course there's my own personal favorite trait of Aquarius - freedom. And if you think about it, we're seeing massive breakdowns of old restrictive structures and ideologies on the planet that have been dominant within the past two thousand years of the Piscean Age - an Age which has been filled with a lot of darkness, destruction and corruption, I might add. Regimes, dictatorships, military force, wars, religious clashes, economic breakdowns and institutions, all coming under fire. And of course, governments and corporations are being held more accountable by the people, thankfully. Humanity is rising up more for all sorts of causes and calling for positive change. Aquarius is the great humanitarian sign, after all. It's also the rebel and the innovator, and we're creating more choices and flexibility for ourselves and our lives,' Rob said.

'What about relationships?'

He smiled. 'Great changes there, and about time really. The transition to this new World Age is inspiring the merging of opposites, wholeness and the reunion of the *true* masculine and feminine energies, both within an individual and in relationships. So partnerships not based on real integrity and honoring of both those energies may struggle, and it could well result in forms of separation, drama and dysfunction.'

'That does seem to have been quite prevalent on earth,' she said, thinking about her own relationship track record.

'And incidentally, this period of change was depicted in many old cultures,' Rob continued. 'The Mayan civilization describe this time as the end of the Fourth Sun. And it's *not* deemed the end of the world, contrary to doomsday theories. Rather, it is the end of an Age dominated by materialism and the ego-consciousness. According to their world cycles it is the beginning of the Age of the Fifth Sun.'

'What does that mean?'

'It's considered to be an age of harmony, where male and female energies will work together in balance. Humanity will be motivated more by *awareness,* and less by fear. Respect for ourselves, others and the planet, will become a high priority. And the desire for real integrity will be present.'

'Real integrity…now that sounds like a great thing,' Isadora said thinking about his words. 'The question is, how to get there?'

'Honestly, Izzy, I think it's about cleaning up ourselves first – our own internal wars, and being in integrity with who we really are as individuals. Taking responsibility for our own stuff and breaking negative and limited cycles that have been handed on to us. We're generations of pattern-breakers.'

'Pattern-breakers?'

'Yes. Recognizing the things that don't work for us, healing inherited dysfunction and outmoded ways, and choosing new paths. It's the only choice we really have.'

'The only choice?'

'Well, the planet is changing, regardless. So the way I see it, hold onto the old way and suffer, or move with the new times. Flexibility creates freedom. And like we really need a planet continually filled with unhappy, dysfunctional relationships…along with all the other negativity.' Rob hesitated a moment before continuing. 'I certainly don't wish to have a relationship like my parents had…some shiny billboard covering up a disconnected and empty reality. I want an honest, truly loving partnership, filled with as much happiness as humanly possible,' he said reflectively.

'I feel the same,' Isadora replied. 'It's destructive and such hard work holding onto an unhappy and unfulfilling relationship.' She glanced down at the ground, for a moment uncertain where to look.

'Like swimming constantly upstream against the current,' he added softly, watching her carefully. 'In this dawning World Age it's likely to be asking for nothing but trouble and pain hanging onto substandard connections of *any* sort. Genuine love and respect, that's a basic benchmark.'

'So if it's not healthy then clean it up and grow, or be on your own. Is that what you're saying?'

'Something like that,' he smiled. 'Create what's possible. Unity and sacred love, that's what the masculine and feminine energies on earth are aspiring towards now.'

'Authentic loving relationships - that has got to be good for children, communities and the world. So this shift into another Age is not a bad thing then, is it?'

'No it's not. Not after all the negativity has come out, or people knuckle down, take responsibility and do some self-exploration. Things tend to get messy with transformation…and the nature of Aquarius is very transformational - a bit like remodeling your home completely.'

'Oh?'

'Yes. It can look like a real mess and be a pain to live in for a while,' he chuckled.

'Definitely sounds like earth at present.' *And how my life has been,* Isadora reflected. 'But it also sounds very encouraging, like there's a lot of hope. Especially if you get a totally remodeled home eventually,' she said.

'Or planet. Yes, I guess it's ultimately encouraging.'

'It sounds exciting and well overdue. Bring it on, I say. Have we actually entered the Age of Aquarius yet Rob, in terms of the heavens?' She looked up at the sky.

'Well, it's not as if it's a linear fixed point in time, but yes, the world is transitioning. The beginning is upon us; the process is already happening.'

'A brand new 2,160 year World Age…that's a big deal. And you know all this stuff, how?'

'Research,' he smiled, 'and my mother.'

Isadora chuckled. 'Thank you,' she said, reaching up and giving him a kiss on the lips. 'It's all so fascinating and inspiring,'

Wrapping his arms around her, he looked down into her eyes. 'I think you should ask me more complex questions if that's how I get thanked.'

'I think I will,' she smiled.

'You make them as challenging as you like,' he said before kissing her again slowly and tenderly.

A wave of pleasure rippled throughout her body. 'Mmm…wow,' she whispered before breaking away fully. 'Terrible time to mention, but shouldn't we be getting back to the hotel to meet Julz and Dan for dinner?'

He glanced down at his watch. 'Yes, we're running a little late. Come on, let's go,' he said taking her hand once more in his.

Chapter Fifty-Two

They were nearing the hotel when Isadora decided to race into a souvenir shop, sending Rob on ahead to let Julie and Dan know she wasn't far behind. She hastily purchased an Ankh necklace for herself, a pretty cartouche pendant and several other items, before heading quickly back to the hotel.

The sky was a slightly dusky blue with the evening drawing in. As she neared the hotel Isadora thought about Rob and how they had become so close in little more than a week. Yet at the same time it felt as if she had known him for a lifetime, such was the ease between them.

It was going to be challenging saying goodbye in several days time, especially as they'd bonded so well and she was happy and calm around him. And particularly after their romance the previous night under the stars on the banks of the beautiful Nile. She felt a small rush of anxiety at the thought of parting company.

Maybe we'll see each other again someday.

'Isadora.' A familiar voice interrupted her thoughts and as she reached the hotel entrance a look of horror and confusion formed instantly on her face.

'Josh? What are you doing here?' She stopped dead in her tracks as he stood up from the steps out front where he'd been seated. Although still handsome, dark rings were present under his eyes and he appeared to be sporting a few days of stubble on his face.

'You didn't answer any of my messages,' he shrugged, as if in explanation.

She flinched backward as he took several more steps towards her, causing him to hesitate. 'Look, I'm sorry if this is a bit of a shock.'

'A bit?!'

'Okay, a lot. You showed me your Egypt itinerary, remember. So I knew you would be in Luxor now. I called Julie's Travel Agency and managed to get the hotel details from them. I flew into Cairo yesterday and caught the train last night.' His hand reached out slowly to touch her cheek. 'I had to see you, Isadora.'

She took another step back.

'Why, Josh? Why now? Why all this way? What's the point?'

'That's why I needed to see you - to explain. I'm so incredibly sorry for how I handled things.'

Isadora was beginning to spin inwardly. Everything felt surreal again as her memories came flooding back like waste flowing in a sewerage pipe. Surely her world couldn't become this unpredictable and messy.

'But you have a child on the way with another woman, Josh. You shouldn't be here.'

'I don't. Have a child, I mean. She miscarried a number of days ago.'

Isadora remained silent for some time. 'I'm sorry to hear.' She rubbed her forehead. 'In any case, you're engaged.'

'I'm not engaged, Isadora. I was never engaged. She lied. She has a tendency to manipulate and lie.'

'But the baby was yours?'

'Yes.' He dropped his eyes for a second. 'That was the truth. I hadn't seen her for a year and it was one night, and it was before I met you. It was a mistake.'

'So you're free now and you're here to appease your guilt?' The words rolled coldly from her mouth before she could stop them.

'Do you really think I would fly this far around the world just to appease my guilt? Come on, Isadora. You know me.' He took the extra couple of steps to reach her and placed his hands gently on either side of her face. 'You know me,' he repeated softly, gazing into her eyes.

She blinked back tears as old feelings for him flooded up.

'I don't know you. We happened so fast and ended so radically, and the shock and pain was....'

'I know. I'm sorry. I'm so very sorry. Please forgive me,' he kissed her forehead softly. 'Forgive me. Please.'

Isadora felt the extremity of her confusion. 'You had all weekend to talk to me, and nothing…after all our time together, our closeness…our intimacy.' Her voice almost broke. 'And you let that heartless woman have her smug way with me, like I was insect crap on a wall.'

'I'm really so sorry.'

'So am I. Because I know you came an awfully long way to say these things, Josh, and I appreciate the huge gesture, but I can't do this.' She removed his hands slowly from her face. 'I can't just change how things are for me now because you had some sort of an epiphany after the event. If that seems harsh, I'm sorry. But I'm not responsible for your choices. That's a big lesson in life I've had to learn myself, lately. So I apologize if it comes as a shock to you,' she paused, 'I really do need to go now, Josh. I do.'

'What? Please, Isadora,' he whispered, his eyes full of emotion. 'I haven't met anyone I've felt for like you for fifteen years. I don't want to lose you.'

Rob's face flickered into her mind in amongst her turmoil, along with his words about swimming against the current. 'It's different now, Josh. We can't change life back. Things are different.'

'What's different? It's been less than two weeks,' he said,

frustration beginning to show in his voice.

'I'm different,' she said gaining strength from her words. 'I'm different. What I went through after seeing you and her together that night in London changed me. And Egypt has changed me. I'm not the same person anymore.'

More than you would ever know, she thought.

'Come on, it's us though. Our connection, it's strong.'

'No, it was strong, but it's broken. It broke near the start, and you broke it.'

'We'll fix it. We'll move on from this,' he said with determination.

'Josh, I've had so many stop-start, half-pie and broken things. I've already seen and know more than I could ever imagine I would have had to. I want the real thing.'

'It *is* the real thing. We can take our time and work through things, or just start again fresh. I can travel with you, to Jordan and Israel…wherever. I've taken some time off work.'

'No you can't do that, Josh. I'm traveling alone. I was always going to be traveling alone. You know that. I don't want you with me.'

'I don't believe that.' He looked hurt.

'You'll have to,' she said, suddenly walking around him and up onto the hotel entrance step before turning back to face him. 'I have to go right now. Julie is waiting for me.'

'It was bullshit, Isadora. My whole theory about life being a *ten*,' he said, turning slowly to face her. 'You were right.'

Isadora saw the look of defeat forming on his face, and an unexpected feeling of compassion rose from within her. 'No Josh, don't say that. It is true,' she said, stepping down off the step and standing before him. 'It's all a ten. Even this. It's all perfect. There's a reason for all things. That was the truth.' She softly touched his arm.

'You think so?' He looked so weary as he stared back into her eyes.

'I know so,' she said, feeling a curiously detached kind of love for him. 'You helped me, and I'm grateful for the gifts you gave me.'

'I didn't help you enough, though.'

'It was the wrong time for us, but that was perfect too…don't you see? It was just how it was, and how it was supposed to be.' She felt all the feelings she had experienced with him flood through her and her heart surged with love for him.

'It wasn't how it was supposed to be at all.'

'We can't change the past, Josh. It happened how it did for a reason. You'll see that someday. There will be a great gift in this for you too.'

'You're the gift I want.'

Isadora avoided his eyes.

'You should really go rest for the night, Josh. You've had a big journey and you look exhausted.'

'Yes, I could probably do with some rest,' he said with resignation. 'I haven't slept much the past week. Can I see you tomorrow? How about breakfast in the morning, I could meet you here around eight? Please…'

Isadora considered long and hard. Dozens of thoughts and ideas passed rapidly through her mind in the space of a few seconds before her intuition settled strongly on one with crystal clarity, and she chose it.

'Okay, Josh. But make it nine.'

***

She was very quiet throughout dinner and Rob noticed. He was beginning to feel her so easily, a little like surgical machinery plugged into a person that monitored every change in temperature, blood pressure and heart rate. Only, the technology in him seemed designed to read all her subtle, or-not-so, shifts in feeling and emotion.

'Are you okay?' He leaned over, whispering softly into her ear so Julie and Dan couldn't hear across the table. 'You're pretty quiet.'

'I'm good...really.' She smiled back at him, but her eyes were distant. 'I'm just a little tired this evening. I think I'll head back to the room and have an early night.'

'Okay, I'll walk you.'

Julie, who had been quietly observing Isadora throughout the whole meal, suddenly and swiftly interjected. 'Hey, Izzy. Are you heading back to the Hotel now?'

'Yes I am,' she said, softly pushing her chair back and standing up.

'I'll walk with you.' Julie said, standing up.

Rob looked surprised.

'Dan, I've been monopolizing you,' she smiled across at Rob. 'Why don't you two have some man time. I'll walk Izzy back.'

'Honestly, Julz. I'll be fine.'

'No, I haven't seen you all day. I'd love to.'

Isadora hesitated. 'Okay. Let's go then.'

Rob felt a peculiar and inexplicable uneasy feeling forming in his gut, but ignoring it he smiled and stood up to give her a warm hug. 'Thanks for such a great day.'

'Yes, it was wonderful.' She beamed back at him.

'Valley of the Kings tomorrow.'

'Now that will be interesting,' Dan interjected. 'I'll see you back at the hotel soon, Julz.'

'Goodnight,' Isadora said.

'I'll see you in the morning, Izzy,' Rob said, feeling confusion at her rapid exit, and also some frustration. He really needed to talk with her and had assumed he would get to walk her back and have quiet time with her that evening.

I guess there's always tomorrow.

But instead he was left with an unfamiliar pining feeling as he watched her walk away.

***

'Everything okay, Izzy?' Julie said, cutting to the chase as they exited the restaurant.

'Sure.'

'You looked a bit distracted over dinner.'

'No, I'm fine,' Isadora responded a little too sharply.

'I've known you for almost two decades, Izzy, and you're not fine. I can smell a rat.'

'Well that's an interesting choice of words.' Isadora's voice was clipped as she began walking faster.

'A rat?' Julie increased her stride to keep up.

'Yes.'

Thinking momentarily, Julie's eyebrows creased together with understanding. 'Oh, damn. You know then,' she said quietly. 'I thought you were a bit cool over dinner.'

'What? You knew?' Isadora turned and looked at her with surprise.

'Well, Dan told me. I'm sorry, I wanted to say something but I wasn't sure.'

'What?' Isadora said, stopping in confusion.

'Well, he noticed how close you were getting with Rob and he told me the truth this morning when we got off the felucca. He reckons Rob is all mucked up from Iraq and needs to sort his head out.'

'What exactly did he tell you, Julz?'

Julie hesitated, now slightly confused herself. 'Well, about the woman waiting for him, in Perth...the one he's apparently about to be engaged to.' She watched the look on Isadora's face go dark in a second.

'Really?' she responded, her eyes beginning to glaze.

'That wasn't the rat you were talking about, was it?'

'No, Julz. It wasn't.'

Chapter Fifty-Three

Julie woke up to bright light in the sparsely furnished hotel room. Her first thoughts were of Dan as she stretched out like a contented cat beneath the starched white cotton sheets, a smile forming broadly on her face. Man, that guy could kiss. She felt hot just thinking about their chemistry. Her second thought, that filtered in immediately after the more pleasant first one, was of deep concern for Isadora.

Joshua bloody Hunter-Gatherer, again! What an insane act of stupidity to follow her here to Egypt. He may just as well have run a truck over Isadora's wounded heart. Julie wanted to give him a piece of her mind. Or better still, set Dan on him like a Rottweiler to a Shitsu.

What the hell was he thinking?!

And what the hell had she done blabbing to Izzy about Rob's partner in Perth.

I really mucked that up. What a mess.

Isadora had begun to bloom on the trip, and in Rob's company. She had forgotten about that idiot Josh and was becoming happy. Sure, they'd had a few strange moments in their travels where Julie wondered if Isadora's head had checked out of planet earth, but she had seen her laughing a lot more in recent days and was pretty certain that it was more than just sunshine that had something to do with it.

Damn Josh…and damn Rob, too!

Glancing across at the time on the clock, Julie was surprised to see it was almost nine in the morning. Finally she'd managed to have a long sleep in. One more night in Luxor and she would have to part ways with Isadora and take that blasted train back up to Cairo. She should sue the company for missing out on the sleeper carriages – those inept people had caused her to feel like a piece of luggage. She would certainly take the matter further when she was back in London. She couldn't fully understand why Isadora needed to continue traveling on her own, but it was clearly important to her. Julie hoped the trip would help free her from old wounds and memories…ties that had bound her too long. Although she didn't understand what her friend was doing, she really had no choice but to trust.

Yawning and stretching again, she rolled over and was surprised to see Isadora's empty bed.

'Izzy?' Julie yelled out to the hollow sounding bathroom and as she did so caught sight of what appeared to be a note sitting perched on the table. Stepping gingerly out of bed, in three long steps she had reached the piece of paper, noticing a pretty cartouche pendant that lay beside it.

'Oh no!' she exclaimed upon reading the note. Hastily grabbing some clothes she raced to the bathroom.

Isadora had gone, a day earlier than scheduled and in an unhappy state. This wasn't good. She would already be on the bus to Hurghada on her way to catch the twelve noon ferry crossing to Sinai.

'Damn and blast!' Julie declared as she raced to the bathroom. 'Not good. Not good!'

She had to move fast.

***

At precisely five minutes past nine, Rob and Dan were finishing a leisurely hotel breakfast when they spotted Julie appearing rapidly down the base of the hotel stairs looking uncharacteristically disheveled. It was hard to miss her as she tripped at the bottom and her light blue singlet was on inside-out and back-to-front. They were amused at the sight. Julie was always immaculately attired and classy looking. So by the time she reached their table, out of breath and oddly dressed, with her blonde hair looking flat on one side and sticking out like a peacock's tail on the other, neither man knew quite where to look.

'Guys, guys, it's Izzy,' she said, panting from her rapid descent down several flights of stairs.

'What is it, Julie?' Rob said concerned.

'She's gone.'

'What do you mean, gone?'

Julie waved the note and Rob snatched it out of her hands to read it.

'I have to go now, Julz. Please don't worry about me, I'll be fine. I will contact you sometime in my travels and let you know I'm safe. This is not about a man, you know that. Remember I said I would choose my life…I'm choosing now. Thank you for being a darling friend. The pendant is for you. With Love, Izzy.'

'She must have left early this morning for Sinai to catch the twelve noon ferry. She'll be on a bus to Hurghada by now.'

'Well, when did the bus leave?' Rob said.

'About eight this morning, I think.'

'So why did she take off so suddenly?' Dan interrupted, 'I didn't think she was leaving until tomorrow or the day after.' He stared at Julie as a look of understanding crossed his eyes. 'You told her?'

Julie rolled her eyes. 'I did. I'm sorry, babe. But I think this is a little more complicated than just that.'

'Told her what?' Rob said staring at them both as guilt washed over their faces.

'I'm sorry, mate.'

It took Rob a few seconds to compute as they both watched him. 'Jessica. You told her about Jessica?'

'I did.' Julie declared. 'It was only fair, Rob. I don't know what you were thinking,' she said with annoyance.

'Shit.' Rob said, looking equally annoyed. 'Jesus, Julie! You *didn't know* what I was thinking! And neither did Izzy.' Quickly dabbing his mouth with the cotton napkin, he screwed up the note and tossed it onto the table as he launched up out of his chair.

'I'm sorry,' Julie said, looking surprised and taken aback at his strong reaction.

'I'm going after her.'

'Rob, it's a long way to Hurghada and chances are slim-to-none you'll make it before the noon ferry.' Dan looked questioningly at his friend.

'I have to try. The bus will be slow. I'm going to grab a few things from upstairs.'

Dan sighed as he stood up. 'Anything I can do to help?'

'Yeah. You can go find me the craziest cab driver in the Middle East.'

'Shouldn't be a problem.' Dan winked, and stood up to give Julie a comforting hug, but as he did so noticed she was staring quizzically across the other side of the breakfast area. 'Are you alright, babe?' He followed her darkening gaze to a man sitting at a table on the far side of the room. 'Julz?'

'Go get the cab, Dan,' she said curtly. 'There's someone I need to have a few words with.'

He noticed she had the kind of steely look in her eye that he already knew, if directed at him, indicated he had screwed up extremely badly. In fact, at that moment she looked more menacing than a terrorist with a loaded AK47 and a lot of bad intent.

Rob, too, had noticed her expression. As he spun towards the stairs heading for his hotel room he locked eyes with a man sitting on the opposite side of the breakfast room.

'Hurry up and get the cab,' Julie directed Dan in an authoritative voice. 'I might be requiring your services.'

***

The bus bumped and rattled its way through the barren desert landscape that appeared to Isadora rather like a lunar surface bathed in bright light. As the vehicle neared the coastline, swells of cobalt blue-green ocean became visible to her, although she barely registered it, instead staring blankly out the window. Her mind was a million miles away.

So much had happened in such a short space of time in Egypt. And now, before she'd barely had a moment to breathe, her new world was unraveling swiftly. Rob was just another appalling repeat of the old pattern. As for Josh, he was the final straw. Having barely slept that night she decided in the end it was time to get away.

God, have I learned anything?

She had intended to meet Josh for breakfast. She'd also intended to spend the day with Rob at the Valley of the Kings. But against all her patterning she put her own feelings ahead of theirs – and left.

I'm not running from my life anymore…I'm choosing it. It's time I trusted myself fully.

Still, she was far from feeling any triumph. Observing the recent events in her life, she simply couldn't recognize herself. If she'd been the lead actress in a film and created the whole script, it would be a highly implausible story. Yet according to Seraph she had actually participated in the entire production and likely written, directed, and produced the whole complicated plot…much to her current horror.

But that means I also have the power to change things in my life for the better.

The spiritual beings had come to her as a form of support. Whether she felt consciously comfortable with that was not the point anymore. They were attempting, from a much higher perspective, to assist her with her limited view of reality. She was now willing to trust that and take a new direction. She'd had enough of dead-end, emotionally destructive, and energetically draining relationships and experiences. She was over giving so much of herself and ending up feeling like a shriveled-up piece of fruit.

I have grown, I have changed, I have learned things. I deserve better.

'Yes you have, dear Isadora.' The angel's voice cut into her thoughts telepathically.

'Seraph?' she said happily as she looked around at the half empty bus. 'I was beginning to think you had disappeared for good.'

'Not forever. However, for now, I have come to say goodbye.'

'Goodbye?'

'Yes, Isadora. You're out of critical condition. My work is done.'

'Done? It's not done, Seraph. I'm on my own now, I need you more than ever,' she said with sudden apprehension.

'I thought we'd covered this…you're never on your own, remember. Besides, you're doing wonderfully yourself now.'

'You think so?'

'I know so. You have another chapter ahead and your new guide will meet you on the other side.'

'But I don't want another guide.' Tears formed in Isadora's eyes. 'I want you.'

'Dear One, there is absolutely no reason to be sad.'

'Of course there is, Seraph.' The tears rolled down her face. 'Now you're abandoning me too. That's all I ever seem to get,' she said feeling a flood of vulnerability wash through her.

'Come come, Isadora. You know that's not the truth, and besides, you've never been abandoned by anyone at all.'

'Yes I have been.'

'By who?'

'Well, starting with my mother. Come on, Seraph. You know the story.'

'No, Isadora, your mother never abandoned you. No one did.'

'No one?' Isadora was stunned.

'Of course not. You assigned the meaning to use it for your own purpose.'

'But she physically left. She fell apart and that was it, game over.'

'And then, perhaps, *you* abandoned *her*.'

'What?! You think I abandoned her? You're crazy!'

'You'll figure it out for yourself some day when you realize why you did it.'

'Why I did it?! Are you completely mad, Seraph?'

'Madness is not generally a characteristic found in Angels.'

'Well I'm totally confused now.'

'Confusion, however, is always a good sign.' Seraph chuckled. 'Love is constant and eternal, Isadora. The only thing that separates humans from divinity is unhealed feelings and emotions and the stories layered over those that cause all the disconnection, pain and suffering. When the feelings and emotions are accepted, fully felt and forgiven, the only thing left is your divine selves.'

Isadora remained silent, absorbing the words carefully.

'Remember when you were on the cliff in Ireland, Isadora?' Seraph continued.

'How could I forget.'

'Do you recall thinking of Everest? The images of yourself strewn about in the snow?'

'Yes,' she sniffed.

'They were versions of yourself and ways of being that have fallen along the way in your life.'

'I get that,' she said with sadness and regret.

'But what you haven't understood was that they fell away, along with connections you shared with them, not because of anything being wrong with you, or anything you did or didn't do - they fell away simply because they didn't serve you. They weren't aligned with who you really are, or your true nature.'

'Really?'

'Truly. It just takes feeling everything and letting go completely to be able to move forward fully.'

'Feeling everything...and letting go...completely. You make it sound like it's easy.' Isadora sighed.

'If you approach it truthfully, it can be. You see Isadora, every heartbreak, every loss...holds *a gift*.'

'A gift?'

'Yes. A gift. With any loss fully mourned a new strength, a new love grows...if you have the courage to have the feeling change.'

'The courage to have the feeling change...' Isadora echoed quietly again.

'Pain doesn't have to be a breaking up, a breaking down, or a closing up...it can be a breaking through, Isadora. A new birth...a new dawn.'

'A new dawn...?'

'Yes, a *bright* new dawn.'

Isadora remained quiet, digesting Seraph's words as the angel continued. 'That's always your potential, and your possibility, now and always.'

'So you think there's a heartbreak I haven't mourned fully, Seraph?' Isadora said quietly.

'If you had, I think you would have received the gifts from it by now.' Seraph paused. 'Do you know Isadora, if you knock over the first domino, all the others fall? It collapses the entire pattern.'

'What do you mean?'

The angel was quiet for so long that Isadora wondered if it had left until she heard Seraph's gentle voice in her ears once more.

'Forgive yourself, Isadora.'

'Forgive myself?' she said with surprise, as her eyes began to unexpectedly fill again with tears.

'Yes. And forgive the story, my friend. It has served you well, but it is no longer required.'

'See, that's the part I just don't get.'

'I hear that a lot.' Seraph chuckled again. 'You will find your way, Isadora. Trust. You are much stronger and wiser than you know or give yourself credit for. Now I must depart, my sweet friend. I have other souls to attend to.'

'Seraph,' Isadora said, with tears beginning to stream readily down her face. 'I never wanted to end my life. Not really. I'm so sorry,' she whispered. 'All I ever really wanted was to live…and to love.'

'I know this, dear Isadora. And now you can.'

'Yes, I can.' She swallowed the lump in her throat. 'You know, I always thought I had to get somewhere, or be somewhere other than exactly where I was. I couldn't feel the moment. I couldn't connect.' Tears rolled down her cheeks. 'Life was always in front of me, or at the *end* of the climb to the top of some great mountain…and there was always another mountain beyond that. There was always another reason to avoid myself…to avoid really feeling.'

'That's sadly not uncommon on earth.'

'I think I'm finally getting it though, Seraph. Life is always happening *right now*…whether I'm sad, or happy. It's all of it, isn't it…it's now.'

'Yes, Isadora, all of it. All of life is sacred. Every moment, every feeling, every breath.'

'Every breath...' Isadora repeated to herself, inhaling deeply as several tears slipped off her face.

'Yes. Every beautiful...precious...breath, Dear One. It's all there is...right here, right now. Life - in all its splendor. If you live with that awareness, eyes facing forward, fully engaged in the moment, the treasure of your birthright is yours.'

Isadora sat quietly, noticing the motion of her breath.

'I'm enormously grateful to you, Seraph,' she sniffed. 'I'll miss you very much.'

'One day you'll see me again, but you will come to love your new guide.'

'That woman?'

'Yes, *that woman*.' Seraph laughed.

'I don't think this is funny.' She wiped her eyes. 'Now I'm being handed over to some former ancient goddess to learn about philosophy, or something like that?'

'She is not just any ancient goddess, Isadora.'

'Well, who is she? I don't even know her name.'

'You never asked.'

'Well, I'm asking now.'

'Her name, Dear One, is Isis.'

Chapter Fifty-Four

Josh watched the blonde woman approach him with a feeling of unease. He'd noticed her fly down the stairs at top speed, tripping at the bottom, and had been mildly amused at the scene. She was dressed as if she had launched straight out of bed throwing the first thing on, badly, and her hair looked a heck of a state. Although clearly a pretty woman, the scowl on her face as she reached him detracted markedly from her good looks. She appeared like a loaded gun good to go off and he wondered, with sudden discomfort, why he was the dot in the center of the target.

And where is Isadora?

'Let me guess. You're Josh?' she announced matter-of-factly on arrival.

'Yes. Do I know you?' he said, amazed at hearing her say his name.

'Thankfully not. I'm Isadora's friend, Julie.'

'Oh, yes. Of course.' He stood up, extending his hand warmly. 'How nice to meet you.'

Julie looked at him with the kind of disdain a feudal lord might greet a servant with. 'I can't say the same, regrettably. You've been the bane of my good friend's life, and now mine too. She's vanished, no thanks to you.'

'What do you mean, vanished?' Josh said with concern.

Instead of answering his question, Julie launched a series of punishing blows about how he had lied and treated Isadora dreadfully. She went on to describe the poor state she had been in before getting on the plane to Egypt. By the time she'd finished roasting him, he was reeling.

'But where is she?' he said.

'She's gone. Well on her way to Sinai by now. She wasn't due to leave today, but she left a note this morning saying she had to go. You shouldn't have come here. You've bloody well mucked her up again.'

His discomfort was increasing by the second. 'I'm sorry, Julie. I did come a very long way to apologize and see her.'

Julie absorbed the fact for a second. 'I guess you did. That's something anyway,' she said with a dismissive tone.

'Julz.' Dan stuck his head inside the main entrance yelling across the foyer, 'I've got a taxi!'

'I have to go,' Julie said, suddenly turning around and exiting at the speed she arrived.

Josh sat down heavily and dropped his head into his hands in despair.

***

Rob was thinking that Dan had found the truly perfect driver as he reached out for something to hold onto and braced himself against the door. The guy was utterly nuts, driving at high speed and cutting corners insanely around every bend on the remote road.

Just as well it's an older car, he thought, glancing over at the speedometer.

The past week had been one of the strangest periods Rob could recall in his life, yet oddly he'd never felt more alive or more connected with who he truly was. Isadora had helped bring him to that place. It was as if she had opened a magical doorway to his heart and given him access to a whole new field of consciousness. He knew it wasn't just the ancient wonders and mysteries of Egypt making him feel so vital. Every cell in his body pulsed with a new awareness. Every event in his life had conspired to bring him to this exact moment just to meet her.

Although he wasn't logically able to make sense of his recent experiences, in his heart he was feeling things he'd never felt before. He was now unexpectedly filled with dread that he would not reach the boat in time, or see her again.

The high-pitched lyrics and mesmerizing beat of Egyptian music filled the taxi and his ears, becoming louder in his head as beads of sweat rolled fluidly down his back and chest. He glanced down at his watch, clenching his jaw with frustration. His guts churned. It was going to be a tight call to reach the boat in time. Looking around at the faded tattered upholstery of the taxi as if looking for some sign of hope, he gripped the door handle and grimaced before motioning to the driver.

'You'll have to go faster, mate. Faster, you must go faster.'

***

Julie sat anxiously in the café by the Nile with her head hung low, tapping her foot nervously. She'd had her third cup of black coffee in an hour as she sat assimilating the earlier conversation with Josh. And despite now having enough caffeine in her system to go clubbing for five hours straight, and also desperately needing the bathroom, she was glued to her chair. Josh had not seemed like a bad guy after all, but Isadora was her only concern. She was worried about her, now more than ever.

As if reading her thoughts, Dan, who had been quietly sitting beside her, laid his hand gently on hers.

'I hope you're not blaming yourself,' he said gently.

'It's not about Rob. I knew things weren't right with her and I should never have put her on the plane. I was only selfishly thinking of my holiday and myself,' she said, glancing up at Dan through guilty tear-filled eyes.

'You didn't do anything wrong. Honestly, honey. Izzy will be fine.'

'Do you think so?' She looked imploringly into his eyes for some sort of redemption.

Dan had always been a sucker for a woman in distress and he placed an arm around her, drawing her warmly into his chest. 'Sure I do.'

'Do you think Rob will reach her in time?' Her voice trembled as the tears finally began to fall in a steady stream.

'I don't know a man who would try harder.'

'He really likes her, doesn't he.'

'Actually darling, I'm beginning to wonder if it's a little more than that.'

***

As Isadora boarded the rusted old cargo boat that was to be her ferry ride across the Red Sea, she felt a sudden eerie feeling much like an animal sensing the coming of an earthquake. Her instinct prickled up, advising her to walk back off the boat, yet the compulsion to move forward into the unknown was overcoming her visceral knowing.

'Seraph?' she said, mentally searching for some reassurance.

But she knew the angel's services had by now been reassigned to other souls. It was very disconcerting for her because, after all, hadn't she traveled all this way by their instruction and arrangement?

Pull it together. You have the answers in yourself.

They wanted me to come here, she thought. So I need to get on the boat.

Just get on the damn boat, Isadora. They didn't guide you here to drown you at sea.

Finally embarking, she sighed heavily, moving to the far side of the vessel where she gazed out at the horizon of water stretching before her.

Trust. I have to trust and have faith, that's what this is about. It's what it's always been about.

As they began slowly moving away from the dock, Isadora heard a slight commotion on the other side of the boat. She could hear Egyptian men laughing and shouting excitedly in the background, but remaining transfixed by the tiny diamonds sparkling on the ocean surface, she searched for glimpses of exotic fish swimming in the warm waters. Sighing once more, she braced herself for the sea voyage ahead.

It's only four hours…how bad can a boat ride be.

Chapter Fifty-Five

Rob flew out of the cab, throwing his daypack onto his back whilst on the move and sprinting toward the wharf. It was just after twelve noon and there was still a chance he could make it. After all, what boat actually left on time. Yelling randomly at strangers for the direction to the ferry for Sinai he could feel the tightness in his chest as his pace barely slackened. Surely it couldn't be that rusted old ship off in the distance that appeared to be inching away from the dock.

As his steps brought him rapidly closer he could see it was indeed the cargo and passenger ferry to Sharm-el-Sheik. He was just fractionally too late…or was he? The boat was several meters from the dock but if he kept his current pace he might actually make it, if he could just grab onto the railing. There was no time left to consider his options, he was at full sprint on the wharf and the only real choice he had was to commit to the jump.

'Jesus!' he yelled, flying through the air as he hit the side of the boat hard and his right hand grasped the base of a railing pole.

But Jesus wasn't Rob's savior that day.

As the ferry pulled further away from the dock, he felt himself sliding helplessly towards the water.

***

Josh picked up the crumpled piece of paper discarded on the hastily abandoned table. He sat down heavily, feeling Isadora disappearing further into the desert with every word he read.

Damn. She's gone.

He absorbed her words thoughtfully.

She needed this. She always needed to take this journey for herself.

A long time passed as he sat deep in thought, considering everything that had brought him to this moment. He realized now the words Isadora had spoken, ironically his own reflected back at him, were the truth. Everything was perfect, even the dull thudding pain inside his aching beating heart. That it hurt so much was simply testimony to the fact he had finally let himself feel for someone completely again, after so many years. He'd let her in, but he didn't get to keep her. Isadora couldn't see it, but her spirit was already more free than she knew. She needed a man who had the strength and security to walk beside that. He simply hadn't been there enough.

Her quest for healing had unwittingly activated his own deeply hidden one. If it weren't for the pain wracking his chest he could have smiled with the happiness of one who had just been handed a golden key for a doorway to a long-lost home. It was a poignant sadness.

There's a part of me that has been lost too. And I have my own journey I need to take.

He felt a soft breeze stirring around him and had a sudden clear knowing that spirit was near. Sitting up tall and still in the chair, he listened with every cell in his body.

Words echoed in a soft whisper around and throughout his being.

No love given is ever lost.

A single tear rolled slowly down Josh's cheek as he registered the words fully.

'Grandpa,' he whispered. 'It's you, isn't it.'

Contemplating, he considered his thoughts before continuing. 'That whole plane journey, and traveling all this way…it was never about getting the girl, was it.' He smiled wryly at his unseen guest. 'It was about me. It was always about me, coming home…to myself.' He pressed his lips together as if the action would somehow hold his emotion in check. 'You're a wise old man, aren't you.'

Josh felt him standing there, clear as day, a hand on his shoulder, an unseen dignified strength hovering nearby.

'Thank you, Isadora. I'll see you again someday,' he said quietly before standing back up.

It was time to go.

The Hopi were calling.

***

Isadora spent time exploring what little of the boat there was to see and concluded it was definitely more of a cargo ship. There were very few passengers aboard and the seating area was an uncomfortable series of benches stretched out around a small open deck with some overhead cover.

They had been moving for over an hour. She watched the sky darken around her with uneasiness as they bobbed their way out into the open waters of the Red Sea. The rolling motion of the boat was increasing and she noticed that as the rain began to fall the vessel started a tipping motion from side to side, causing several travelers on the opposite side of the deck to huddle together and make her wish she too had someone to sit with.

The most disturbing thing for her was that she had begun to experience motion sickness and her stomach was not the slightest bit happy about it. In a short space of time she found herself dropping to her hands and knees on the deck and unexpectedly began to vomit violently. Ignored by the few other passengers fending for their own safety, Isadora realized she was now truly on her own. As the storm and movement of the boat worsened she grabbed a metal bench leg to stop herself from sliding around on the wet deck.

The ship quickly settled into a terrifying pattern of tipping completely starboard and port, affording Isadora a horrifying view of the wild dark ocean either side. Sea spray flew randomly into her face and her clothes were becoming wet. Her knuckles were ice cold and white from gripping the bench leg tightly and her body continued to slide on the surface of the deck. The stench of her own vomit reeked in her nostrils and burned in the back of her throat. She had no real seafaring experience, but even still, Isadora knew the situation was not good. If only she had listened to her intuition and not boarded the vessel.

But I must be meant to be here. Why?

Wedging a foot into another bench leg to stop herself from sliding about, she lay petrified on the deck watching the ocean appear either side of the boat at gravity-defying angles and prayed frantically for the journey to be over. In order to distract herself from her now anxious breathing she began thinking about Seraph's parting words.

The angel had told her if she knocked over the first domino the others would fall – implying that an entire life pattern could be healed. But she was still so confused by what that all meant.

Let's see… I abandoned my mother and created a heartbreak story for some deeper purpose; and there's still something I have to forgive.

Sadness welled up unexpectedly within her. She couldn't fathom why she would abandon anyone she loved and needed, although it did make sense to her now that she would seek out other experiences of abandonment to resolve the original one. Yet to hear that underneath she was the one actually doing the abandoning for her own purpose had thrown her completely.

It doesn't make sense...if I was the one abandoning, why? Why?

The boat rolled once more at a steep angle to the sea spreading massive waves of fear throughout Isadora's body. For a moment she recalled Seraph saying Isis would meet her *on the other side.* Did that actually mean when she was dead?

No! Isadora thought, suddenly very determined. That was not what Seraph meant. The boat would make it to the other side. It was always going to make it to the other side, and she could lie there fossilized in fear, or she could Trust.

And then she got it.

In that moment, Isadora understood something quite simple that she had never recognized or accepted about her mother, or herself, until that point.

It was freedom she wanted. She wanted to be free. But she couldn't make the journey...it was so much harder back then...and she had too much fear and not enough faith.

Tears began to pour steadily down Isadora's face at the deep dawning realization.

I couldn't save her, I couldn't carry her, and I couldn't bring her back...not the way I wanted her to be. So I abandoned her.

A wall shattered at the realization.

It was freedom I wanted too.

And there it was, just like that. All the buried guilt, shame and sorrow, and her unquenchable thirst for forgiveness.

'Dear Isadora, you did the best you could with the knowledge and awareness you had.' Seraph's gentle voice rippled through her mind.'

'But I failed her.' The deepest pain wrenched her heart.

'You didn't fail her at all. You didn't fail any other human being. You simply made the mistake of *closing your heart*...and with that, you failed yourself.'

'Surely I should have been able to do something,' she sobbed.

'You were so young. And it was never your job to rescue her. It was not your choice to make.'

Tears streamed freely down Isadora's face as she listened to Seraph's compassion-filled voice.

'No love given is ever lost...*it is always held in trust until it's able to be received.*'

The angel was quiet for what seemed like the longest time as Isadora struggled to speak.'

'Until she's able to receive the love, you mean?' she said in a choked voice.

'No, my friend...until *you* are.'

'Me?' Isadora flinched inwardly. Tears stung her eyes. 'I don't understand,' she said, noticing a curious feeling forming inside her. Everything around her appeared to slow right down. She glanced across at the empty deck, observing the wild stormy seas smashing against the side of the boat as if a silent film were being played on a screen around her. There was no sound anywhere. Nothing. Just a very disturbing quiet.

'Love is everywhere, Isadora.'

'It's not everywhere,' she snapped defensively. 'It's not!' She was filled with dread as a strange feeling inside her grew larger by the second.

'You only need choose to feel it, Isadora. Choose to *receive* it.' Seraph said softly.

'I can't.'

'Can't or won't?'

'I can't! she roared as if in warning to an unseen enemy to step back. 'I can't...!'

'Yes, you can.'

The feeling forming in her chest had become overwhelming. Her clothes were now soaking wet, her hair a matted tangled mess, and she was gripping the bench leg so tight that it was cutting into her hands. Her entire body shook.

'I just can't.' Her voice trembled.

'Why? What's there, Isadora?'

'I'm…too…afraid.' It was terror. 'I'm just too…damn…afraid.' Her voice trailed off.

'Go to that place then. Move into the fear. What's there?' Seraph said.

Isadora felt herself retract rapidly into a dark cavern where she felt the enormity of the feeling buried deep inside her at full force. 'I don't deserve it.' She recoiled in revulsion at her own sense of unworthiness. 'I don't…deserve love,' she sobbed.

Seraph was silent for what seemed like an eternity. Until finally, in the most gentle of voices, the angel spoke. 'Then go there too. Move right into the heart of that feeling and see what's there.'

In less than a second, time seemed to collapse all around Isadora. She saw her entire life panoramically laid out about her - every moment from birth and before that. She saw the mirror of her mother and her fears reflected back at her; and her mother before her…and hers before her. Her entire female ancestry connected despairingly to one another - a chain of unmet needs and unspoken pain passed on as a burdensome legacy. All their fears echoing throughout time from some long forgotten origin. All trapped; all encumbered with unworthiness. Yet each carrying a torch and dreaming of a life of dignity and grace to return home to. Isadora reeled in horror at the recognition as she sucked in cool air. She saw the part of her that was the same, how her self-judgment and guilt had condemned and imprisoned her, binding her inextricably to her female lineage.

Tears of sadness rolled down her cheeks as she felt their crushed hopes and dreams, the suffering, the injustice and hardship of their lives - their limited choices and numbed-out rejected feelings. Her own wounded feminine consciousness, lying speared throughout time.

'I feel as though having a happy life would be dishonoring in some way.' Isadora whispered, cringing at the sudden realization and the crippling guilt she felt inside.

'Ironic, isn't it.' The angel chuckled softly. 'Yet if you do allow happiness, you'll gift your mother. You'll gift all your ancestors, your family and the world, across time and space. You can receive more, and you can give and be more in this life. You can set them all free…' She heard Seraph's gentle voice. 'Free yourself. One domino…that's all it takes.'

'Why now?' Why? she whispered quietly.

'Because your soul has yearned for this time, Isadora…across the Ages. You have waited for that possibility to truly exist in life again. And now it does. Now you can.' Seraph paused. 'Accept what was. Be open to *what Is*.'

The next words were to be the last she would hear from the angel for a very long time. 'Take the gift of freedom that was always your destiny and use it wisely, my dear friend.'

As the boat passed slowly through the storm, inching closer to the coast of Sharm-el-Sheik, Isadora did just that. She let in all the love that had been held in trust for her; she released the past; she broke the chain. And she claimed her true freedom.

She forgave herself.

Epilogue

Julie lay in bed listening to the birds chirping happily outside in the early morning spring air, enjoying Dan's arms wrapped tightly around her as she thought about Isadora. Six weeks had passed since her own arrival back from Egypt and there had only been sporadic contact from her friend throughout that time. Isadora had seldom responded to any of Julie's email messages, but she had sent several postcards, one from Jordan and another from a Greek island. Then finally, an email over a week ago from Turkey saying she would be arriving back in London tomorrow.

It had been quite a whirlwind week since then, what with Dan's arrival and surprise news. So she hadn't had much time to think about her friend, until now. Dear Izzy. She hoped she'd found what she needed in her travels and finally had some peace. It had been such a crazy time in Egypt, most especially in Luxor with Josh's appearance, Isadora's sudden disappearance, and Rob's hot pursuit. He'd returned later that night looking rather forlorn and had barely uttered a word all the way back to Cairo before departing for Perth. Julie had written an email to Isadora telling her what he had done to reach her. She realized how much he must have come to care about Izzy in a short space of time. And Josh, too, had traveled all that way to see her.

Why don't I get men running after me like that?

She felt Dan stirring and turned her body to look over at him as he opened his eyes.

That's right, I did, she smiled.

'Now there's a sight,' he said, 'an angel to wake me.'

'You're so sweet,' Julie said, stroking the side of his face.

'You are,' he smiled. 'You look wide awake. What's going on in that beautiful head of yours?'

'I've been thinking about Izzy.'

'You'll be looking forward to seeing her.'

'I am, so much. I'm wondering how she's been…how she'll be,' Julie said softly.

'When are you going to tell her?'

'About us?'

'Well, that too. But do you think we should let her know about Rob before she arrives here?' Dan said.

'I really don't know if that's a good idea, darling. It didn't work so well the last time.'

'Well, let's not think about it right now. In fact, I have a much better idea,' he said rolling onto her and kissing her passionately.

Julie responded immediately, pressing her body against his, and all thoughts of Isadora vanished in a millisecond.

***

Sometime late in the afternoon of the next day, Isadora pushed her trolley towards the entrance of the International Arrivals area at London Heathrow Airport. She had loved the flight back and even relished the landing. She smiled broadly, looking and feeling totally relaxed and at ease. Walking with a spring in her step, her emerald eyes sparkled like jewels set in her tanned and glowing face. She walked tall in a long flowing blue dress with an ankh pendant around her neck and her dark hair cascading freely in waves down her back. Six weeks had passed and she felt like a whole new person.

A transformed human being, she thought.

The weeks abroad had served her incredibly well, as had Isis, her friend. The world was a very different playground for her now.

Emerging into the Arrivals Hall, she searched the waiting crowds for Julie.

'Izzy!' She heard the shout.

No mistaking that voice. Now where is she?

'Izzy!' There was Julie's voice again.

She saw her friend's unmistakable blonde head bobbing her way to the front of the crowd, and suddenly bursting through a gap, Julie ran the extra few meters and launched herself warmly at Isadora.

'Izzy, thank God. It's so good to see you!' She hugged her tightly.

'And you, Julz.'

'You look fantastic!' Julie exclaimed, stepping back and looking her up and down. 'I'll have whatever you've been having. But don't tell me it's some Greek God of a man because, guess what?!' She held up her left hand that was now sporting a gorgeous diamond engagement ring on it.

'Wow, how wonderful!' Isadora beamed at her with surprise. 'Congratulations. But who?'

Julie turned around. 'Him of course!' Dan's head was clearly sticking up above the majority of the crowd as he made his way toward them.

'Izzy, great to see you again,' he said warmly, giving her a big bear hug.

'And you, Dan. Congratulations, I'm so ecstatic for you both. When did this happen? Where, how?' Isadora laughed.

'Come on, we'll tell you all about it in the car and over dinner at my place.' Julie said hooking her arm around Isadora's. 'We have a whole lot of catching up to do, don't we.'

***

Isadora had showered and changed at Julie's. She was sitting relaxing on the comfortable sofa and enjoying the spring warmth flowing through the open balcony doors when the doorbell rang. Julie and Dan were both in the kitchen rattling around and making lots of noise so she didn't think twice before getting up to open it.

'There's someone here, Julz. I'll get it.' She shouted towards the kitchen, not noticing that it suddenly went deathly quiet.

As she opened the door, Rob was standing there, brandishing flowers and champagne and looking a little sheepish.

'Welcome back, Izzy.' Aside from extending the bouquet to her with a soft smile, he didn't move.

'Rob?' She was completely taken aback.

'Buddy!' Dan exclaimed walking into the living room. 'Great to see you, man. Come on in,' he said, shaking his friend's hand and giving him a hug and a warm pat on the back.'

'Rob, how wonderful to see you!' Julie said, throwing herself at him warmly.

'Now, isn't this a great reunion,' Dan beamed.

Isadora slipped quietly into the background and was clutching the flowers as she looked at Rob with complete surprise. She recalled the email Julie had sent her while she was in Jordan telling her that he'd chased her all the way to Hurghada in a taxi after she left, just narrowly missing her boat.

'Dan, I think something is burning. Quick,' Julie hastily pushed him toward the kitchen. 'You two go and have a drink on the balcony,' she directed with authority before removing the champagne from Rob's hand, snatching the flowers from Isadora, and disappearing into the kitchen.

Isadora was suddenly nervous as they made their way outside. The sky revealed a bright pink sunset as they leaned against the balcony wall facing one another.

'Beautiful evening,' Rob said.

'Perfect.' She looked into his clear blue eyes and all the memories of Egypt rushed back.

He stared quietly at her for a while. 'You fled Egypt in a hurry.'

'Yes, I guess I did really, didn't I,' she smiled shyly.

He paused, 'But you didn't say goodbye.'

'No. I'm sorry,' she said a little awkwardly. 'So you've come all this way to celebrate Dan and Julie's engagement?'

'No, I didn't know they were engaged until now,' he said grinning.

'Oh, really? Sorry, I've let the cat out of the bag,' she responded, flustered and confused. 'So what did you come all this way for?'

'Well, isn't that obvious,' he paused, gazing into her eyes. 'I came for you.'

'But I thought…'

'I know what Julie told you in Egypt, but you left before giving me a chance to tell you how I felt. There's no one in the world for me more than you, Izzy,' he said, sliding his hand in behind the small of her back and moving closer.

He will come for you, Seraph's words echoed in her mind. *When you are ready, he will come for you.*

'Are you sure about that, Rob. I mean, I'm not your average sort of a girl.'

'I never aspired to average, Izzy. You're something special.'

'I'm quite different, though,' she said with some apprehension.

'You are the Bright Light of Isis,' he said leaning in to kiss her.

'What?!' she replied, stunned.

'Your name, Isadora. Your name. It means *Light of Isis.*

'Isadora Bright. *Bright Light of Isis*,' she whispered, as tears of recognition filled her eyes. 'I had no idea.'

'Google it,' he smiled. 'Do I get a kiss now?' he smiled, drawing his mouth down close to hers.

'Yes,' she whispered happily as she felt his lips on hers.

'Dinner is almost ready!' Julie yelled from the kitchen.

'You've got to love that woman's sense of timing, don't you.' Rob pulled back from her, shaking his head good-naturedly as they laughed together.

His expression suddenly changed to one of seriousness as he glanced at her with hesitation.

'What is it, Rob?' she said with curiosity.

'Izzy, in front of the Sphinx, something happened to you, didn't it?'

'What do you mean?'

'I mean, you kind of tripped off somewhere and then you said something about *the architects returning*.'

'I did?'

'Yes. I think you know you did.' His voice was gentle. 'You're tapping into something, aren't you?'

Isadora was inwardly taken aback before finding words to respond. 'I don't know what you mean.'

'Come on, sure you do. Something was happening to you in Egypt. You saw something in the King's Chamber, you experienced something in front of the Sphinx, and that woman you were talking to at the Temple of Isis, who was she?'

'You saw her?' Isadora said with shock.

'Shouldn't I have?' He looked at her inquisitively.

She froze, uncertain of what to say.

'Just so you know, nothing shocks me, Izzy.'

'Really?' She looked unsure.

'I specialize in brain surgery for a living.'

She smiled at him. 'Yes, you do.'

'You might have quite a gift, you know,' he said tipping her chin up and looking down into her eyes.

'What if that gift sets me apart.'

'More the reason to embrace it, I say. That's how new frontiers are found and created in life, Izzy. By people accessing their innate gifts and talents.'

'Maybe. Or maybe you just get hunted out of town,' she said quietly.

'Only by the ignorant. Others will get who you are and what you bring to life.'

'I don't know about that.'

'I do. So tell me now, the *architects returning*, who are they? You know, don't you.'

She stared into the beautiful blue of his eyes seeing nothing but love looking back, and exhaled heavily before she said the words.

'We are, Rob. *We* are the architects returning.'

For a second he was speechless. 'What? You and I?'

'Not just us,' she smiled. 'There are many of us, all over the world. We've been on this earth countless times before and have been especially primed to return now, at the beginning of a brand new World Age cycle.'

'Jesus,' he said, as the impact of her words hit him. 'Why?'

'To return the ancient knowledge, technologies, healing and wisdom of our time, to the planet at this critical juncture...to oversee a new dawn.'

'Phew.' He took a deep breath. 'I guess that's a pretty big deal if it only rocks around every two thousand years or so.'

'The ancient ones thought so...we thought so...long ago.'

'So you're saying we planned, designed, and created the Sphinx, the Giza Pyramids...all of it.'

'Yes.'

'What for?'

She chuckled looking up into his eyes. 'So we would remember.'

'That's it? To impress ourselves with ourselves lifetimes later, and cause us to seek answers. No other great dramatic purpose like time travel or something exciting like that?'

'No,' she smiled. 'Not really.'

'Shit,' he said flabbergasted.

'Well you have to admit, it's a pretty bold, sophisticated, and enduring reminder to leave for yourself.'

He laughed. 'Yes, it's a heck of a statement.'

'It is.'

'Couldn't we have just left ourselves a note saying *Remember Who You Are. Remember Your Greatness*?'

'We did. It just happens to be a giant pyramid post-it note on the surface of the earth,' she grinned. 'Besides, it is serving its purpose. There are hundreds of thousands of human lights switching on to shine the way for the bright new dawn. The world is waking up again, humanity is healing, people are remembering...wisdom, truth, forgiveness, peace, love...'

'Yes, they are remembering love.' He leaned down and kissed her deeply. 'You know, I've been thinking...,' he said as his lips eventually parted from hers.

'Oh dear.'

He smiled. 'There are other very interesting old archeological sites around the world and I could sure do with another exotic holiday soon, with you at my side, exploring the mysteries of life and the universe.'

'You could now, could you?' Isadora's green eyes twinkled mischievously.

'Yes, I could.'

'I'm sure we can make that happen.'

'Come on you two lovebirds, dinner's ready,' Julie interrupted, poking her head out onto the balcony, 'and it's your favorite, Middle Eastern! Come on, chop chop.' She smiled at them as Rob took Isadora's hand in his.

'Light of Isis...my sacred love,' he said, kissing her again tenderly before guiding her off the balcony.

For a second, Isadora caught the reflection behind her in the glass door as she walked back inside. It was just for the briefest moment, but Seraph was looking back at her and she was certain the angel was smiling.

----- THE END -----

ABOUT THE AUTHOR

Louise Beker is a writer, bodywork practitioner and yoga instructor. She has spent over twenty years discovering, exploring, and experiencing core healing principles with gifted teachers and practitioners around the world. This is her first novel. She resides in Auckland, New Zealand.